P9-CSH-162

THE FORCES IN AMERICAN ECONOMIC GROWTH SERIES

The Railroads

WITHDRAWN

The Railroads

THE NATION'S
FIRST BIG BUSINESS

Sources and Readings

COMPILED AND EDITED BY

Alfred D. Chandler, Jr.
THE JOHNS HOPKINS UNIVERSITY

Harcourt, Brace & World, Inc.
NEW YORK · CHICAGO · SAN FRANCISCO · ATLANTA

To Mimi

THE FORCES IN AMERICAN ECONOMIC GROWTH SERIES

THE FORCES in *American Economic Growth* series *provides a documentary record of the building of the American economy. Each book in the series concentrates on the economic force or forces that generated the most compelling pressure for change at key junctures in American history. In each volume the men responsible for change speak for themselves. By presenting such a record the editors hope to enhance the reader's sense of economic reality, his awareness of underlying historic currents, and his ability to investigate and interpret business and economic change and growth.*

The series attempts to achieve this goal by providing illustration and by permitting analysis. The documents presented are intended to show how new patterns of economic action occurred and how American entrepreneurs, managers, engineers, financiers, business analysts, workers, and labor-union leaders carried on their various activities at different periods of history. The record provides more than mere illustration. The documents have been collected and presented in a way to encourage analysis and interpretation. They raise questions of why and what as well as how. Why did new ways come when they did and in the way they did? What stimulated and what hindered change? What was the role of personality in producing innovation and bringing economic growth?

The series, in short, supplies the record, the source materials, that a reader can use to form his own judgment about the nature of economic and historical change. It will allow him to be his own historian and his own interpreter of the changing American business and economic scene.

ALFRED D. CHANDLER, JR.

CONTENTS

PART I

The Railroads as Promoters
of Economic Change

PART II

The Beginnings of
Modern Corporate Finance

PART III

The First Modern
Corporate Management

PART IV

The Beginnings of
Modern Labor Relations

PART V
New Ways of Competition

PART VI
The Beginnings of Modern Governmental Regulation of Business

PART V

The Railroads

A GENERAL INTRODUCTION
TO THE READINGS

The Mid-Nineteenth-Century Transportation Revolution

IN 1830, 23 miles of railroad track were being operated in the United States; by 1890 that figure had grown to 166,703 miles, as cities and villages were linked across the land. The swift and widespread adoption of the railroad, together with the telegraph and ocean-going steamship, forged a transportation revolution that profoundly altered existing patterns of American agriculture, industry, and commerce. Besides stimulating national production and income, the new forms of transportation, particularly the railroad, helped to create new economic methods and institutions that were essential in guiding and shaping the American drive to industrialism. New ways of moving and communicating across land and sea helped to lay the foundations of the modern American economy and to transform the nation into the world's greatest industrial power. The large corporation, the craft union, the investment banking house, and the regulatory commission all moved toward their modern form in meeting the financial and operational needs of the new instruments of transportation.

Although improvements came before mid-century, the really revolutionary changes in American transportation and communication appeared in the dozen or so years before the Civil War. Turnpikes and canals had been constructed in sizable numbers earlier in the century, and steam power had been applied to river transportation, especially on the western waters, since the War of 1812. Yet in the mid-1840's natural waterways still carried the lion's share of American commerce, and sails remained the primary mover of goods and passengers over any extended distances, as they had been since the days of Greece and Rome.

Then, after 1846, the railroad, the ocean-going steamship, and the telegraph became almost overnight the standard methods of transportation and communication. The railway quickly replaced the canal as the primary means of "artificial" or overland transportation. In 1840 the nation had 3,326 miles of canals and 2,818 miles of railroads. When the decade closed, only 400 more miles of canal had been built as compared to nearly 5,000 miles of railroad track. Most of the latter was completed in the second half of the decade, for in the closing years of the forties began the nation's first really great railroad boom. During the fifties, when more canals were abandoned than built, nearly 22,000 miles more of track were constructed. By the outbreak of the Civil War the basic railroad network east of the Mississippi had been completed. And the critical part of this mileage was finished between 1849 and 1854 (see map).

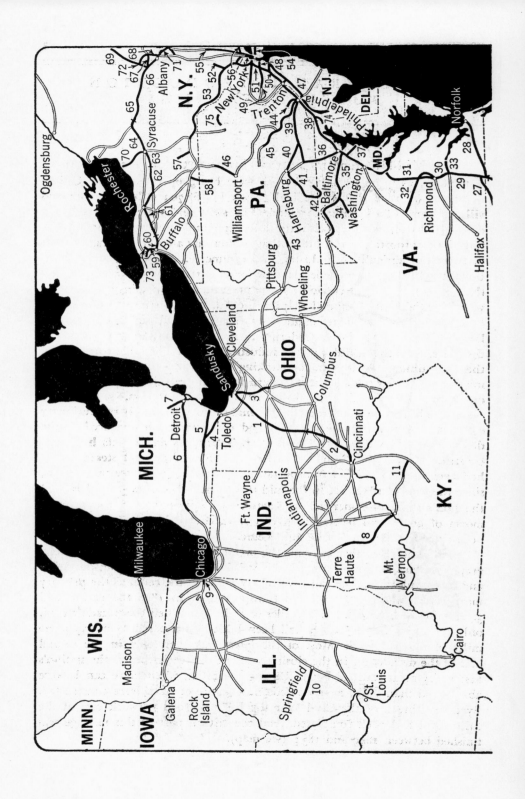

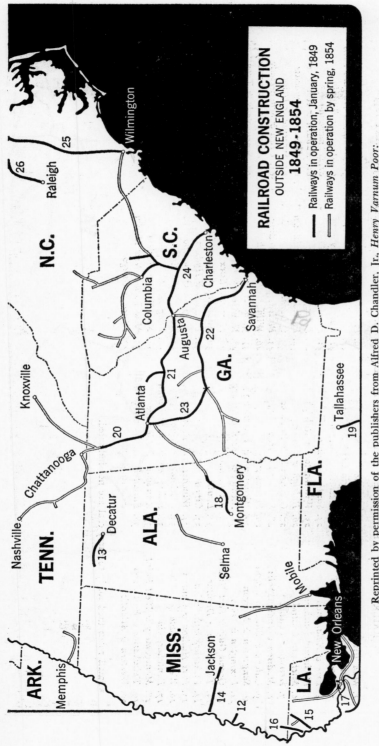

RAILROAD CONSTRUCTION

OUTSIDE NEW ENGLAND

1849-1854

—— Railways in operation, January, 1849

══ Railways in operation by spring, 1854

Reprinted by permission of the publishers from Alfred D. Chandler, Jr., *Henry Varnum Poor: Business Editor, Analyst, and Reformer* (Cambridge, Mass.: Harvard University Press), opposite p. 84. Copyright, 1956, by the President and Fellows of Harvard College.

RAILROADS OF THE UNITED STATES (OUTSIDE NEW ENGLAND) IN OPERATION, JANUARY 1849 [a]

1. Mad River & Lake Erie
2. Little Miami
3. Mansfield & Sandusky
4. Erie & Kalamazoo
5. Michigan Southern
6. Michigan Central
7. Detroit & Pontiac
8. Madison & Indianapolis
9. Galena & Chicago Union
10. Sangamon & Morgan
11. Lexington & Ohio
12. Grand Gulf & Port Gibson
13. Tuscumbia & Decatur
14. Vicksburg & Brandon
15. Port Hudson & Clinton
16. West Feliciana
17. Pontchartrain
18. Montgomery & West Point
19. Tallahassee & Port Leon
20. Western & Atlantic

21. Georgia
22. Georgia Central
23. Macon & Western
24. South Carolina
25. Wilmington & Raleigh
26. Raleigh & Gaston
27. Greensville & Roanoke
28. Seaboard & Roanoke
29. Petersburg
30. Richmond & Petersburg
31. Richmond, Fredericksburg & Potomac
32. Louisa
33. City Point
34. Winchester & Potomac
35. Baltimore & Ohio
36. Baltimore & Susquehanna
37. Annapolis & Elkridge
38. Philadelphia, Wilmington & Baltimore

39. Philadelphia & Columbia
40. Harrisburg & Lancaster
41. Cumberland Valley
42. Franklin
43. Portage
44. Philadelphia, Norristown & Germantown
45. Philadelphia & Reading
46. Williamsport & Elmira
47. Camden & Amboy
48. New Jersey
49. Morris & Essex
50. Elizabeth & Somerville
51. Paterson & Hudson
52. Paterson & Ramapo
53. New York & Erie
54. Long Island
55. New York & Harlem
56. New York & New Haven
57. Ithaca & Owego

58. Tioga
59. Buffalo & Niagara Falls
60. Attica & Buffalo
61. Tonawanda
62. Auburn & Rochester
63. Auburn & Syracuse
64. Syracuse & Utica
65. Utica & Schenectady
66. Albany & Schenectady
67. Schenectady & Troy
68. Rensselaer & Saratoga
69. Saratoga & Washington
70. Oswego & Syracuse
71. Western
72. Saratoga & Schenectady
73. Lockport & Niagara Falls
74. New Castle & Frenchtown
75. Carbondale

[a] Small roads used solely to carry coal are not indicated.

In these very same years steam power quickly replaced sail on the major ocean routes, particularly on the all-important North Atlantic runs. On January 1, 1848, Samuel Cunard inaugurated the first steam packet line on the "Atlantic Shuttle" between New York and Liverpool. Others quickly followed. Then in the fifties the growing use of the iron hull and screw propulsion increased the size, speed, and efficiency of individual steamships. By the coming of the Civil War, the best paying runs had all been taken over by the steamship. Although the British led in the adoption of the new form, American registered steam tonnage rose rapidly from a mere 5,631 in 1847 to 97,296 in 1860.

The telegraph added still another fundamental dimension to the mid-century revolution. Samuel F. B. Morse built with government support the first experimental telegraph line between Baltimore and Washington in 1844. By 1847 the new instrument's technical difficulties had been ironed out enough to permit its commercial development. Then as the railroad began to extend, so too did the telegraph. Indeed the two spread nearly simultaneously across the continent. Railroad managers found the telegraph an invaluable aid to safe and efficient train operations, and the telegraph promoters realized that the railroad provided a highly convenient right of way. So, many lines were built under carefully worked out contracts between telegraph and railroad companies. Because the telegraph was easier and cheaper to build, it soon outran the railroad in the still unsettled areas of the West. By 1860 some 50,000 miles of wire had been strung in the United States and by the outbreak of the Civil War telegraphic communication reached from the Atlantic to the Pacific.

The railroad, steamship, and telegraph made transportation and communication faster, cheaper, and more certain than it had ever been before. The telegraph provided almost instantaneous communication to nearly every part of the nation, while the railroad and steamship permitted a fast and regular movement of mail. This more assured regularity allowed the Post Office to initiate the use of postage stamps in 1847 and to drop postage rates in 1851 from 5¢ for 300 miles to 3¢ for 3,000 miles. Business could now be transacted by mail far more easily and efficiently than it ever had been in any earlier period.

Of still more significance was the impact these new forms had on the movement of goods and passengers. Speed and volume increased immediately. The railroad reduced the time required for a trip from New York to Chicago from more than three weeks to less than three days. In the winter, when the canals and rivers were frozen, the passage west by stage coach had taken even longer. For freight the shipping time had been greater than for passengers, and in the winter months only the lightest and most valuable type of freight could be moved at all.

The steamship made as fundamental though less dramatic cuts in the time of the transatlantic passage. In the years before 1848, the specialized sailing packets made the trip from Liverpool to New York in from sixteen to eighty-three days, with thirty-five days being an average run. The steamships immediately sliced the average time of the westbound run in half, and by 1860 travelers already considered a two-week passage a slow one. This sharp reduction in the time of a round-trip passage on land or water meant that a single train or steamship could carry much more freight between its termini in a given time period than could one canal boat or sailing ship. The former could make two or more round trips while the older carrier was making a single one. Moreover, in the 1850's the volume of freight carried by a single steamship or pulled by a single locomotive was continuously being enlarged. As a result, in almost no other period in American history did the volume of traffic moved increase so sharply as it did in the dozen or so years before the outbreak of the Civil War.

Besides expanding the volume of traffic, the new forms of transportation permitted a regularity and a certainty in travel and in the movement of goods that had never before existed. Trains had to be run on a fairly exact schedule if only to prevent accidents. Storms, drought, ice, or mud had much less effect on the scheduling and running of trains than they did on river boats, canal boats, and stage coaches. Steamships on the Atlantic runs were able to maintain schedules much more easily than sailing ships operating at the mercy of the shifting winds and tides.

It was this new regularity, speed, and volume of transportation that so profoundly affected the American farmer, merchant, and manufacturer during the decade or so before the Civil War. The railroad helped open the Western prairie to settlement. With the steamship it assured quick movement of the prairie's basic crop, wheat, and its processed product, flour, to the urban markets of the East and of Europe. Only after 1846 did grain become a significant American export.

The railroad, with its certainty and its speed in the moving of goods, encouraged the rise of wholesalers and middlemen in all parts of the nation. Moreover, these wholesalers now became jobbers who bought and sold the goods in their own name rather than acting as agents selling on commission for others. The primary reason for this change was that the merchants no longer had to accept the risks of carrying large inventories. If their shelves became depleted, they could telegraph the manufacturer and usually expect delivery by rail within a few days. The wholesalers preferred the new arrangement as it permitted them to control the mark-up, which they could not do as commissioned agents, and to adjust stocks more closely to the fluctuations of local demands. The manufacturer was, of course, delighted to sell his product immediately rather than having to tie up capital in goods that might sit for months in the commission agent's warehouses or on his own shelves.

The manufacturer was affected by the transportation revolution in even more significant ways. The new volume and regularity of transportation made possible the swift rise of the factory in the United States. Prior to the mid-forties the modern factory, employing regularly as many as two hundred hands, existed only in the textile or closely related industries. Then in the 1850's the rapid expansion of the market and the assurance of a regular and constant flow of raw and semifinished materials permitted many manufacturers for the first time to replace the shop and the "putting out" methods of production with that of the factory. In that decade, shoes, clothing, clocks, watches, sewing machines, agricultural implements, machine tools, and small arms for the civilian market as well as such basic materials as iron and brass all began to be mass produced.

Of the three elements of the new transportation, the railroad was the greatest force for economic change. It affected the economy in ways far beyond those of increasing the regularity and volume of traffic and reducing the costs of transportation. Railroad companies required far more initial capital investment than did telegraph or steamship lines, and railroad construction and operation called for many more workers and managers than did the other two forms of transportation and communication. It is not surprising, therefore, that railroad operation added much more than did the operation of the other two elements to the national income in terms of wages, salaries, and dividends. Moreover, the railroad became a much larger market for the products of American industry than did the steamship or the telegraph. By the 1850's the former was the largest single market for iron and a major market for coal, wood, machinery, felt, glass, rubber, and brass.

The Railroads as the Nation's First Big Business

Actually, it can be argued that the railroads made still another and even more significant contribution to American economic growth. Besides increasing the volume and regularity of transportation, adding to the national income, and becoming a brand-new market for American industry, they created new patterns of economic and business action and new institutional forms. Growth depends on the organization of economic activities as much as it does on inputs of capital, labor, and technological improvements. And the railroads were the first American business to work out the modern ways of finance, management, labor relations, competition, and government regulation. Railroad promoters and managers pioneered in all these areas, not because they were a particularly intelligent or perceptive breed of entrepreneurs, but because they had to. Their capitalization, their plant and equipment, their running expenses and labor force were much larger than those of any other business of that day.

Size and complexity of operations required new ways and new forms. The massive financial requirements of the railroads caused the centralizing and institutionalizing of the nation's investment market in New York City. They opened new opportunities for American financiers, bankers, and speculators. The operational demands of the new roads called forth the first large administrative structures in American business, which became manned by some of the nation's earliest professional managers. The desire of skilled workers, whose livelihood depended totally on the whims of their managers, to obtain some control over their own economic destinies encouraged the growth of the modern craft union. The new unions in turn fostered the modern methods of collective bargaining between the representatives of management and labor.

Size and complexity affected the development of external relations as well as internal organization. Competition between a handful of corporate giants burdened with high operating costs that did not vary with the volume of business available was certainly a brand-new economic phenomenon. Prices became based more on costs and less on any impersonal market demand. Cooperation became as valued as competition. The need to assure a continuous flow of traffic over a number of separate lines as well as the threat of repeated price cutting brought collaboration between managers. When the resulting rate agreements failed to control competition, railroad men organized formal regional associations to pool traffic or profits. And when these federations also failed, senior executives began to build—through construction, merger, and purchase—great self-contained railroad systems. Because such cooperation, federation, combination, and consolidation violated existing economic concepts and political doctrines, they engendered a demand for public and government regulation of the corporation. The result was the creation of a new type of economic institution, the regulatory commission.

The several institutions initially developed to meet the need of railroad construction and operation—the regulatory commission, the craft union, the large corporation, and the investment banking house—soon became integral parts of the American economic scene. They all played a critically important part in the continuing growth of the American economy in the years after the building of the railroads was completed and the methods of railroad finance, operation, competition, and regulation had been routinized. To provide a knowledge of how and why these new institutions were formed, and of the business and economic methods they generated, is one of the primary purposes of this book of readings.

The selections presented here will be most useful if the two basic periods in American railroad history are kept clearly in mind. The dividing line between these periods was the severe economic depression of the 1870's. Before that depression most railroaders were concerned with the construction and expansion of new and existing facilities. After that time they turned their attention to a constant search for new traffic to use existing facilities.

The first period was, then, one of growth; the second, one of competition. The period of growth really began with the construction boom of the late 1840's. Construction continued apace throughout the fifties, held back only slightly by the depression following the panic of 1857. After 1865 construction, retarded by four years of war, again surged forward. Railroads in the South were re-laid as tracks moved swiftly into the trans-Mississippi west. By the time the depression of the seventies struck, every important American town had its railroad connections.

After the depression the only significant new routes to be opened to railroad transportation were those connecting the Mississippi Valley with the Pacific coast. The rest of the construction completed in the eighties and nineties essentially filled in the basic network. This did not mean that construction slowed. In fact more railroad mileage was built in the 1880's than in any other decade in American history. But the impetus for construction after the depression came from the pressures of competition, and more from a desire to retain an existing volume of traffic than to expand it. Since so many railroads decided that their economic well-being depended on building (or buying) their own tracks into all the important commercial centers of the regions they served, competitive construction led to a massive duplication of existing facilities.

The change in the railroad world from expansion to competition in the 1870's affected nearly all the ways of doing business. Intensified competition brought the associations and consolidations that in turn led to the demand for government regulation. The rise of the great consolidated systems raised new problems of finance and increased the role of the investment banking house in American railroading. The management of the huge new systems became immensely more complex. Finally depression, competition, and the resulting reduction in pay and lay-offs of personnel helped to transform the railroad brotherhoods from fraternal and mutual-aid societies into instruments of economic power. Their members began to use the union to improve their wages, hours, and conditions of work through collective bargaining supported by the threat of a strike.

By the 1890's the American railroad network was practically completed. Individual railroad systems had come to cover about the same territory as they do today. By then the brotherhoods were fully established as collective bargaining agencies, and the Interstate Commerce Commission was already playing a role in rate-making and railroad regulation. The patterns of railroad finance, administration, labor relations, and government regulation had been stabilized. In the meantime the rising industries producing for the great new urban market were beginning to adopt and modify the institutions and patterns of economic activities initially developed by the railroads. From the 1880's on the city and industry replaced the railroads as prime promoters of change and growth in the American economy.

The following readings focus on the railroads as pioneers in the ways of modern big business. They concentrate on institutional innovation more than on quantitative economic growth and do so by letting the innovators speak for themselves. The first set of readings does, however, emphasize the impressive impact the railroads had on agriculture, industry, and commerce and on the quantitative growth of the economy. It should thus provide a proper introduction to the later sections, which deal with the coming of new forms of finance, management, labor relations, competition, and government regulation. The significance of the initial readings and those that follow require a quick summary view of the quantitative growth of the American railroad network and of the larger individual companies within it. The statistics to follow indicate that growth.

RAILROAD STATISTICS

TABLE 1. RAILROAD MILEAGE AND EQUIPMENT: 1830 to 1890

YEAR	MILEAGE ROAD OPERATED (Dec. 31)	ROAD OWNED[a]	ALL TRACK (Dec. 31)	LOCO-MOTIVES	EQUIPMENT[b] REVENUE CARS TOTAL	PASSENGER	FREIGHT	BAGGAGE, MAIL, EXPRESS
1890	166,703	163,359	208,152	31,812	1,090,869	21,664	1,061,952	7,253
1889	161,276	159,934	202,088	30,566	1,080,665	21,471	1,051,141	7,053
1888	156,114	154,222	191,376	29,006	1,032,182[c]	20,247	1,005,108	6,827
1887	149,214	147,953	184,935	27,275	976,772[c]	19,339	950,889	6,554
1886	136,338	133,565	167,952	26,108	870,602	18,365	845,912	6,325
1885	128,320	127,689	160,506	25,662	828,058	16,497	805,517	6,044
1884	125,345	125,119	156,414	24,353	820,954	16,644	798,399	5,911
1883	121,422	120,519	149,101	23,405	800,741	16,230	778,663	5,848
1882	114,677	114,428	140,878	21,889	750,933	14,934	730,435	5,564
1881	103,108	103,530	130,455	19,911	667,218	13,947	648,295	4,976
1880	93,262	92,147	115,647	17,949	556,930[c]	12,789	539,255	4,786
1879	86,556	84,393	104,756	17,084	496,718	12,009	480,190	4,519
1878	81,747	80,832	103,649	16,445	439,109	11,683	423,013	4,413
1877	79,082	79,208	97,308	15,911	408,082	12,053	392,175	3,854
1876	76,808	76,305	94,665	15,618	399,524	14,621[d]	384,903	—
1875	74,096	74,096	—	—	—	—	—	—
1874	72,385	72,623	—	—	—	—	—	—
1873	70,268	70,651	—	—	—	—	—	—
1872	66,171	57,323	—	—	—	—	—	—
1871	60,301	51,455	—	—	—	—	—	—
1870	52,922	—	—	—	—	—	—	—
1869	46,844	—	—	—	—	—	—	—
1868	42,229	—	—	—	—	—	—	—
1867	39,050	—	—	—	—	—	—	—
1866	36,801	—	—	—	—	—	—	—
1865	35,085	—	—	—	—	—	—	—
1864	33,908	—	—	—	—	—	—	—
1863	33,170	—	—	—	—	—	—	—
1862	32,120	—	—	—	—	—	—	—
1861	31,286	—	—	—	—	—	—	—
1860	30,626	—	—	—	—	—	—	—
1859	28,789	—	—	—	—	—	—	—
1858	26,968	—	—	—	—	—	—	—
1857	24,503	—	—	—	—	—	—	—
1856	22,076	—	—	—	—	—	—	—
1855	18,374	—	—	—	—	—	—	—
1854	16,720	—	—	—	—	—	—	—
1853	15,360	—	—	—	—	—	—	—
1852	12,908	—	—	—	—	—	—	—
1851	10,982	—	—	—	—	—	—	—
1850	9,021	—	—	—	—	—	—	—
1849	7,365	—	—	—	—	—	—	—
1848	5,996	—	—	—	—	—	—	—
1847	5,598	—	—	—	—	—	—	—
1846	4,930	—	—	—	—	—	—	—
1845	4,633	—	—	—	—	—	—	—
1844	4,377	—	—	—	—	—	—	—
1843	4,185	—	—	—	—	—	—	—
1842	4,026	—	—	—	—	—	—	—
1841	3,535	—	—	—	—	—	—	—
1840	2,818	—	—	—	—	—	—	—
1839	2,302	—	—	—	—	—	—	—
1838	1,913	—	—	—	—	—	—	—
1837	1,497	—	—	—	—	—	—	—
1836	1,273	—	—	—	—	—	—	—
1835	1,098	—	—	—	—	—	—	—
1834	633	—	—	—	—	—	—	—
1833	380	—	—	—	—	—	—	—
1832	229	—	—	—	—	—	—	—
1831	95	—	—	—	—	—	—	—
1830	23	—	—	—	—	—	—	—

[a] Prior to 1882, includes elevated railways.
[b] Prior to 1881, includes elevated railways.
[c] Agrees with source; figures for components do not add to total.
[d] Includes baggage, mail, and express.

TABLE 2. MILES OF RAILROAD BUILT: 1830 to 1925 [a]

YEAR	MILES	YEAR	MILES	YEAR	MILES	YEAR	MILES
1925	644	1905	4,388	1871	6,660	1850	1,261
1924	579	1904	3,832	1870	5,658	1849	1,048
1923	427	1903	5,652	1869	4,103	1848	1,056
1922	324	1902	6,026	1868	2,468	1847	263
1921	475	1901	5,368	1867	2,541	1846	333
1920	314	1900	4,894	1866	1,404	1845	277
1919	686	1899	4,569	1865	819	1844	180
1918	721	1898	3,265	1864	947	1843	288
1917	979	1897	2,109	1863	574	1842	505
1916	1,098	1896	1,692	1862	720	1841	606
1915	933	1895	1,420	1861	1,016	1840	491
1914	1,532	1894	1,760	1860	1,500	1839	386
1913	3,071	1893	3,024	1859	1,707	1838	453
1912	2,997	1879	5,006	1858	1,966	1837	348
1911	3,066	1878	2,428	1857	2,077	1836	280
1910	4,122	1877	2,280	1856	1,471	1835	138
1909	3,748	1876	2,575	1855	2,453	1834	214
1908	3,214	1875	1,606	1854	3,442	1833	116
1907	5,212	1874	2,584	1853	2,170	1832	191
1906	5,623	1873	5,217	1852	2,288	1831	99
		1872	7,439	1851	1,274	1830	40

[a] [Miles for 1880 to 1892 not included in original table.]

TABLE 3. RAILROAD PASSENGER AND FREIGHT SERVICE: 1865 to 1890

YEAR	PASSENGER SERVICE				FREIGHT SERVICE					
	PASSENGER REVENUE	PASSENGERS CARRIED	PASSENGER MILES	REVENUE (PASSENGER-MILE)	FREIGHT REVENUE	TOTAL REVENUE TONS CARRIED[a]	TON-MILES CARRIED, ALL ROADS	REVENUE PER TON-MILE	REVENUE TON-MILES PER TRAIN-MILE	TON-MILES CARRIED, 13 RAILROADS
	$1,000	1,000	Mil.	Cents	$1,000	1,000	Mil.	Cents		Bil.
1890	272,321	520,439	12,522	2.174	734,822	691,344	79,193	0.927	163.99	—
1889	259,439	494,808	11,965	2.169	665,962	619,166	68,677	0.970	159.91	—
1888	251,356	451,354	11,191	2.246	639,201	590,857	65,423	0.977	159.36	—
1887	240,543	428,226	10,570	2.276	636,666	552,075	61,561	1.034	156.16	—
1886	211,930	382,285	9,660	2.194	550,359	482,245	52,802	1.042	150.99	—
1885	200,884	351,428	9,134	2.199	509,691	437,040	49,152	1.057	143.59	17.83
1884	206,791	334,571	8,779	2.356	502,870	399,075	44,725	1.124	133.58	16.81
1883	206,837	312,687	8,541	2.422	539,510	400,453	44,065	1.224	125.86	17.09
1882	188,137	289,031	7,688	2.447	485,778	360,490	39,302	1.236	128.81	16.23
1881	173,357	—	—	—	551,968	—	—	—	—	16.06
1880	147,653	—	—	—	467,749	—	—	—	—	14.48
1879	142,336	—	—	—	386,676	—	—	—	—	13.07
1878	124,637	—	—	—	365,466	—	—	—	—	10.68
1877	125,205	—	—	—	347,705	—	—	—	—	8.75
1876	136,121	—	—	—	361,137	—	—	—	—	8.74
1875	139,105	—	—	—	363,960	—	—	—	—	7.84
1874	140,999	—	—	—	379,467	—	—	—	—	7.73
1873	137,384	—	—	—	389,036	—	—	—	—	7.48
1872	132,309	—	—	—	340,932	—	—	—	—	6.42
1871	108,899	—	—	—	294,430	—	—	—	—	5.57
1870	—	—	—	—	—	—	—	—	—	4.92
1869	—	—	—	—	300,000	—	—	—	—	4.22
1868	—	—	—	—	—	—	—	—	—	3.44
1867	—	—	—	—	—	—	—	—	—	3.03
1866	—	—	—	—	—	—	—	—	—	2.62
1865	—	—	—	—	—	—	—	—	—	2.16

[a] Revenue tons carried for 1870 are 72,500,000 tons; for 1861, 55,073,000 tons.

TABLE 4. RAILROAD PROPERTY INVESTMENT, CAPITAL, INCOME, AND EXPENSES: 1850 TO 1890

[In thousands of dollars]

YEAR	PROPERTY INVESTMENT AND CAPITAL					INCOME AND EXPENSES			INTEREST AND DIVIDENDS	
	INVESTMENT IN RAILROAD AND EQUIPMENT	STOCK, MORTGAGE BONDS, EQUIPMENT, OBLIGATIONS, ETC.			STOCK PAYING DIVIDENDS	TOTAL TRAFFIC EARNINGS	OPERATING EXPENSES	NET EARNINGS	DIVIDENDS PAID	INTEREST PAID ON FUNDED DEBT
		TOTAL	CAPITAL STOCK	BONDED DEBT						
Excluding elevated railways										
1890	8,789,222	10,020,925	4,500,472	5,055,225	—	1,086,040	—	342,071	83,576	224,500
1889	8,598,081	9,576,940	4,447,104	4,784,173	—	991,935	—	317,867	79,532	216,878
1888	8,344,305	9,281,915	4,392,287	4,585,472	—	950,520	—	207,307	78,943	205,288
1887	7,799,472	8,595,041	4,146,958	4,155,028	—	931,373	—	331,174	80,013	202,000
1886	7,254,995	8,089,268	3,956,377	3,853,748	—	822,192	524,880	297,312	80,094	182,885
1885	—	7,775,858	3,778,610	3,740,255	—	765,311	498,822	266,489	77,672	179,681
1884	—	7,617,986	3,726,655	3,647,313	—	763,307	—	266,514	93,204	107,286
1883	—	7,423,040	3,675,793	3,479,412	—	807,113	—	291,588	101,579	171,414[a]
1882	—	6,960,649	3,478,914	3,214,084	—	—	—	—	—	—
Including elevated railways										
1890	—	10,122,636	4,640,240	5,105,902	1,721,094	1,097,847	—	346,921	85,076	226,800
1889	—	9,680,942	4,495,099	4,828,366	1,790,842	1,002,926	—	322,123	81,263	218,974
1888	—	9,369,399	4,438,411	4,624,035	1,769,773	960,256	—	301,631	80,243	207,124
1887	—	8,673,187	4,191,562	4,186,943	1,805,488	940,151	—	334,989	91,573	203,790
1886	—	8,163,149	3,999,509	3,882,966	1,675,670	829,941	—	300,604	81,654	189,036
1885	7,037,627	7,842,533	3,817,698	3,765,727	1,304,802	772,559	—	269,494	77,672	187,426
1884	6,924,554	7,676,399	3,762,617	3,669,116	1,658,919	777,396	—	270,891	94,415	178,058
1883	6,684,756	7,477,866	3,708,061	3,500,880	1,713,702	823,773	—	208,367	102,053	173,140
1882	6,035,090	7,016,750	3,511,036	3,235,543	1,673,791	770,210	—	280,317	102,031	159,232
1881	5,577,997	6,278,595	3,177,375	2,878,424	—	701,781	—	272,407	93,344	128,587
1880	4,653,609	5,402,038	2,708,673	2,530,875	—	613,734	—	255,558	77,115	107,866
1879	4,416,511	4,872,018	2,395,647	2,310,489	—	525,621	—	216,545	61,681	112,238
1878	4,166,332	4,772,297	2,292,258	2,297,791	—	490,103	302,528	187,575	53,629	103,161
1877	4,180,192	4,806,202	2,313,279	2,255,319	—	472,909	301,933	170,977	58,556	98,821
1876	4,086,653	4,468,592[b]	2,248,359	2,105,141	937,025	497,258	310,805	186,453	68,040	93,560
1875	—	4,658,209	2,198,601	2,459,607[c]	—	503,066	—	185,506	74,294	—
1874	—	4,221,764	1,990,997	2,230,766[c]	—	520,466	330,895	180,571	67,043	—
1873	—	3,784,543	1,947,639	1,836,904[c]	—	526,420	342,609	183,811	67,121	—
1872	—	3,159,423	1,647,844	1,511,579[c]	—	465,241	—	165,754	64,418	—
1871	—	2,664,628	1,481,450	—	—	403,329	—	141,746	56,457	—
1870	—	2,476,893	—	—	—	—	—	—	—	—
1869	—	2,041,226	—	—	—	—	—	—	—	—
1868	—	1,869,529	—	—	—	—	—	—	—	—
1867	—	1,172,881	756,223	416,658	—	334,000	228,700	105,300	32,125	—
1863	—	1,149,481	—	—	—	190,000	—	—	—	—
1861	—	763,678	—	—	—	130,000	—	—	—	—
1860	—	318,126	—	—	—	—	—	—	—	—
1855	—	—	424,792	299,263	—	84,250	42,802	—	—	—
1851	—	—	—	—	—	—	—	—	—	—
1850	—	—	—	—	—	39,566	—	—	—	—

a Includes other interest.   b Sum of capital stock, bonded debt, and $55,092,192 Pacific R.R., U.S. subsidiary bonds.   c Includes other debt.

TABLE 5. RAILROAD EMPLOYMENT AND WAGES: 1890-1910

YEAR	EMPLOYEES (IN THOUSANDS)	WAGES (IN THOUSANDS OF DOLLARS)
1910	1,699	1,143,725
1909	1,503	988,324
1908	1,436	1,035,438
1907	1,672	1,072,386
1906	1,521	900,802
1905	1,382	839,945
1904	1,296	817,599
1903	1,313	757,321
1902	1,189	676,029
1901	1,071	610,714
1900	1,018	577,265
1899	929	522,968
1898	875	495,056
1897	823	465,602
1896	827	468,825
1895	785	445,508
1894	780	—
1893	874	—
1892	821	—
1891	784	—
1890	749	—

TABLE 6. RAILROADS IN 1855—150 MILES AND OVER

NAME OF COMPANY	LENGTH OF ROAD	TOTAL COST OF ROAD & EQUIP.	GROSS EARNINGS	NET EARNINGS
Western, Mass.	155	$ 9,953,258	$1,763,944	$ 718,703
New York Central	534	28,523,913	6,563,581	3,162,126
New York and Erie	464	33,439,431	5,488,993	2,627,118
Pennsylvania	256	17,158,495	3,409,192	1,977,533
Sudbury and Erie	269	2,075,650	In progr.[a]	—
Baltimore and Ohio	382	22,218,849	3,711,453	1,601,090
Manasses Gap	165	In progr.	—	—
Wilmington and Weldon	162	—	—	—
Wilm'gton & Manchester	171	2,330,877	339,800	151,064
Greenville & Columbia	165	1,999,080	214,865	206,774
South Carolina	203	7,133,848	1,363,008	788,862
Georgia	211	4,416,991	906,694	532,110
Georgia Central	191	3,833,140	1,280,570	645,774
Memphis and Charlest'n	288	3,563,362	176,484	102,016
Mobile and Ohio	527	3,666,991	In progr.	—
Miss. Central	188	628,303	In progr.	—
New Orl., Opelousas & G. W.	350	1,825,812	In progr.	—
Nash. and Chattanooga	151	3,843,694	316,000	112,177
Atlantic & Gt. Western	254	613,231	In progr.	—
Cleveland and Toledo	200	5,124,629	736,272	396,986
Mad River and L. Erie	205	4,446,661	—	—
Ohio and Penn.	187	5,670,700	1,111,626	662,117
Tol., Wabash & St. Louis	242	—	In progr.	—
Cin., Logansport, and Chicago	255	2,080,433	In progr.	—
New Albany and Salem	288	6,643,189	645,827	371,402
Chicago and Rock Isl'd	182	5,214,152	In progr.	—
Chicago and St. Louis	220	—	1,077,312	—
Chic., St. Paul & F'd du Lac	178	3,625,000	In progr.	—
Galena and Chicago	298	5,866,263	1,506,710	942,231
Illinois Central	707	17,698,099	In progr.	—
Terre Haute and Alton	173	3,537,424	In progr.	—
Detroit and Milwaukee	185	1,966,969	In progr.	—
Mich. Central	282	10,300,147	2,215,283	879,656
Mich. South'n & N. Ind.	475	11,645,208	2,410,000	875,000
Green Bay, Mil. & Ch.	155	1,193,765	In progr.	—
Milwaukee and Miss.	200	2,704,593	465,051	307,632

[a] [In progress, i.e., under construction.]

TABLE 7. RAILROADS IN 1883—500 MILES AND OVER

RAILROADS	LENGTH OF LINE OPERATED [a]	ENGINES	CARS PASS.	CARS BAGG., MAIL & EXP.	CARS FREIGHT	COST OF ROAD AND EQUIP.	GROSS EARNINGS	NET EARNINGS
N. Y. Central and Hudson R.	953	655	460	176	25,181	147,804,779	30,363,991	9,613,397
N. Y., Lake Erie and W'ern	1,026	569	354	113	29,534	159,155,124	22,802,247	7,357,664
Pennsylvania	1,314	795	463	145	20,079	61,771,025	32,017,813	13,696,400
Philadelphia and Reading	1,077	907	802	120	54,368	42,482,722	28,275,973	13,906,168
Baltimore and Ohio	595	637	342	89	17,510	54,044,480	11,579,839	5,432,183
Chesapeake and Ohio	512	169	41	26	4,934	61,449,814	3,906,792	1,306,858
Norfolk and West.	501	107	36	21	2,205	31,334,572	2,812,777	1,103,203
Central of Ga.	730	60	64	72	1,932	12,400,000	3,613,856	1,275,332
Mobile and Ohio	527	81	32	13	1,259	20,852,281	2,271,059	630,033
E. Tenn., Va. & Ga.	1,025	158	87	33	3,746	83,699,918	3,776,754	1,318,284
Nashville, Chatta. & St. L.	554	83	40	19	1,862	16,511,912	2,283,523	1,008,668
Louisville and Nashville	746	374	204	88	10,416	67,385,426	5,879,116	2,869,686
Lake Shore & Michigan S.	1,340	553	174	117	16,492	84,000,000	18,513,656	7,511,803
N. Y., Chicago & St. Louis	523	108	36	14	6,694	70,504,635	2,327,684	638,389
Michigan Central	1,468	396	1,186	82	11,094	30,759,378	14,009,767	4,268,128
Chic., St. Louis & Pittsb.	581	190	68	40	3,170	40,506,255	4,044,876	837,322
Ohio and Miss.	616	114	62	33	2,302	38,668,800	4,250,150	980,321
Wabash, St. Louis & Pacif.	3,540	614	251	123	20,016	117,625,082	16,915,121	3,584,195
Chicago and Alton	850	228	99	34	6,528	23,584,747	8,810,610	3,930,652
Chicago and Northwestern	3,465	578	296	128	18,114	135,088,904	24,081,834	10,009,318
Chic., Burlingt'n and Quincy	3,255	542	253	97	18,860	137,729,911	26,116,369	12,613,891
Chic., Rock Island & Pac.	1,381	309	154	49	7,489	57,720,673	12,189,903	5,080,087
Illinois Central	1,928	340	223	86	8,169	37,475,076	13,064,743	6,069,492
Indiana, Bloomington & W.	697	110	74	39	3,414	24,727,266	3,022,366	1,109,692
Chic., Milwaukee & St. P.	4,549	657	311	196	19,712	146,093,665	23,659,823	9,881,785
Chic., St. Paul, Minn. & Om.	1,192	181	72	39	4,841	49,993,541	5,515,285	1,891,458
Northern Pacific	1,497	289	118	56	7,450	149,693,520	7,855,459	2,518,529
St. Paul, Minn. & Manitoba	1,203	201	108	52	4,753	44,812,236	9,148,524	4,805,531
Burlingt., Cedar Rapids & N.	702	78	27	24	2,798	18,175,635	2,863,555	895,378
Union Pacific	1,821	342	201	78	66	157,391,04 0	21,002,542	10,648,002
Atchison, Top. & Santa Fe	1,821	349	167	70	9,371	96,629,182	14,117,348	7,369,130
Missouri Pacific	990	155	85	29	4,622	39,950,939	9,153,731	4,175,266
Missouri, Kansas & Texas	1,368	161	50	36	4,115	66,448,676	7,843,511	3,197,008
St. Louis and San Francisco	735	85	31	28	2,879	41,384,219	3,896,565	2,073,436
St. Louis, Iron Mount & S.	905	138	60	45	4,692	52,743,550	7,904,683	3,690,120
Galve'n, Harrisb. & San A.	746	113	77	23	3,149	49,707,720	3,686,767	1,416,721
Houston and Texas Central	522	6	31	21	1,771	26,531,095	3,251,876	1,508,105
Internat'l & Gt. Northern	775	74	36	19	1,477	27,867,110	3,435,969	954,252
Texas and Pacific	1,487	165	73	24	2,847	62,404,552	7,045,652	1,648,007
Denver and Rio Grande	1,559	242	108	81	5,797	58,271,089	7,361,546	2,618,434
Oregon Railway & Navig.	550	51	21	8	957	30,856,995	5,946,363	2,896,930
Central Pacific	3,004	235	267	59	4,661	148,871,325	24,744,421	8,094,149
Atlantic and Pacific	605	30	55	15	1,000	46,017,320	—	—

[a] Figures often for main line only. See note with Table Source, p. 18.

SOURCES

TABLE 1. U.S. Bureau of the Census, *Historical Statistics of the United States, Colonial Times to 1957* (Washington, D.C., U.S. Government Printing Office, 1960), p. 427.

TABLE 2. U.S. Bureau of the Census, *Historical Statistics of the United States, Colonial Times to 1957* (Washington, D.C., U.S. Government Printing Office, 1960), p. 428.

TABLE 3. U.S. Bureau of the Census, *Historical Statistics of the United States, Colonial Times to 1957* (Washington, D.C., U.S. Government Printing Office, 1960), p. 428.

TABLE 4. U.S. Bureau of the Census, *Historical Statistics of the United States, Colonial Times to 1957* (Washington, D.C., U.S. Government Printing Office, 1960), p. 428.

TABLE 5. U.S. Bureau of the Census, *Historical Statistics of the United States, Colonial Times to 1957* (Washington, D.C., U.S. Government Printing Office, 1960), p. 437.

TABLE 6. Compiled from *American Railroad Journal,* 1856.

TABLE 7. Compiled from "Statement of the Mileage, Capital, Operations, etc., of the Railroads of the U.S., for 1883," *Poor's Manual of Railroads,* 1884. This source often includes statistics only for a road's main line. Rarely is a road's total mileage indicated. In 1883, for example, the New York Central fully controlled the Lake Shore; the Michigan Central; the New York, Chicago and St. Louis (the Nickel Plate); the Cleveland, Columbus, Cincinnati and Indianapolis (474 miles); the Canadian Southern (434 miles); and some smaller roads. The total mileage it operated was well over 5,000 miles. The Pennsylvania's mileage listed includes only the Philadelphia to Pittsburgh division. In addition it operated 2,338 more miles east of Pittsburgh and 3,211, west of that city. Other small lines gave it a total of close to 7,000 miles. The Baltimore and Ohio ran more than 600 miles of branches in the East and controlled the Ohio and Mississippi for a total of close to 2,500 miles. The Erie's branches added over 600 miles to the track it operated.

PART I

The Railroads As Promoters of Economic Change

INTRODUCTION

⟦ THE RAILROAD began to have a revolutionary effect on the American economy in the decade of the 1850's. Although the locomotive had its first run in America in 1830, only a year after George Stephenson had proven the practicality of applying steam to moving goods and passengers overland, the railroad remained for many years a novel and relatively inefficient means of land transportation. By 1850, however, uniform methods of construction, grading, and bridging had been perfected. The iron *T* rail of today had come into common use, and the boiler on wheels pulling stage coaches had taken on a modern look. The locomotive had its cab, sandbox, cowcatcher, driver wheels, swivel or bogie truck, and equalizing beams. The coaches had become "long" cars carrying sixty passengers on reversible seats. The box, cattle, lumber, and other freight cars were smaller but otherwise little different from those used today. ⟧

During the 1840's severe economic depression as well as technological deficiencies slowed the adoption of railroad transportation. By the close of 1841, 3,500 miles of road had been constructed. By the end of 1848, there was still less than 6,000 miles of track in the United States, and most of the mileage built during the intervening period was in New England, the region least affected by the depression. Then, between 1849 and the coming of the Civil War, railroad mileage expanded five times, so that 30,600 miles of track had been completed by the end of 1860. ⟧

These few years, then, witnessed the construction of the basic railroad network east of the Mississippi River. Particularly significant were the completion of the four great east-west trunk lines and the very rapid railroad-building in the Old Northwest. Between 1851 and 1854 the Erie, the Baltimore and Ohio, the Pennsylvania, and the New York Central all provided roads under single managements between the Atlantic seaboard and the Western waters. The Old Northwest, which in 1849 had only 600 miles of track, enjoyed a system of 10,000 miles by 1860. In 1849 Chicago had only one short line. By 1854 that city had become the leading railroad center in the United States with several alternate routes to the Eastern seaboard and with rail connections to four places on the Mississippi River (see map).

⟦ As part of its impact on the American economy, this sudden growth of a new transportation system stimulated the swift settlement of the Old Northwest. One railroad analyst, Henry Varnum Poor, told an audience in 1854:

The pioneer, as he moves forward over the prairie of the west, carries with him the railway—as necessary to his life as are the axe and the plough. The railway keeps pace with the frontier line of settlement; so that the crop of this year of a frontier farm, in the great march of civilization, has only to be held to the next, to be sent whizzing to the Eastern market at a speed of thirty miles to the hour.

The railroad opened this area partly by making it reasonably accessible to settlers, but even more, as Poor stressed, by giving its agricultural crops cheap and quick access to Eastern and European markets. The resulting "Northwestern surge" was in Allan Nevins' opinion "the most decisive for the American future" of all the developments of the critically decisive decade of the fifties. By 1860 Illinois, Indiana, and Wisconsin had replaced Pennsylvania, Ohio, and New York as the leading wheat-growing states in the Union. They had also become major livestock producers. These areas that were so quickly opened to commercial agriculture became at once important markets for goods manufactured at home or abroad and also for tea, sugar, coffee, and other foods imported from more tropical climates.

These new flows of wheat, manufactured goods, and imported foodstuffs altered the course of American commerce. Before the railroad boom of the 1850's the commercial axis of the United States ran between New Orleans and New York. The great majority of the agricultural products of the vast Mississippi Valley went east via New Orleans, and a sizable portion of manufactured and other products moved west through the same port. By 1860 Chicago had replaced New Orleans as the emporium of the West, and the east-west routes were beginning to carry as much traffic as did river and coastal shipping. The trunk lines even took over much of the trade of the Southwest. For example, the Pennsylvania Railroad running between Pittsburgh and Philadelphia carried in 1857 very little cotton. In 1858 it transported 5.7 million pounds. The next year the figure had risen to 17.9 million and in 1860 to 28.7. By the outbreak of the Civil War cotton was a major business for the Pennsylvania.

The railroad brought as significant changes to America's industries as it did to its agriculture and commerce. In the first place, the railroads became a major market for iron and other industries. By the 1860's they were taking close to half the iron rolled in the United States, and as late as 1880 three-fourths of the steel produced in this country went into rails alone. More significant than output was the revolution that the new demand for iron in large quantities caused in its making. The use of coal to mass-produce iron had been practiced abroad ever since Henry Cort developed his process in Britain at the end of the eighteenth century. In the United States, however, the market remained the village blacksmith and the town artisan who wanted a high-quality malleable wrought iron best produced by charcoal and the forge. Iron-making establishments had remained small, with the furnace near sources of wood and ore and the forge and finishing mill located close to transportation. The railroad created the first demand that was large enough to permit the adoption of mass-production methods. Anthracite coal or coke made from bituminous coal replaced charcoal in the blast furnace, while the coal-using reverberatory furnace took the place of the forge. The mills now had all processes carried on in one location. And nearly every one of the new large integrated mills, which appeared for the first time in the second half of the 1840's and in the 1850's, concentrated on the production of rails. Also, the railroad-engendered iron mills and the railroads themselves intensified the demand for bituminous coal, so that the amount mined rose from 2.7 million tons in 1847 to 9.1 million in 1859. The railroads too became large users of machine tools, of copper, glass, India rubber, felt, and animal and mineral oils.

Nevertheless, the second or indirect influence of railroads on American industry was probably more profound than their direct impact as a great new market. The railroads, by bringing down costs of transportation, lowered the final cost of manufactured goods in a number of industries and so increased the demand for their products. Still more important was the continuous and relatively steady flow of raw materials into and finished goods out of American factories that the coming of the railroad, telegraph, and steamship made possible. The adoption of mass-production methods, particularly in the making of consumer durables, had been prevented before 1850 by the slowness and the uncertainty in the movement of goods and the communication of commercial dispatches. This was particularly true in the winter months when the canals were frozen and storms harried the coastal waters. As in the case of iron, mass-production techniques had long been known. The methods developed about 1800 by Eli Whitney for making small arms through the assembling of interchangeable parts were used before the late 1840's only to fill large government contracts for guns and pistols. Then during the 1850's, as the railroads and steamships opened up new markets and assured steady supplies of materials, these techniques were adopted to mass-produce shoes, clothing, clocks, watches, locks, sewing machines, harvesters and other agricultural implements, and also guns and revolvers for customers other than the American military forces.

To measure statistically the full impact of the transportation revolution in which the railroads played the leading role is an extremely difficult task. The stimulus the railroads gave to the westward movement, to the expansion of wheat and cattle production, to the coming of new commercial routes, and to the adoption of mass-production methods in the manufacture of iron and consumer durables is almost impossible to pin down with precise, meaningful figures. But while economists may argue as to the extent to which the railroads affected the nation's income and product, few deny that the railroad was a significant force in the growth of the American economy during the second half of the nineteenth century.

The following readings illustrate and document this significance, particularly in the years following 1850. The first selection, entitled "Influence of Railroads upon Agriculture," was published in the introduction to the volume on agriculture in the Census of 1860. It reveals the great importance contemporaries gave to the influence of railroads on the development of agriculture and the course of commerce in the United States. While its analysis of prices is somewhat naive by current standards, most of the data the census supplies are useful and relevant.[1] The second set of selections indicates the direct effect the railroads had on industry by providing a new market for the iron trade. In the first of these readings, Louis C. Hunter, an authority on the history of iron, describes the "revolution in the iron industry" that occurred after 1845 and demonstrates the critical part played by the railroads in these changes. Hunter's remarks are followed by an analysis of the iron market in the early 1870's that was printed in one of the industry's standard manuals. It emphasizes the value the iron manufacturers placed on

1 A careful analysis of price changes and their beneficiaries can be found in Thomas S. Berry, *Western Prices Before 1861* (Cambridge, Mass., 1943), especially Chapters 5, 7, and 8.

the railroad demand. Space does not permit the presentation of readings on the indirect effect of the new form of transportation on American industry. Instead, a passage has been selected from Walt W. Rostow's *Stages of Economic Growth,* one of the most important recent studies on growth. Rostow suggests the vital role played by railroads not only in the economic development of the United States but also of many other parts of the world. In the first of these passages he defines what he means by the "take-off" into self-sustained growth and in the second he indicates where and how the railroad was the "leading sector" in this "take-off."

THE READINGS

1] Their Impact on Agriculture and Commerce

. . . .

W E NOW proceed to show the positive advantages which all departments of agriculture have derived from the construction of railroads.
So great are their benefits that, if the entire cost of railroads between the
Atlantic and western States had been levied on the farmers of the central
west, their proprietors could have paid it and been immensely the gainers.
This proposition will become evident if we look at the modes in which
railroads have been beneficial, especially in the grain-growing States. These
modes are, first, in doing what could not have been effected without them;
second, in securing to the producer very nearly the prices of the Atlantic
markets, which is greatly in advance of what could have been had on his
farm; and, third, by thus enabling the producer to dispose of his products
at the best prices at all times, and to increase rapidly both the settlement
and the annual production of the interior States. A moment's reference to
the statistics of internal commerce will illustrate these effects so that we
can see the vast results which railroads have produced on the wealth and
production of the country.

1. If we examine the routes and tonnage of the trade between the Atlantic cities and the central western States, we shall find some general
results which will prove the utter incapacity of all other modes of conveyance to carry on that trade without the aid of railroads. Between Lake
Erie on one side and the Potomac on the other, the commerce between
the east and west is altogether carried on by way of several great arteries,
which are these, viz.: the Erie canal, the Oswego canal, the Champlain
canal, the Central railroad, the Erie railroad, the Pennsylvania railroad,
and the Baltimore and Ohio railroad. There are no other great channels
of conveyance between the east and the west, and in fact no other routes
appear practicable. However large an amount of product or merchandise
may be carried by the lakes, it must be shipped to or from Buffalo, Oswego,
or Ogdensburg. However multiplied may be the routes by rail or canal,
by which products may arrive at Buffalo, Pittsburg, Wheeling, or Parkers-
burg, all the freights carried over them going east must pass over these
great routes. We have, therefore, the means of determining accurately the
relative transportation by different routes and modes. The different modes

FROM U.S. Census Office, "Influence of Railroads upon Agriculture," *Census of 1860,
Agriculture* (Washington, D.C., 1863), pp. clxv–clxix.

are all reduced to two—canals and railroads. The proportion of tonnage on these several lines of conveyance, as reported in 1862, was as follows:

CANALS

	TONS
Erie canal	2,500,762
Oswego canal	852,920
Champlain canal	650,000
Aggregate	4,003,682

But, we must observe that the Oswego canal joins to the Erie canal, and its tonnage, arriving at or leaving Albany, is included in that of the Erie canal. In fact, the tonnage of the canals, which is counted at Albany, is only that of the Erie and the Champlain, and of the latter but a small portion goes to or from the west. We have at the utmost, then, the carriage on canals between the Atlantic cities and the west of 3,150,000 tons.

RAILROADS

	TONS IN 1862
Pennsylvania railroad	1,792,064
Erie railroad	1,632,955
New York Central railroad	1,387,433
Baltimore and Ohio (estimated)	1,200,000
Aggregate tonnage of these lines	6,018,452

We observe that in 1862 the tonnage of the six great arterial lines of transportation between the east and west amounted to over nine millions of tons, of which only one-third were carried by water. We must recollect that this was the case when the Erie canal of New York had been enlarged and refitted with the express purpose of transporting the products of the west, and was supplied with five thousand canal-boats. It is evident, therefore, that railroads not only carry two-thirds of the freights to and from the west at the present time, but that such is the rapid increase of western products, and the surplus carried to Atlantic or foreign markets, that the time is near when all that can be carried by water will be but a small proportion of the whole. The transportation by wagons is no longer possible to carry the surplus products of the interior States to either foreign or domestic markets. In fine, in the absence of railways the cultivation of grain beyond the immediate wants of the people must cease, or the surplus perish in the fields. Such was exactly the state of things in the west before the general introduction of railroads. The great grain-fields of Ohio, Indiana, Illinois, and beyond the Mississippi, have been mainly cultivated because railroads made their products marketable and profitable. In one word, railroads did what could not have been done without them.

2. Railroads secured to the producer very nearly the prices of the Atlantic markets, which was greatly in advance of any price which could possibly be obtained in western markets. It might be supposed that if the carriage

of a bushel of grain from Sandusky to New York was reduced from forty cents a bushel to twenty cents, the gain of twenty cents would inure, in part at least, to the consumer; but experience shows this is not the fact. This gain of twenty cents inures to the producer. In proof of this it will be sufficient to adduce two or three well-known facts. The prices of flour and meat at New York (estimating them at the gold standard) have not been reduced in the least, notwithstanding the immense quantities of the products of grain imported into that city. On the other hand, the prices at Cincinnati, on the Ohio, have doubled, and in some articles, such as pork, have trebled. The great bulk of the gain caused by the cheapness of transportation has gone to the producer. This depends on a general principle, which must continue to operate for many years. The older a country is, the more civic and the less rural it becomes; that is, the greater will be the demand for food, and the less the production. The competition of the consumer for food is greater than that of the producer for price. Hence it is that Europe, an old country, filled with cities, makes a continual demand on this country for food. Hence it is that New England and New York, continually filling up with manufacturers, artisans, and cities, must be supplied with increased quantities of food from the interior west; and hence, while this is the case, prices cannot fall in the great markets. Hence it is that the cheapening of transportation inures to the benefit of the agricultural producer. New England consumes more than a million barrels of western flour. The transportation is cheapened a dollar per barrel; and thus, in New England alone, in the single item of flour, a million of dollars, net profit, is put into the pockets of the western farmer by the competition of railroads; for a large portion of this flour is carried over the Massachusetts Western railroad. It is entirely true that the manufacturer of New England shares, on his side, in the gain of cheap transportation; but we are here considering simply the influence of railroads on agriculture.

In the western markets the gain to the farmer is palpable in the enhanced prices of every article. At Cincinnati, in 1848 and 1849 (which was the beginning of the greatest railroad enterprises), the average price of hogs was $3 per hundred. In 1860 and 1861 it was double that, and has continued to increase. This was a net gain to the farmers of Ohio alone of from three to four millions of dollars. In the entire west it was a profit of more than twenty millions on this single animal; for, if there were now no railroads, this product could not be carried to market except on foot, which would take away half the value. No further illustration of this point need be made. Take the market prices of New York and Boston, on the Atlantic, and of St. Louis and Cincinnati, in the west, at an interval of twenty years, and it will be seen that the cheap prices of the west have gradually approximated to the high prices of the east, and this solely in consequence of cheapening the cost of transportation, which inures to the benefit of the farmer.

3. By thus giving the farmer the benefit of the best markets and the highest prices, railroads have increased the agricultural productions of the interior States beyond anything heretofore known in the world. We have already shown that this increased production, or rather its surplus, could

not have been carried to market without the aid of railroads, more than two-thirds of the whole being carried off by that means. Let us now reverse this operation, and we find, on the other hand, that railroads have stimulated and increased production. The northwestern States are those in which the influence of railroads on agriculture is most obvious. In the five States of Ohio, Indiana, Illinois, Michigan, and Wisconsin there were comparatively few miles of railroad prior to 1850; but from 1850 to 1860 the construction of roads was most rapid. In 1850 there were only 1,275 miles of railroad in those States, but in 1860 there were 9,616 miles. Let us now examine the products of those States in 1850 and 1860, and see how the progress of railroads has sustained and stimulated agricultural production. The following table shows the increase of the principal vegetable and animal production in the five States of Ohio, Indiana, Illinois, Michigan, and Wisconsin in the ten years from 1850 to 1860:

	IN 1850 (IN BUSHELS)	IN 1860 (IN BUSHELS)	INCREASE PER CENT
Wheat	39,348,495	79,798,163	100
Corn	177,320,441	280,268,862	58
Oats	32,660,251	51,043,334	50
Potatoes	13,417,896	27,181,692	100
Cattle	3,438,000	5,371,000	59

This increase is decidedly beyond that of the population; showing that the products of agriculture are, in those States, profitable. The aggregate of grain products in those States was:

| In 1850 | 255,240,444 bushels [1] |
| In 1860 | 422,369,719 bushels [1] |

What part railroads have had in carrying this product to market we shall see by ascertaining the surplus, and the manner in which it was transported. The commissioner of statistics [2] for the State of Ohio, in his report to the legislature of Ohio, estimates (in the actual carriage of railroads and canals) that *three-fifths* of the value of agricultural products of Ohio are exported, excepting, of course, pasturage, fruits, garden products, &c. In 1859–'60, twelve millions of bushels of wheat were exported from that State, and an equal proportion of corn, reduced into other forms, such as fat cattle, hogs, pork, lard, whiskey, cheese, &c. Three-fifths of the aggregate grain production of these five States (1860) will give two hundred and fifty millions of bushels of grain. This is vastly greater than the whole tonnage of canals and railroads, and would, therefore, seem incorrect. This, however, is not so. The heaviest article (corn) is reduced to a fourth, perhaps, less weight by being changed into whiskey, pork, and cattle. The same is true of oats, and thus the ten millions of tons represented by the canals and railroads may cover all the surplus which finds the extreme

1 Includes wheat, rye, corn, oats, barley, and buckwheat.
2 Edward D. Mansfield.

eastern markets. A large quantity of the surplus products of these States is consumed in way-markets. We see now, that, since railroads carry two-thirds of this immense export, they represent nearly or quite the same proportion of the capacity of those States to raise any surplus, and therefore two-thirds of the profit made upon it. If we now consider the question of the profits of agriculture, the case becomes still stronger. The actual cash value of the products carried to market from these five States (that is, the surplus) is two hundred millions of dollars, and it is safe to say that one-half this sum is due to the influence of railroads. There are some interesting facts on this subject, to some of which we will briefly allude. Take, for example, the prices of both products and lands in the interior States, and compare them at different periods. Forty years ago (1824–'25) the surplus products of Ohio had already accumulated beyond the means of transportation. In consequence of this fact, wheat was sold in the interior counties, for 37 cents per bushel, and corn at 10 cents. After the New York canal (Erie) was finished, in 1825, and the Ohio canals several years later, these prices were raised more than fifty per cent; but when two or three of the main railroad lines were finished in 1852–'53, the rise in prices and the amount carried forward to the eastern markets were even more increased. To show, in some measure, the effect of the improved means of transportation on the value of produce in the interior, we make the following table of prices at Cincinnati at several periods:

		IN 1826 [3]	IN 1835	IN 1853	IN 1860
Flour	$3.00 per barrel		$6.00	$5.50	$5.60
Corn	0.12 per bushel		0.32	0.37	0.48
Hogs	2.00 per cwt		3.12	4.00	6.20
Lard	0.05 per pound		0.08	0.08½	0.11

We find that in 1860 the price of flour was nearly double that of 1826; the price of corn nearly four times as much; the price of hogs three times as much, and the price of lard double. From 1835 to 1860 (when the railroads were completed), under the influence of railroad competition with canals the price of corn advanced 50 per cent, and that of hogs 100 per cent. Perhaps no articles can be selected which furnish a more complete test of the value and profits of farming in the States of the northwest than that of these staples, corn and hogs.

But there is another respect in which the influence of railroads is almost as favorable to agriculture as that of cheapening the transportation of produce. It is that of cheapening the transportation, and therefore reducing the prices of foreign articles and eastern manufactures consumed by the farmers of the interior. We need not adduce tables to illustrate this; for it is quite obvious and well known that this has been the effect, though perhaps not to so great an extent as the reverse, in the case of produce. In 1839–'40 sugar was just the same price as in 1857 and 1858; but the average price of coffee from 1833 to 1838 was three cents higher than it was from 1853 to 1860. On the whole, the prices of articles carried from the

3 The prices of 1826 are from "Drake & Mansfield's Cincinnati, 1826."

east to the west were diminished, while those from the west to the east were increased. Again, the influence of railroads on the value of farming lands is too great and striking not to have been noticed by all intelligent persons. We have, however, some remarkable instances of the specific effect of certain railroads; we have, for example, the immediate effect produced on the lands of Illinois by the Illinois Central railroad. That company received from the government a large body of land at a time when the government could not sell it at a dollar and a quarter ($1.25) per acre. Since then the company has constructed its road and sold a large part of those lands at an average of $11 per acre, and the greater part of the lands of Illinois is fully worth that. Notwithstanding the rapid growth of population, the larger part of this advance is due to railroads. The following table shows the advance (by the census tables) of the cash value of farms in the five States mentioned in the ten years from 1850 to 1860:

	1850	1860
Ohio	$358,758,602	$666,564,171
Illinois	96,133,290	432,531,072
Indiana	136,385,173	344,902,776
Michigan	51,872,446	163,279,087
Wisconsin	28,528,563	131,117,082
Aggregate	671,678,075	1,738,394,188
Increase in ten (10) years		$1,066,716,113

It is not too much to say that one-half this increase has been caused by railroads, for we experience already the impossibility of conveying off the surplus products of the interior with our railroads. Putting the increase of value due to railroads at a little more than one-third, we have four hundred millions of dollars added to the cash value of farms in these five States by the construction of railroads. This fact will be manifest if it is considered that the best lands of Illinois were worth but a dollar and a quarter per acre prior to the construction of railroads, and are now worth twenty dollars.

We need not pursue this subject further. If the effect on the central western States has been so great, it is still greater in the new States which lie beyond the Mississippi. They are still further from market, and will be enriched in a greater ratio by the facilities of transportation. Indeed, railroads are the only means by which the distant parts of this country could have been commercially united, and thus the railroad has become a mighty means of WEALTH, UNITY, and STABILITY.

2] Their Impact on Industry

a] THE CHANGE IN IRON MANUFACTURE

. . . .

THE FINAL stage in the centralization of the iron manufacture, the establishment of blast furnaces at the rolling-mill centers of the country, was dependent on two factors: the adaptation of mineral coal as a smelting fuel and access to new and ampler ore supplies. The substantial beginnings of this stage date from the forties and fifties, but it was not until the decades following the surrender at Appomattox that the transition gained momentum. The shift from charcoal as a blast-furnace fuel got under way first in the iron region of eastern Pennsylvania during the thirties, stimulated by the growing scarcity of charcoal and the availability of anthracite coal, and was made technically practical through the use of the hot blast. By 1860 nearly 100 blast furnaces in eastern Pennsylvania used anthracite coal as fuel and in the country as a whole the output of anthracite iron had passed that of charcoal iron.

The introduction of bituminous coal proceeded more slowly in the trans-Appalachian region. The delay in its adoption was not due simply to the abundance of timber (contrary to the accepted view, cheap timber did not mean cheap charcoal), nor to prejudice of consumers and producers but, above all, to the fact that wrought iron made from coal or coke pig iron was not so well adapted to the agricultural uses to which iron was put in the West as the charcoal-smelted product. For general blacksmithing purposes, the toughness, malleability and capacity for welding of charcoal-smelted iron made it much preferred to that made from coal or coke pig iron. The latter product first found general acceptance in rolling mills engaged in the manufacture of rails. By 1860 bituminous coal and coke were well established as blast furnace fuels in the major pig-iron districts of the West.

The successful introduction of coal in blast-furnace practice removed a major obstacle to the scale of operation heretofore imposed by both technical and transportation difficulties connected with the use of charcoal. Typical weekly yields of 25 to 30 tons of iron from the old-style charcoal blast furnaces were before 1860 dwarfed by yields of as high as 300 tons from the much larger furnaces developed to make use of mineral coal. With greatly enlarged furnace capacity and the trend toward centralization of pig-iron production in rolling-mill centers, the problem of supply of raw material shifted from fuel to ore. The widely distributed but shallow

FROM Louis C. Hunter, "Revolution in the Iron Industry," in Harold F. Williamson, ed., *Growth of the American Economy*, 2d ed. (Englewood Cliffs, N.J., 1951), pp. 177–79. © 1951, by permission of Prentice-Hall, Inc., Englewood Cliffs, N.J.

deposits of ore that served the rural pig iron industry were quite inadequate to the great and expanding needs of the coal and coke blast furnaces. At first the enlarged blast-furnace plants were located near the more extensive ore deposits of the older iron districts, but an industry capable of meeting the needs of a nation in process of industrialization could not attain permanency until the great ore ranges of the Lake Superior country were discovered and made accessible. Not only was the ore of the five great ranges from Marquette to Mesabi present in masses of near-mountain proportions, some of which were admirably adapted to exploitation by opencut and stripping methods, but its metallic content was much above that of the ores of the older iron districts, often half to twice again as large.

The problem of transporting the ore to the rising iron districts of eastern Ohio and western Pennsylvania some 600 to 1,000 miles away was solved by two major innovations: the development of specialized ore steamships and extraordinarily efficient ore-handling equipment at loading and unloading docks on the Great Lakes, and by the construction of ore-carrying railroads to and from the lake ports. Not until the completion of the original Soo Canal in 1855 did the development of the Superior ores get under way. By 1860 nearly one-tenth, 10 years later fully one-fourth of the pig iron manufactured in the United States was made from Lake Superior ore. The center of iron production, which had long rested in eastern Pennsylvania, moved gradually to the trans-Appalachian region. Pittsburgh, with inexhaustible supplies of unsurpassed coking coal at its doorsteps, prepared to assume the dominant position in the nation's iron industry. The erection of its first blast furnace in 1857, using coke fuel and ore drawn by water and rail from the distant ore fields of Missouri and Lake Superior, marked the beginning of a new era in the iron manufacturing of the entire country.

Associated with the changes in technique of production were changes in the use of and demand for iron. Blacksmith's bar and nail iron receded steadily in importance before iron in the variety of forms and shapes required for industrial purposes, above all those growing out of the introduction of steam power in transportation. By 1850 if not earlier the railroad had become the leading industrial outlet for iron and within 10 years after the Civil War one-half of the iron consumed in the United States was employed in railroad construction and maintenance. The manufacture of rails for the rapidly expanding railway network of the country led to a virtual revolution in blast-furnace and rolling-mill practice. Early rails were merely heavy strap iron, differing only in size from the ordinary run of merchant bar turned out by the typical rolling mill. As the demand for rails assumed vast proportions and strap rails gave way to rails with U- or T-shapes, specialized rail mills on a large scale were established to meet the demand. The rolling of shaped rails called for new and specialized rolling equipment and enlarged power plants as well as iron of a quality better adapted to the manufacture of rails and more economical than that suited to merchant bar. Some of the largest rail mills operated their own blast-furnace plants to supply them with crude metal.

The first rail mills were erected in the middle forties and 10 years later a full score were in operation, of which the largest were located in Pennsylvania, where two-thirds of the total product in the country was rolled prior to 1860. West and south of Maryland the rail mills were small in number and capacity and were engaged chiefly in rerolling worn rails. In 1860 the annual output of these mills totaled 235,107 tons, absorbing close to one-fourth of the pig iron of the country and surpassing bar iron in importance. Outstanding among the rolling mills of the fifties were the Phoenix Rolling Mills in eastern Pennsylvania, and the Cambria Iron Works in western Pennsylvania. Of the three rolling mills comprising the Phoenix plant, the rail mill with its 36 heating and puddling furnaces and three trains of rolls quite overshadowed the other two works, turning out 18,592 tons of rails in 1856. The Cambria Works at Johnstown, Pennsylvania, was the largest integrated rail mill in the country. Its 30 puddling furnaces were supplied with pig metal by one charcoal and six coke furnaces, and from its four trains of rolls in 1857 came 17,808 tons of rails. The first wrought-iron girders were rolled in the decade before the Civil War, but the age of structural iron was still in the future.

b] THE GROWTH OF THE IRON TRADE

A REVIEW of the few portions of the iron trade presented in this volume, presents some startling facts for the consideration of even those who are tolerably well acquainted with the magnitude of our industry. Without claim to absolute accuracy, but with every possible effort to that end, and basing our statements upon those of individual manufacturers taken in the aggregate, we present here a record of *seven hundred and thirty-five* blast furnaces, all capable of making iron, and most of which are engaged in its production for a greater or less portion of the year. These are located in twenty-four different States, and possess, according to the statements of their owners, a capacity of *four million six hundred and twenty-four thousand nine hundred and eighty-nine tons* (4,624,989 tons) of pig-iron annually. The natural inference from a statement of such magnitude is, that our capacity must be fully up to our ability of consumption, and that, when the amount of our imports is taken into consideration, is in excess; hence, that the iron trade must flag. Not so.

An experienced manufacturer has shown us that the total mileage of railroads in the United States, was, January 1st, 1873	80,194
The mileage constructed during 1873 is estimated at	3,000
Giving a total mileage to date of	83,194

FROM Thomas Dunlap, "The Iron Market," in *Wiley's American Iron Trade Manual of the Leading Iron Industries of the United States* (New York, 1874), pp. 10–12.

This number of miles of railroad required for construction and equipment per mile as follows:

	TONS
For track	100
For locomotives	25
For cars	20
For sundries	5
Total iron required per mile	150

Eighty-three thousand one hundred and ninety-four miles of road, at 150 tons per mile, have therefore required and used, up to January 1st, 1874, 12,479,100 tons of iron. The amount annually required to keep this mileage of road and equipment in repair, was estimated by good judges at 10 per cent of the gross consumption originally. Actual statistics since have shown it to be not under 14 per cent, at which ratio the repairs demanded by the above 12,479,100 tons already consumed in railroads, represents an annual requirement of 1,747,074 tons of iron. Leaving out of the question for the present the item of increased annual mileage, since the financial troubles of 1873 have temporarily restrained the construction of railways, we add, from the same source, a few of the other principal iron-consuming industries. These figures, while approximately correct, are beneath the mark, but serve to bear out our statement. There are annually demanded of iron for—

	TONS
Gas and water pipes	190,000
Stoves and hollow ware	250,000
Mowers and reapers (actual for 1872)	33,000
Other agricultural implements	150,000
Ship-building (far too low)	40,000
Miscellaneous castings	600,000
Sewing-machines (actual in 1872)	33,083
Nuts and bolts	250,000
Nails and tacks	250,000
Architectural iron	150,000
	1,946,083
Add for railways, as above	1,747,074
Add for increase in industry since 1872, 5 per cent of consumption	97,304
	3,790,461
Allowing the ratio of railway increase to be only 5 per cent for 1874, which would represent only a little over 4,000 miles of road to be built in that year, we have to add for this at the rate of 150 tons per mile	623,850
Total	4,414,311

Now, when we take into consideration the fact that this admitted blast-furnace capacity of 4,624,989 tons does not represent an actual production of over 2,695,434 tons, and at best cannot possibly represent more than a production of 3,000,000 tons, we have a consuming demand of 1,414,311 tons to be supplied from importation and scrap-iron re-melted or heated. The importations of pig metal for the fiscal year ended June 30, 1873, were but 241,356 tons. Hence we may safely estimate, from a purely commercial basis, guided by the rules of natural demand, and keeping in view the constantly increasing requirements of iron for all uses as a substitute for wood, that the blast-furnace capacity of our country cannot possibly be in excess of our home necessities, much less, without a marked increase, afford a surplus for exportation. The value and importance of this product to our people, may be more clearly understood by computing the money value of the material and product in currency. A production of 2,695,434 tons represents a consumption of 5,390,868 tons of ore, which, at the very moderate valuation of $6 per ton, equals an expenditure of $32,345,208. It further represents a consumption of 4,043,151 tons of fuel, which, at $2.50 per ton, cost $20,215,573; and of limestone, of $1,347,717. The usual furnace estimate for labor is $3 per ton, which would represent for the above product $8,086,302, and for interest, repairs, contingencies, etc., $4 per ton, of $10,781,736, or a total expenditure made by this industry, in the production of 1873, for its material, etc., of $72,776,536, or over half the interest on our national debt. The money value of this product, averaging the price of all kinds of pig metal for the year at $35 per ton—a fair estimate when the price of charcoal iron and the product is considered—will represent a total money value added to the products of industry, of $94,340,190. Nothing could more clearly indicate the importance of the industry than these figures, and when the immense area of our country abounding in mineral deposits and yet entirely undeveloped is considered, it is clear that even this value is as nothing to that of the next decade.

Next in order as represented in this volume, is the wrought-iron product, which is represented by 309 rolling mills in active operation, located in 23 States, and showing a *capacity* of 2,823,700 tons of rolled iron. Of this capacity, 1,470,500 tons are rails, and the remainder, 1,273,200 tons, bar, plate, sheet, hoop, and other rolled iron.

The production of rails in 1873 is estimated to have been 850,000 tons, and of other rolled iron, 980,000 tons, giving a total of 1,830,000 tons of iron made by rolling mills in the year. This would represent a money value for rails, at $70 per ton, of $59,500,000, and of other rolled iron, at $100 per ton, a low figure, of $98,000,000, or a total value of $157,500,000, which, added to the value of the pig metal produced in 1873, viz., $94,340,-190, gives a total value of $251,841,190, to which is to be added an additional value of $50 per ton on 120,000 tons of rails, which were of BESSEMER steel, at $120 per ton, or $6,000,000, making a grand total of $257,841,190 to be credited to these two branches of the iron trade alone—a money value which may well astonish those not familiar with the great industries here represented. Taking, however, the figures of rolled iron in detail, we find reported and estimated by the Iron and Steel Association as follows:

	TONS
Merchant bar and rod iron	400,000
Sheet and plate	250,000
Hoop	30,000
Nails and spikes	200,000
Axles, etc.	100,000
	980,000

Append to these the actual selling prices for November, the lowest rate
of any month of 1873, and we find the following actual market value for
the product at the seaboard at that date to have been—

	TONS	PER TON	TOTAL
Bar and rod iron	400,000	$ 75	$30,000,000
Sheet and plate iron	250,000	150	37,500,000
Hoop iron	30,000	145	4,350,000
Nail and spike iron	200,000	95	19,000,000
Axles, etc.	100,000	140	14,000,000
Total valuation			104,850,000
Add value of rails			65,500,000
Value of all rolled iron for 1873			$170,350,000

And this at the lowest prices of the year, which total added to the pig
metal also taken at same date, will give $264,690,190.

.   .   .   .

3] Their Impact on the Economy

The Achievement of Regular Growth

WE TURN now to analyse narrowly that decisive interval in the history
of a society when growth becomes its normal condition. We consider
how it comes about that the slow-moving changes of the preconditions period, when forces of modernization contend against the habits and institutions, the values and vested interests of the traditional society, make a
decisive break-through; and compound interest gets built into the society's
structure.

. . . Take-offs have occurred in two quite different types of societies;
and, therefore, the process of establishing preconditions for take-off has
varied. In the first and most general case the achievement of preconditions
for take-off required major changes in political and social structure and
even in effective social values. In the second case take-off was delayed not
by political, social and cultural obstacles but by the high (and even expanding) levels of welfare that could be achieved by exploiting land and

FROM Walt W. Rostow, "The Take-off," *The Stages of Economic Growth* (Cambridge, Eng.,
1960), pp. 36–38, 52–53, 55–56. Reprinted by permission of Cambridge University Press.

natural resources. In this second case take-off was initiated by a more narrowly economic process as, for example, in the northern United States, Australia and, perhaps, Sweden. And, you will recall, as one would expect in the essentially biological field of economic growth, history offers mixed as well as pure cases.

The beginning of take-off can usually be traced to a particular sharp stimulus. The stimulus may take the form of a political revolution which affects directly the balance of social power and effective values, the character of economic institutions, the distribution of income, the pattern of investment outlays and the proportion of potential innovations actually applied. Such was the case, for example, with the German revolution of 1848, the Meiji restoration in Japan of 1868, and the more recent achievement of Indian independence and the Communist victory in China. It may come about through a technological (including transport) innovation, which sets in motion a chain of secondary expansion in modern sectors and has powerful potential external economy effects which the society exploits. It may take the form of a newly favourable international environment, such as the opening of British and French markets to Swedish timber in the 1860's or a sharp relative rise in export prices and/or large new capital imports, as in the case of the United States from the late 1840's, Canada and Russia from the mid-1890's; but it may also come as a challenge posed by an unfavourable shift in the international environment, such as a sharp fall in the terms of trade (or a war-time blockage of foreign trade) requiring the rapid development of manufactured import substitutes, as with the Argentine and Australia from 1930 to 1945.

What is essential here is not the form of stimulus but the fact that the prior development of the society and its economy result in a positive, sustained, and self-reinforcing response to it: the result is not a once-over change in production functions or in the volume of investment, but a higher proportion of potential innovations accepted in a more or less regular flow, and a higher rate of investment.

The use of aggregative national-income terms evidently reveals little of the process which is occurring. It is nevertheless useful to regard as a necessary but not sufficient condition for the take-off the fact that the proportion of net investment to national income (or net national product) rises from, say, 5% to over 10%, definitely outstripping the likely population pressure (since under the assumed take-off circumstances the capital/output ratio is low),[1] and yielding a distinct rise in real output *per capita*. Whether real

---

[1] Capital/output ratio is the amount by which a given increase in investment increases the volume of output: a rough—very rough—measure of the productivity of capital investment; but since the arithmetic of economic growth requires some such concept, implicitly or explicitly, we had better refine the tool rather than abandon it. In the early stages of economic development two contrary forces operate on the capital/output ratio. On the one hand there is a vast requirement of basic overhead capital in transport, power, education, etc. Here, due mainly to the long period over which investment yields its return, the apparent (short-run) capital/output ratio is high. On the other hand, there are generally large unexploited back-logs of known techniques and available natural resources to be put to work; and these back-logs make for a low capital/output ratio. We can assume formally a low capital/output ratio for the take-off period because we

consumption *per capita* rises depends on the pattern of income distribution and population pressure, as well as on the magnitude, character and productivity of investment itself.

As indicated in the accompanying table, we believe it possible to identify at least tentatively such take-off periods for a number of countries which have passed into the stage of growth.

TABLE 1. SOME TENTATIVE, APPROXIMATE TAKE-OFF DATES

COUNTRY	TAKE-OFF	COUNTRY	TAKE-OFF
Great Britain	1783–1802	Russia	1890–1914
France	1830–60	Canada	1896–1914
Belgium	1833–60	Argentina[c]	1935–
United States[a]	1843–60	Turkey[d]	1937–
Germany	1850–73	India[e]	1952–
Sweden	1868–90	China[e]	1952–
Japan[b]	1878–1900		

a The American take-off is here viewed as the upshot of two different periods of expansion: the first, that of the 1840's, marked by railway and manufacturing development, mainly confined to the East—this occurred while the West and South digested the extensive agricultural expansion of the previous decade; the second the great railway push into the Middle West during the 1850's marked by a heavy inflow of foreign capital. By the opening of the Civil War the American economy of North and West, with real momentum in its heavy-industry sector, is judged to have taken off.

b Lacking adequate data, there is some question about the timing of the Japanese take-off. Some part of the post-1868 period was certainly, by the present set of definitions, devoted to firming up the preconditions for take-off. By 1914 the Japanese economy had certainly taken off. The question is whether the period from about 1878 to the Sino-Japanese War in the mid-1890's is to be regarded as the completion of the preconditions or as take-off. On present evidence we incline to the latter view.

c In one sense the Argentine economy began its take-off during the First World War. But by and large, down to the pit of the post-1929 depression, the growth of its modern sector, stimulated during the war, tended to slacken; and, like a good part of the Western world, the Argentine sought during the 1920's to return to a pre-1914 normalcy. It was not until the mid-1930's that a sustained take-off was inaugurated, which by and large can now be judged to have been successful despite the structural vicissitudes of that economy.

d Against the background of industrialization measures inaugurated in the mid-1930's the Turkish economy has exhibited remarkable momentum in the past five years founded in the increase in agricultural income and productivity. It still remains to be seen whether these two surges, conducted under quite different national policies, will constitute a transition to self-sustaining growth, and whether Turkey can overcome its current structural problems.

e As noted in the text it is still too soon to judge either the present Indian or Chinese Communist take-off efforts successful.

.   .   .   .

are assuming that the preconditions have been created, including a good deal of social overhead capital. In fact, the aggregate marginal capital/output ratio is likely to be kept up during the take-off by the requirement of continuing large outlays for overhead items which yield their returns only over long periods. Nevertheless, a ratio of 3:1 or 3.5:1 for the incremental capital/output ratio seems realistic as a rough bench-mark until we have learned more about capital/output ratios on a sectoral basis.

Leading Sectors in the Take-off

The overall rate of growth of an economy must be regarded in the first instance as the consequence of differing growth rates in particular sectors of the economy, such sectoral growth-rates being in part derived from certain overall demand factors (for example population, consumers' income, tastes etc.); in part, from the primary and secondary effects of changing supply factors, when these are effectively exploited.

On this view the sectors of an economy may be grouped in three categories:

1. Primary growth sectors, where possibilities for innovation or for the exploitation of newly profitable or hitherto unexplored resources yield a high growth-rate and set in motion expansionary forces elsewhere in the economy.

2. Supplementary growth sectors, where rapid advance occurs in direct response to—or as a requirement of—advance in the primary growth sectors; for example coal, iron and engineering in relation to railroads. These sectors may have to be tracked many stages back into the economy.

3. Derived-growth sectors, where advance occurs in some fairly steady relation to the growth of total real income, population, industrial production or some other overall, modestly increasing variable. Food output in relation to population and housing in relation to family formation are classic derived relations of this order.

In the earlier stages of growth, primary and supplementary growth sectors derive their momentum essentially from the introduction and diffusion of changes in the cost–supply environment (in turn, of course, partially influenced by demand changes); while the derived-growth sectors are linked essentially to changes in demand (while subject also to continuing changes in production functions of a less dramatic character). . . .

At any period of time it appears to be true even in a mature and growing economy that forward momentum is maintained as the result of rapid expansion in a limited number of primary sectors, whose expansion has significant external economy and other secondary effects. From this perspective the behaviour of sectors during the take-off is merely a special version of the growth process in general; or, put another way, growth proceeds by repeating endlessly, in different patterns, with different leading sectors, the experience of the take-off. Like the take-off, long-term growth requires that the society not only generate vast quantities of capital for depreciation and maintenance, for housing and for a balanced complement of utilities and other overheads, but also a sequence of highly productive primary sectors, growing rapidly, based on new production functions. Only thus has the aggregate marginal capital/output ratio been kept low.

Once again history is full of variety: a considerable array of sectors appears to have played this key role in the take-off process.

The development of a cotton-textile industry sufficient to meet domestic requirements has not generally imparted a sufficient impulse in itself to launch a self-sustaining growth process. The development of modern cotton-textile industries in substitution for imports has, more typically, marked the pre-take-off period, as for example in India, China and Mexico.

[Rostow then discusses the famous exception of Britain's industrial revolution.]

The introduction of the railroad has been historically the most powerful single initiator of take-offs.[2] It was decisive in the United States, France, Germany, Canada, and Russia; it has played an extremely important part in the Swedish, Japanese and other cases.

The railroad has had three major kinds of impact on economic growth during the take-off period. First, it has lowered internal transport costs, brought new areas and products into commercial markets and, in general, performed the Smithian function of widening the market. Second, it has been a prerequisite in many cases to the development of a major new and rapidly enlarging export sector which, in turn, has served to generate capital for internal development, as, for example, the American railroads before 1914. Third, and perhaps most important for the take-off itself, the development of railways has led on to the development of modern coal, iron and engineering industries. In many countries the growth of modern basic industrial sectors can be traced in the most direct way to the requirements for building and, especially, for maintaining substantial railway systems. When a society has developed deeper institutional, social and political prerequisites for take-off, the rapid growth of a railway system, with these powerful triple effects, has often served to lift it into self-sustained growth. Where the prerequisites have not existed, however, very substantial railway building has failed to initiate a take-off, as for example in India, China, pre-1895 Canada, pre-1914 Argentina, etc.

It is clear that an enlargement and modernization of armed forces could play the role of a leading sector in take-off. It was a factor in the Russian, Japanese and German take-offs; and it figures heavily in current Chinese Communist plans. But historically the role of modern armaments has been ancillary rather than central to the take-off.

2 For a detailed analysis of the routes of impact of the railroad on economic development see Paul H. Cootner, *Transport Innovation and Economic Development: The Case of the U.S. Steam Railroads* (1953), unpublished doctoral thesis, M.I.T. (Cambridge, Mass.).

PART II

The Beginnings of
Modern Corporate Finance

INTRODUCTION

❡ As CREATORS of new institutions and new patterns of business activities, the railroads probably played a more important role in the growth of the American economy than they did by more directly stimulating national income and productivity. For railroad promoters and managers were the first Americans to build and administer the really large business enterprise. Nearly all the unique problems that they faced and nearly all the resulting new patterns of economic actions were related directly to the unprecedented size of the individual railroad corporations.

The first problem every railroad promoter or executive faced was the raising of formidable amounts of money. This challenge became particularly acute with the sudden expansion of the railroad network after 1850. For not only did many different roads begin simultaneously to seek funds, but the individual companies were larger and in need of more capital than the earlier ones. In 1849 no railroad company in the United States operated more than 250 miles of road, and only a few ran more than 100 miles. By 1855 at least sixteen (see Table 6), railroads were working over 200 miles of road, and the four trunk lines were moving at least twice as much traffic as the largest road in the country had moved five years earlier. Similarly, only two roads were capitalized at as much as $10 million in 1850. By 1859 at least ten had a capital account of that size, and five had sold

securities totaling twice that amount. No other business enterprise had ever required money in that kind of magnitude. The largest and most successful canals—New York's Erie and Champlain —had been built for about $7.5 million. Turnpikes and steamboats were, of course, much less expensive. In fact a new, fully equipped river steamboat cost about as much as a single mile of well-built railroad. In 1850 very few of even the largest manufacturing companies required as much as a million dollars to finance.

In their earlier years many railroads, like canals, had relied on financial aid from state governments. The depression of the late 1830's and early 1840's, however, convinced many disgruntled taxpayers that state-supported internal improvements resulted only in high taxes with little improvement in transportation to show for them. Many state constitutions were then amended to prohibit the use of state funds to finance railroads or canals. In the 1850's, promoters therefore turned to local county, town, or city aid or to the federal government. In that decade and the next Congress made lavish land grants to a number of Western roads. Although these grants became a major political issue and so still loom large in American history texts, federal aid assisted in the building of only 8 per cent of the nation's railroad system.[1] State, munic-

[1] Those interested in evaluating the significance of federal aid should read Vernon

ipal, and county aid was in the long run more significant than federal assistance. As in the case of federal land grants, local public funds often provided the initial impetus to build a new road.

Nevertheless, private investors contributed much more capital to the construction of American railroads than did public bodies. Of course, private investors were the final purchasers of most state and local securities sold to finance railroads and canals but, from the 1850's on, by far the largest share of railroad financing came directly from private sources. At first the private investors were usually individuals living in a road's termini or along its line who believed they had much to gain from its construction. They normally purchased shares of stock in the road, often paying for them by providing land or labor. Except in the more industrial and urban Northeast, local capital was rarely enough to complete construction. Most railroad promoters and builders had to resort to the distant investor who lived far from the line of the road, either in the Eastern cities or in Europe. Such an investor was much more interested in a steady return on his money than in improving transportation facilities. He usually rejected stock in favor of bonds, which appeared to offer a more certain return. As a result nearly all American roads, again except in the Northeast, were capitalized more by bonds than by stock. Moreover, the continuing demand for funds led roads in the 1850's to issue many different kinds of bonds. First-, second-, and third-mortgage bonds, debenture, convertible, and even real-estate bonds were issued and traded before 1860. Preferred stock too was first used as a device for financing

R. Carstensen, ed., *The Public Lands: Studies in the History of the Public Domain* (Madison, Wisc., 1963), pp. 121–79.

railroad construction, although it only became widely adopted in the 1890's, when it was used as a substitute for bonds in the many reorganizations of that period.

The sudden need of many railroads for large sums of money in the early 1850's not only brought into use a variety of financial instruments but also created or expanded the activities of a number of financial institutions. Local banks played an important part in providing capital to railroads, and local stock exchanges began to trade in railroad securities. But since outside capital was so essential to provide the necessary funds, the centralizing and institutionalizing of the nation's money and investment markets on Wall Street was a far more significant development. In winning financial supremacy over Boston and Philadelphia (Chicago in 1850 was still a frontier town), New York had the advantage of being the nation's largest commercial port and the city with the closest and most numerous ties to the capital-exporting countries of Europe. Nevertheless, its sudden rise as the nation's financial center in the early 1850's resulted from a concatenation of specific events that occurred in the late 1840's, including the Irish and German famines, the Mexican War, the European revolutions of 1848, the California gold rush, and the over-expansion of railroad and manufacturing in both England and New England.

Because New York took the lead in financing American railroads, its Stock Exchange rapidly expanded after 1850 as securities of railroad corporations in all parts of the country began to be listed and traded on its floor. At the same time the modern investment banking house made its first appearance. Since the promoters of many roads in the South and West could not possibly have tracked down all of the Eastern and European investors they needed, and since such investors were often unable to evaluate the securities offered to them, leading private banking and mercantile firms began to specialize as middlemen in railroad finance. They bought and sold railroad securities, acted as financial agents for a number of roads, and served as investment advisers to men with surplus capital.

From the 1850's on, the investment banker played a critical role in American railroading and in the overall development of the American economy. In a very real sense, he allocated the investment capital available in America and Europe among its many seekers. Because he controlled the flow of funds, he often had much to say about the affairs of the roads he helped to finance. When a road overextended itself financially, his position became paramount. Thus, from the depression of the late 1850's to that of the mid-1890's, investment bankers arranged for the financial and often the administrative reorganization of American railroads.

By the latter part of the century, J. Pierpont Morgan had become the most powerful of these investment bankers. Morgan carried out the regular functions of his trade—the buying and selling of securities, the underwriting of new issues, and the advising of clients on their investment portfolios. His greatest contribution to American railroading and indeed to the American economy was, however, the financial and administrative reorganization of the many roads that had overextended themselves and fallen into bankruptcy during and after the fierce competition of the 1870's and particularly of the 1880's. Investors asked Morgan to revive financially the roads whose mortgages they held. In such a reorganization Morgan and his partners usually reduced the large bonded debt, consoli-

dated smaller lines into the larger centralized system, and sought to lessen the threat of competition by buying into adjoining roads. Successful in railroad consolidation, Morgan soon began to play a similar role in American industry. His firm assisted in the formation of General Electric, United States Steel, International Harvester, Allis-Chalmers, and other industrial giants. And where Morgan led, other investment bankers soon followed.

Morgan's enormous financial power and prestige rested on the confidence of investors. Morgan's roads paid while others did not. Even more significantly, investors invariably compared Morgan's performance to those of bankers and brokers who put their own immediate profit ahead of the interests of either the railroads or investors. Jay Gould, Jim Fiske, Russell Sage, Calvin Brice, George I. Seney, and William P. Clyde had given Wall Street a deserved reputation for chicanery and shady deals. These men quickly learned that high profits could be made from railroads in other ways than providing transportation. They used their inside positions to manipulate stock prices, and they bought and sold roads in the South and West without ever leaving their Wall Street offices. Thus when Morgan began negotiating to reorganize a bankrupt road William P. Clyde spoke up. "Well, Mr. Morgan, I've bought Richmond Terminal at 7 or 8 and sold it at 15 twice in the last few years. I see no reason why I shouldn't do it again. So I fear I cannot join with the others in asking you to deal with the property."

Financiers more reputable than Clyde joined with the speculators to form construction companies to build railroads and formed land companies to buy land, town sites, or mineral properties along the line of their roads. For example, a construction company made up of some of a projected railroad's directors would contract to build that road for a lump sum to be paid for by the road's securities. The construction company would use these securities as collateral for the actual cash needed for construction. Since the stock they had received as payment gave them control of the road itself, they could raise the price to be paid for construction whenever it pleased them. As the profits came from construction, these directors were not disturbed when the road became bankrupt in trying to pay off its high construction costs. In such a way these ancillary activities often yielded more profit than the roads themselves. After the completion of the railroad network and the reorganization of many railroad systems, opportunities for speculation and exploitation by insiders lessened. Long before that time, however, such speculative manipulation had raised a loud and clear cry for reform.

An intimate relationship between the railroads and courts and legislatures throughout the land intensified this demand for reform. Such a connection was inevitable since every step in building and financing a railroad required legislative sanction. Even if a railroad did not seek public support, it needed corporate charters, often in several states, if it was to raise money through sales of stocks and bonds or to take land by eminent domain. Moreover, because the corporation had never been used before on such a widespread scale as a means of controlling such large amounts of men, money, and materials, the charters were often vague and imprecise as to permissible policies and procedures. Indeed it was this very vagueness and imprecision that gave many a railroad financier or speculator his opportunity to exploit a privileged position as a director or transfer agent. Even after the rules of the game had been more

carefully defined, particularly in general incorporation laws for railroads, the need for legislative sanction and support remained.

This need attracted railroad promoters, financiers, or their agents to the state capitals and even to Washington. Often a railroad like the Pennsylvania or the Camden and Amboy was said to control its state legislature. Just as often different railroad "parties" contended with one another for privileges or protection from the legislature. State senators and representatives might legitimately support one railroad party or another, as legislative favors could profoundly affect the economic and business fortunes of their local communities. Too often, however, they were willing to be convinced of their interest by an outright bribe. Even though protests against such corruption and collusion between railroads and legislators grew loud, the resulting demands for reform had relatively little impact until large groups of merchants and farmers became directly affected by rate and service discrimination resulting from railroad competition. Then moral indignation reinforced self-interest to play a significant part in bringing the passage of the initial regulatory legislation.

The readings presented in this section indicate why and how the railroads pioneered in the complex ways of modern corporate finance. In the first selection two experts on railroad finance, Frederick A. Cleveland and Fred W. Powell, survey its constructive and exploitive aspects. They describe both public and private sources of support and indicate the methods and instruments used in this financing. They also indicate the workings of "inside" construction and land companies.

The selections following that by Cleveland and Powell trace in more detail the historical development of railroad financing and particularly of the institutionalizing and centralizing of the nation's investment and speculative activities on Wall Street. The first of these comes from the *American Railroad Journal,* whose editor, Henry Varnum Poor, reported each week from New York during the early 1850's about the railroad's most essential requirement—money for construction. Poor's editorials not only described the ways of marketing securities in the rapidly growing investment market but warned both railroad men and investors against the new breed of speculators. He urged the railroad builders and both foreign and American investors to use "responsible American houses" that were beginning to specialize in marketing securities for railroad companies and in purchasing them for men seeking sound investments. In Poor's opinion no firm was more responsible and more reputable than Winslow, Lanier and Company, one of the very first modern investment banking houses in this country. The next selection is taken then from the autobiography of that firm's senior partner. James F. D. Lanier, an influential Indiana banker who moved to New York in 1848, tells how his house pioneered in marketing the securities of new Western roads and how, after the depression of 1857, it carried out one of the earliest financial reorganizations of a large railroad.

The third and fourth selections indicate both the constructive and destructive aspects of railroad finance in the years following the Civil War. Then financiers like Daniel Drew and Jay Gould realized Poor's worst fears about the potential dangers from the speculator and manipulator. On the other hand, J. P. Morgan and Company carried out the more legitimate activities originally developed by Lanier on a wider and much grander scale. The selections by Charles Francis Adams, Jr., from the classic "A Chapter of Erie," written in 1869, picture two types of plungers. One, represented by Daniel Drew, cared only for stock manipulation; the other, Commodore Vanderbilt, had a broader vision. He used Wall Street to make money but also to build a large, powerful, and profitable business empire. Vanderbilt, as Adams pictured him, had the drive, ruthlessness, and optimism that characterized the empire builders who did so much to mold the American industrial economy. Adams also describes the corrupt alliance between railroads and state legislatures as it existed in its most flagrant form. "A Chapter of Erie" was itself one of the earliest and most effective protests against the corrupting influence of speculative directors. The fourth selection indicates how Morgan, pursuing the role initially created by Lanier, helped financially to revive a large number of bankrupt roads, including those exploited by speculators such as Drew, Gould, Fiske, Brice, and Clyde.

THE READINGS

1] Financing Construction

Promotion and Underwriting

· · · · · · · · · · · · ·

The Nature of the Financial Support Obtained

In General. The different kinds of financial support which have been attracted to railroad enterprises are of three broad classes: subsidies, funds contributed by investors, and funds contributed by speculators. Subsidies have been granted in various forms by individuals, by local and state governments, and by the national government. Investors in railroad securities have not always been individuals; during the early period many a local and state government advanced capital not alone to give needed support to a much needed transportation project but on the theory that it would acquire a right to participate directly in the profits of a lucrative business when the railroad should be constructed and in operation. Generally speaking, investors are of two classes: those who have put their money into local projects with which they are personally familiar, and those who have taken shares or bonds representing properties which have been investigated or are represented by financial agencies. Speculation has contributed a large share. The capital which has found its way into the market through speculative channels has not come from any particular class of individuals. There have always been professionals who have purchased securities with the idea of unloading on a rising market, and there have always been victims of the exaggerated representations of promoters.

Individual Subsidies. Individual subsidies have been given in the form of subscriptions to cover the expense of surveys, releases of rights of way, and donations of land, stone, gravel, timber, and other materials. Many individual subscriptions were nothing but subsidies. Such were the subscriptions made in response to appeals upon the basis of public benefit rather than private profit; such also were the subscriptions of merchants whose desire was for larger and more active business, and the subscriptions of farmers who were attracted by the prospect of higher prices for their products and easier access to market. These subscriptions were paid not only in money but also in land, labor, and materials, and by notes secured by farm mortgages.

Local Subsidies. Local subsidies have been granted in all sections of the country to an extent which is practically impossible of determination. All

FROM Frederick A. Cleveland and Fred W. Powell, "Promotion and Underwriting" and "Finances of Construction," *Railroad Finance* (New York, 1912), pp. 30–33, 50–62, 64. Copyright 1912 by D. Appleton & Co., 1940 by Fred Wilbur Powell. Reprinted by permission of Appleton-Century.

communities wished to share in the business prosperity which followed the opening of new railroad connections, and cities and towns needed little urging upon the part of promoters to induce them to become financially interested in their projects. They have endorsed the bonds of railroad companies, and exchanged their bonds for bonds of railroad companies and for railroad shares. Local subsidies have also been given in the form of donations of money, bonds, and lands. Throughout the West it was once the common practice to donate land for station sites and yards.

State Subsidies. States, also, have given generous support to railroads. Maryland was heavily interested in the Baltimore and Ohio, New York in the New York and Erie, and Massachusetts in the Western railroad. Virginia early adopted the policy of taking three-fifths of the share capital of all railroads within its borders, and Louisiana similarly subscribed to the extent of one-fifth. For a short time Ohio subscribed to one share for every other subscription for twice that amount to the share capital of railroads within the state. Few Northern states, however, gave aid in the form of share subscriptions. The loan of credit was the most widely used form of state subsidy in all parts of the country. Massachusetts authorized loans to the amount of over $11,000,000 to eight railroads; New York, of over $8,000,000 to nine railroads. During the reconstruction period in the South, legislatures voted away the credit of their states to an extent which ultimately gave but little range for choice between repudiation and insolvency. States have also guaranteed city bonds issued in aid of railroads; they have advanced loans out of special funds and out of the general treasury. Some of these loans bore no interest. Other forms of state aid were: direct appropriations to pay the expense of surveys, interest payments on railroad bonds, surrendered claims, and grants of land. Texas, which retained its public lands upon annexation to the United States, granted over 32,000,000 acres to railroads and internal improvements, chiefly railroads. Most of the state constitutions now forbid any loan of state credit, and many of them forbid state subscriptions to the shares of corporations. Over half, also, forbid local aid of any sort.

National Subsidies. National aid to railroads began with a provision in the tariff of 1830 for a drawback upon duties paid upon imported railroad iron; and from 1832 to 1842 complete exemption was allowed upon rails. In this way the railroads had profited to the extent of nearly $6,000,000 by 1843 when the system was abolished. Beginning in 1835 congress granted to certain railroads rights of way through the public lands, and in 1853 the privilege was made general. In 1850 congress granted lands to Illinois, Alabama, and Mississippi, to encourage the construction of a line of railroad from Mobile to Cairo and from Cairo to Chicago and Galena. The Mobile and Ohio and the Illinois Central were the final recipients of this bounty. With the act of 1850 began the system of congressional land grants to railroads through the medium of the states as trustees or agents of the transfer. As the railroads extended out into the territories, they received grants of land directly from congress. Altogether there were seventy-nine land grant railroads, and the lands within the limits of the original grants amounted to nearly 200,000,000 acres. This total has been reduced by forfeitures to less than 160,000,000 acres, title to nearly 110,000,000 acres of which has been established. The Northern Pacific alone received an acreage of about 44,000,000; an amount equal to the combined grants of the Union Pacific, Central Pacific, and Southern Pacific. The Atchison system received 17,000,000 acres; the Illinois Central, over 2,500,000 acres; and the Mobile and Ohio, over 1,000,000 acres.

Loans of Credit. Congress also granted direct financial aid by loaning $64,623,512 to six railroads to encourage the construction of a through line to the Pacific. The Pacific railroad acts of 1862 and 1864, besides granting large tracts of lands from the public domain, provided that thirty-year United States bonds be delivered as sections of the line should be completed. These bonds were secured by mortgage upon the railroad property. In accordance with these laws, $27,236,512 was received by the Union Pacific, $25,885,120 by the Central Pacific, $6,303,000 by the Kansas Pacific, $1,970,560 by the Western Pacific, $1,628,320 by the Sioux City and Pacific, and $1,600,000 by the Central Branch Union Pacific.

. . . .

Finances of Construction

Definition. Construction may be considered as the building of all the fixed properties used by a railroad in conducting the business of transportation. It pertains, therefore, to the roadway and structures as distinguished from rolling stock and other equipment. In its fullest sense it comprehends grading, tunneling, construction of bridges, trestles and culverts; purchase and laying of ties, rails, and other parts of the roadway including ballast; building and equipping of stations and office buildings, shops, and engine-houses, as well as water front structures and power plants. It also includes engineering, supervision, and inspection, and the acquiring of fee title to lands and right of way. Cost of construction may be understood as made up of outlays for building operations, plus interest on outlays during the construction period, less deductions for salvage and for charges for transportation during construction; in other words, the net expense to the railroad corporation.

Construction Financed Through Sales of Shares. Construction of the early local railroads was generally financed by means of the proceeds of sales of corporate shares. It was the practice to begin with subscriptions to share capital by persons interested in local manufacturing or commercial enterprises or by local investors who had accumulated savings or inherited small estates. These subscriptions were paid in cash; the shareholders as proprietors of the corporation thus held the chief beneficial interest in the properties, and they chose the directors from among their number in much the same manner as officers were chosen at a town meeting. This is particularly true of the New England railroads. The Eastern railroad of Massachusetts was built as far as the New Hampshire line by 1840, and the cost, amounting to $1,365,000, was met through sales of shares.[1] The Boston

[1] Annual report, 1875.

and Lowell was also built out of the proceeds of share sales; and no bonds were issued until nearly twenty years after the opening of the road.[2] In central New York, the Syracuse and Utica railroad was built at a cost of $700,000, or $100,000 less than the amount of subscribed share capital.[3] This was the method common to the railroads of the Atlantic seaboard states prior to 1840. Even the Pennsylvania railroad was begun with the idea that sales of shares would provide all the capital needed, but the task proved too great for the available investment funds of Philadelphia, and to prevent unprofitable delays the policy of the company was changed so as to limit the mortgage indebtedness to the amount of the share capital.

Supplementary Bond Issues. [In New England] the use of bond issues as a means of raising capital for construction was usually the result of miscalculation. Lack of engineering experience, indefiniteness of plans, estimates based upon the analogy of the turnpike; these were some of the most common causes of exhaustion of funds before completion of the work of construction. There arose, therefore, the problem of supplementary financing. Sometimes it was possible to obtain additional funds through the issuance of new shares, but where the local supply of investment capital made this impossible, there was no alternative but to issue long time obligations secured by mortgage giving to the new contributors prior claim against the corporate estate.

With all the unforeseen demands for additional capital, however, the bonded debt of the first American railroads was small indeed. Before 1850 the construction capital of roads built in New England was almost wholly obtained from sales of shares. This is clearly shown by their annual reports to shareholders. In 1849 the Providence and Worcester had outstanding $424,000 in bonds as against $1,166,000 in share capital. The Delaware, Lackawanna, and Western in 1854 had a paid share capital of $1,958,000 and a funded debt of only $900,000; the New Jersey railroad in 1855 reported a debt of only $317,000, with a share capital of $1,294,000; and the Cincinnati, Hamilton, and Dayton in 1855 showed a similar condition, with $965,000 in bonds and $2,100,000 in shares. When in 1848 it was proposed to extend the Louisa railroad into Richmond, only $40,000 could be raised from new subscriptions to capital shares, and the directors therefore issued bonds which they personally indorsed.[4]

Generally speaking, the disposition of the shareholders was to keep the indebtedness down to a small proportion of the total capital, and so insure control. This attitude was reflected in the report of the directors of the Michigan Central in 1854, when in discussing the necessity of providing for the floating debt either by an issue of bonds or by the sale of more shares they said, "We prefer the last named measure, and shall only resort to a further issue of bonds in case we find it impossible to sell our stock at par." And the Boston and Providence, though compelled to resort to an issue of bonds, gradually reduced its debt until in 1865 it amounted to only $21,500.

2 Annual report, 1853.
3 Wager, "Syracuse and Utica Railroad," Oneida Hist. Soc., *Transactions*, I, 153.
4 "Hist. of the Chesapeake and Ohio," 8.

Exchange of Shares for Land, Labor, and Materials. In the Middle West there was insufficient local capital in a form readily convertible into cash. The capital of the community was represented largely by farm improvements. The products of the farm, the forest, and the mine could not be readily marketed and converted into cash until after the introduction of improved methods of transportation. It was therefore impossible to finance railroad construction through cash subscriptions to shares. In recognition of this condition, there was resort to barter, or exchange of the shares of railroad companies for land, labor, and materials. To obtain the money needed, shares were exchanged for farm mortgages and other credit obligations which might be discounted. Thus, while the construction of the Bellefontaine and Indiana and of the Indianapolis and Bellefontaine lines was financed for the most part through the sale of capital shares, subscriptions were paid largely in land, and to some extent in labor and materials.[5] The weakness of this practice is at once apparent. It limited the activities of the management, and frequently caused loss to the farmers, with the result that the railroads were embarrassed through hostile legislative and administrative action.

Share Capital for Roadbed; Bonds for Rails and Equipment. When promoters were able to procure sufficient local subscriptions to share capital to complete the roadbed, they had a basis for credit which enabled them to dispose of bonds to provide for the rails and equipment. This was the plan followed by many railroads in the South and in the Middle West.[6] It was a natural and almost necessary method in communities where local capital was inadequate, and where subsidies were not available in amounts sufficient to serve as a guarantee to the non-resident investor. The use of bonds as a means of providing for original capitalization almost invariably indicated the presence of outside capital.

Subsidies as Collateral Aids to Capitalization. Subsidies have played an important part in the financing of construction. Before the railroad period, the lottery was in common use as a means of aiding enterprises which were public in their nature. But after the corporation had come into common use as an agency for assembling capital and controlling large enterprises, public sentiment changed; and the lottery privilege was granted in aid of but one or two railroad projects.[7] Popular interest was aroused sufficiently to warrant more substantial aid, and when share subscriptions were inadequate, or when additional evidence of support was desired as a means of attracting outside capital through the sale of bonds, public subsidies in the form of subscriptions to shares or of guarantees of bonds were granted by both state and local governments. There were also public and private subsidies in the form of donations of land for right of way and for yards and station sites, not to mention the larger grants of lands which were to be sold to raise funds for construction work. Perhaps the most important factor in keeping the capital cost of American railroads down to a figure

5 Cleveland and Powell, "Railroad Promotion," 198–201.
6 *Ibid.*, 197–8.
7 *Ibid.*, 167.

which is low by comparison with the railroads of Europe has been the American practice of donating lands for right of way. Another factor which has contributed to lower capital cost in the United States has been the power given to railroad corporations to obtain rights of way by eminent domain, whereas in England they were compelled to obtain their land by private bargaining.

Bonds Favored by Investors. Failure to build within estimates, calls for assessments to put in proper condition the inferior work turned over by contractors, and delays in the payment of dividends, eventually led investors to regard railroad shares as of uncertain value, and to put their savings into railroad bonds. Bonds, although they often proved to be in excess of the value of the property, were believed to be adequately secured not only by the priority of the claim held against the estate, but also by the prospective value of the territory which would be developed by the road. This attitude of mind led to an entirely new system of financing construction, as has been set forth by John P. Davis:

Railway bonds had much resemblance to government securities; the railways did not appear, at first blush, to be dependent on the efforts of individuals, but rather on the condition of the tributary country, and their income was quite similar to the taxes paid to the government. The investor in railway bonds seemed to be putting his faith not in a Vanderbilt or Gould, but in the manufacturers, farmers, producers, and consumers of the tributary territory upon which the roads depended for their success. The autocratic influence of "railroad managers" had not been appreciably exerted. The disastrous results of competition and "rate wars" had not yet been felt. If a railway could not pay the interest on its bonds, rates could be increased, and if it could pay the interest on its bonds, it could by a little more pressure on the tributary territory be made to pay some interest even on stock and more bonds. Thus the value of railways came to be determined not by the expense of building them, but by the amount of bonds and stock that their tributary territory could carry.[8]

Bonds Sold at Discount; Shares Given as Bonus. The facility with which public subsidy bonds and bonds of the railroads themselves were sold, suggested to promoters the possibility of building entirely out of the proceeds of bonds, keeping the shares for themselves as a source of future profit. The share capital was subscribed as before, in conformity with the law, but only a nominal cash payment was made to defray the expenses of obtaining the charter and of forming the preliminary organization. The bonds were then sold at ruinous discounts, or exchanged at extravagant prices for construction work, services, and materials. Shares were often given as a bonus to facilitate the placing of the bonds. In the end the promoters had control of the property, which had cost them little or nothing, and this property was mortgaged far in excess of its value. Their control over the share capital made it possible for them to declare unwarranted dividends, and thus to advance prices and so afford themselves opportunity to unload at a profit. The next logical step for the corporation was bankruptcy; and in the process of reorganization the bonds were scaled down

8 Davis, "Union Pacific," 197.

or subjected to heavy assessment. Such was the common course of railroad construction after about 1850.

Land Bonds. Land grant railroads have made every effort to sell their lands to provide funds for construction; but sales have usually been slow until after the completion of the road, and land bonds have been frequently issued instead. Sometimes the lands were included with the other property as part of the security for the first mortgage bonds, as in the case of the Mobile and Ohio.[9] Usually, however, a separate issue of securities was made. Thus the Chicago, St. Paul, and Fond du Lac issued $3,600,000 of land grant bonds,[10] and the Toledo, Wabash, and Western issued $450,000 of "real estate" bonds.[11] The Illinois Central set aside the greater part of its lands as security for the first mortgage bonds, and also reserved a large acreage as security for interest. The report for 1856 shows that while the company had $16,878,000 of bonds outstanding, only $3,258,000 had been paid in on its share capital. Receipts from the sales of lands were sometimes mortgaged, as in the case of the Atchison, Topeka, and Santa Fé, which in 1874 issued "land income" bonds.

Net Earnings Applied to Construction. With the early New England roads, the construction of which was financed by sales of shares, the practice was to use the net earnings from operation of the completed sections to pay dividends. After the introduction of bond construction, however, the practice was changed, the net earnings on the completed portions being generally applied to the property as an offset to cost. Many of the roads at the time they were completed had a large floating debt in the form of contractors' bills, unadjusted claims, and construction notes. These obligations, properly chargeable as part of the cost, in some instances were met by appropriations from earnings; in others they were funded by bond issues. Some of the companies attempted to carry them along without distinguishing between the floating debt incurred for construction and the floating debt incurred in operation.

Agencies of Construction

Construction Directly by the Railroad. In some instances construction was carried on by the railroad corporation itself as a construction company; as for example the Camden and Amboy, which reserved the work upon some of the more difficult sections of the road in order that they might be more quickly completed.[12] Generally speaking, however, there was resort to contracts. Circumstances have sometimes forced railroads into the work of construction. In the building of the Coal and Coke railway of West Virginia, because of the failure of the contractors, it was necessary for the company to take over one unfinished section of the road and with its own forces carry it to completion.[13]

9 *Amer. Railroad Jour.*, XXV, 515.
10 Annual report, 1857.
11 Annual report, 1856.
12 *Hazard's Register of Pa.*, VII, 361.
13 Annual report, 1905.

Early Railroads Built by Small Contractors. The earliest railroads were built by small contractors, but the results of this method were often unsatisfactory. As soon as the line was completed sufficiently to allow the operation of trains, it was surrendered to the company, which had then to make large additional expenditures to place the property in proper condition. After the completion of construction work upon the Boston and Maine, the directors reported: "Most of the work on the road was, at first, done by contract, and, of course, was less perfect than that done by the company. A great deal of the masonry, built by contract, has been rebuilt,—many whole bridges and culverts have been built in a much more substantial and thorough manner than they were at first; and on account of the imperfect manner in which the roadbed was graded and dressed, as originally done, it has become necessary to raise large portions of it from one to two feet; giving it a new dressing of gravel to protect it from frost, and keep the superstructure in surface. . . . The ties . . . used are larger and better than those laid down generally when the road was first built." [14]

Large Contractors and Construction Companies. At a very early period, construction work was let to large contractors, who would engage to build an entire line, subletting different sections to small contractors. Some of these companies also engaged to supply the equipment. In most instances they received part payment in securities of the road, and often in public subsidy bonds. Contracts on the New York and Erie were let subject to the provision that part payment would be made in shares at the market price.[15] In such instances part of the shares were carried in the treasury until they were issued under the terms of construction contracts. Contractors on the South Western railroad of Georgia received two-thirds of their payment in bonds and one-third in shares at par.[16]

Contract Work Paid for in Securities. Upon the Greenville and Miami railroad, half of the contractors' bills were paid in cash and half in shares and bonds of the company.[17] The North Missouri railroad appropriated for payment for construction, subsidy bonds issued by the state of Missouri, bonds of the city and county of St. Louis, and a small amount of capital shares.[18]

. . . .

The Dependent or "Inside" Construction Company. With the extension of railroads into the undeveloped portions of the West and South, the promise of adequate returns from operation was not sufficient to make the securities of the railroad company attractive to those to whom appeal was made for construction capital. Promoters therefore had to share with contractors, grants of government land and subsidy bonds of counties and

14 Annual report, 1849.
15 Report of the committee appointed to investigate the New York and Erie, 44–6. (1842.)
16 Annual report, 1853.
17 Annual report, 1853.
18 Annual report, 1855.

municipalities, or resort to the organization of subsidiary railroad construction companies. In consequence, the railroads in those sections of the country have been generally built not because they were needed, but because promoters saw opportunity for large immediate profits by building them. The customary procedure has been well described as follows:

The railway builder, urged on by the people whose towns, factories, and farms would be benefited by increased facilities of transportation, soon found, shrewdly enough, that he could usually build his road from the bonuses of the future patrons of the road, and the proceeds of the bonds that eastern investors, encouraged by glittering reports of the communities through which it was to pass, would invest in; then he would have the stock of the road and the privilege of operating it for the profit of his venture; if the road should be prosperous, his stock would be valuable; if not, he could at least contrive by some means to declare a dividend or two and unload his stock.[19]

Large Profits of Promoters. By strict interpretation of law as announced in judicial decisions, the amount of securities which may be issued has been limited to funds or properties acquired. But the freedom permitted in determining and stating cost has left the officers practically without limitation. The cost, as interpreted by those in control, was the amount of the capital issues. Except for charter restrictions there was no limit to the amount of bonds and share capital which promoters as directors of a railroad company might issue to themselves as proprietors of an inside construction company in payment for the road. Thus the par or nominal value bears little or no relation to the actual cost of the property. To Newton Booth we are indebted for this description of the manner in which railroads were built:

For many years it has not been the American fashion for the owners of railroads to put their own money into their construction. If it had been it would have insured a more conservative and businesslike use of that species of property. The favorite plan has been to get grants of land, and loans of credit from the General Government; guarantees of interest from the State governments; subscriptions and donations from counties, cities and individuals; and upon the credit of all this, issue all bonds that can be put upon the market; make a close estimate as to how much less the road can be built for than the sum of these assets; form a ring . . . for the purpose of constructing the road, dividing the bonds that are left; owning the lands, owning and operating the road until the first mortgage becomes due and graciously allowing the Government to pay principal and interest upon the loan of her credit, while "every tie in the road is the grave of a small stockholder." Under this plan the only men in the community who are absolutely certain not to contribute any money are those who own and control it when it is finished. The method requires a certain kind of genius, political influence, and power of manipulation, and, furnished one clew to the reason why railroads "interfere in politics." The personal profit upon this enterprise is not a profit upon capital invested, but the result of brain work—administrative talent they call it—in a particular direction.[20]

19 Davis, 198.
20 Booth, "The Issue of the Day;" speech at San Francisco, August 12, 1873: 4–5.

Use of Privileged Information for Personal Profit. Promoters gained or lost upon their ventures in railroad construction as they were able to unload their inflated securities upon the public; but there were many other opportunities open to them which seldom failed to bring a profit. There were the land grants, which they sometimes dissevered from all connection with the other property of the road, and sold or leased. There were also opportunities for large profits from operations in real estate. As individuals, promoters would purchase sites for shops, stations, and terminals before their location was publicly announced, and then turn the land over to the railroad at a large advance in price. In the same manner they would sometimes obtain town sites, and divert the route of the railroad to afford themselves opportunity to sell out to settlers. In locating the line of the Milwaukee and Mississippi railroad, Byron Kilbourn refused to cross the Wisconsin river at Newport, but chose instead a vacant site, owned by him and bearing his name, a few miles up the river. To-day, nothing remains of the town of Newport, while Kilbourn has about half the population which Newport had before the building of the railroad.

Speculative Land Companies. In many instances promoters have formed land companies for the purpose of carrying on their speculative operations. Upon the St. Joseph and Denver City, there was the Kansas and Nebraska Land company; and upon the Northern Pacific, the Lake Superior and Puget Sound Land company so sapped the resources of the railroad company as to contribute materially to its downfall in 1873.

Type of Construction Company Contracts. Examples of construction company contracts could be cited at great length. The Logansport, Crawfordsville, and South Western railroad agreed with its director-contractors to turn in all the municipal subsidy bonds, capital shares, and bonds. About $1,000,000 was actually paid out on account of construction, and for this, over $4,000,000 of securities were issued. The Morgan Improvement Company, made up of directors and others in the Gilman, Clinton, and Springfield railroad, took the contract for construction. Its actual expenditure was $1,500,000, but the cost to the railroad company was $2,000,000 in first mortgage bonds, $1,400,000 in shares, and $598,000 in municipal subsidy bonds.

.   .   .   .

Wisconsin Central. The Wisconsin Central, originally the Portage, Winnebago, and Superior railroad, was built by a construction company at the head of which were the president and general manager of the railroad. The directors of the railroad company on accepting the work were forced to admit that it was worth less than its cost. They thought it necessary, however, to report:

The officers of the Construction Company, by the terms of their contract, were to receive no compensation whatever except their respective salaries, which were fixed in their contract, and they never have, to the best of our knowledge and belief, received in any manner any profits or private gain or advantage, directly or indirectly, from their connection with this work. They contracted originally not even to invest in any way in property along the line of the road while it was in their charge; and your Directors believe that they have fulfilled this agreement in the most exact and honorable manner, both in its letter and spirit.[21]

Whatever may be the facts behind the statement, it is noteworthy as indicating the general practice in railroad construction at that time.

2] The Institutionalizing of the Nation's Investment Market on Wall Street in the 1850's

a] THE NEW WALL STREET MARKET

Wall Street Trading

. . . .

IN THE field of speculation prices are somewhat lower than at the close of last week. Railroad bonds are negociated at about the old rates, the best class of 7 per cent western bonds selling from 85 to 90 net. It is difficult to give the net of sale at auction. There is so much gammoning required to carry off a public sale handsomely, that only the sellers know how much it costs. Our friends must not suppose that because they see quotations all the way from 90 to 100, they can readily sell their own securities at that rate, no matter how good they are. These quotations are often the tricks of the trade, and they show the mark that particular cliques or parties wish to bring out some security at, rather than the price that any person is willing to pay. These quotations are merely an introduction of some stock to the public, before which it makes its bow, and then retires to be brought forward again in some suitable occasion. This process of training is kept up till the stock has become familiarized to the public and the public to the stock, and if it is good looking, and makes a good appearance, some person will come along who will take a fancy for it, buy it up at a good price, and take it out of the market. Stocks are purchased in Wall street, just as horses are at the Tattersals. The young and fresh ones in both cases, for what can be made upon their growth and improvement. The old and damaged ones are bought up for the purpose of giving them time to recruit, to slough over old sores, after which they come out as fresh as new, to tempt the unwary and inexperienced. The figure may be carried still further, and used to show the danger of too public an exhibition of the securities, that a person may have to sell; for as in the case of the sale of a horse, all will give it a bad name in hopes of being able at some time to buy it

---

21 Annual report, 1878.

FROM ["Wall Street Trading"] and "Negotiation of Railroad Securities at Home and Abroad," *American Railroad Journal,* January 25, 1851, and July 3, 1852.

at a low price, so with stocks and bonds; the lower their first sale the greater the amount to be made by their rise.

It may not be inappropriate to state here the usual manner in which securities are negociated. We have already spoken of sales at auction. These are considered safe to be tried only under peculiar circumstances. If one man is seen running through the streets, no person would think of following him. But let ten start together, and every person in sight will join in the chase. If these ten halloo the rest will halloo in sympathy; and if the leaders act in concert, they will soon acquire such an influence over the feelings of those following, as to have them almost entirely under their control, and ready for any dare devil exploit that may have been planned. Persons are in this way easily brought into a state, when they "go it blind," indifferent, unconscious even, of any blows or contusions they may receive. So with selling railroad securities at auction. The great mass of operators will of course unite to break down the sale; and will do so, unless it is strongly supported. A few strong names must be selected to lead off, to puff and blow, and manufacture a public sentiment in favor of the what to be sold; to form the nucleus, and start off in the race, and the number and spirit of those that will follow, will bear an exact proportion to the apparent zeal and confident assertion of the leaders. After the public sentiment is brought up to the proper point, the managers must attend the sale, start and sustain the bids at a proper point, and take for the sellers what cannot be disposed of *bona fide*. All this process, as may be well supposed, costs something; so much, that sales made in this manner are only resorted to where a very large amount is to be disposed of. Securities sold at auction often bring more than those sold at private sale, but the expense is great, and the risk still greater. If the parties fail to make a good *hit,* the security loses *caste,* and must then be disposed of as a second hand article.

When securities are disposed of at *private* sale, the broker or operator to whom they are committed, makes up a *party* of his friends, among whom they are divided, each taking 5, 10, or $20,000; for, notwithstanding we have some pretty capacious maws in Wall street, it can boast of but few individuals who severally could comfortably digest a mass of bonds of $500,000, without having the functions of his business stomach somewhat deranged. Even such a person prefers a variety of dishes to a surfeit of one. As soon, therefore, as the seller, with the greatest secrecy and confidence, imparts his scheme to the money lender or broker, he communicates with an electric dispatch the same to some twenty or thirty others. The whole party must know and discuss the matter, as much as the principal who stands between them and the seller. If the seller, for the purpose of trying the market, and finding out what he can expect to sell for, goes to other operators, he strikes the wires which carry his secrets around another circuit, composed of an equal number of names. In this manner, a person may not have been a day in Wall street before every important man on 'change will understand his whole scheme as well as the seller does himself. He has thus shown his whole hand, without knowing a card held on the other side. Now we do not pretend to say, that such a person may not be very well used by the party whom he may finally employ; but those whom he does not are at the same time possessed of his plans, and may have a great interest in defeating him. His scheme may interfere with some project of their own, even if they are governed by no more selfish object. No person wishes to invest his money in a security that is not popular with *all* parties—that will not always sell without requiring any efforts on his part to give it credit. The frowns of a half dozen leading operators are often sufficient to damn a good security, which would at once have gone into public favor under the smiles of the same persons. So long, therefore, as purchasers have a plenty of room for choice, they prefer securities that are well known to those which must be pushed and crowded into favor by efforts of their own. Another evil which results from the exposure of a scheme in the manner stated is the fact, that unless securities are "placed" soon after they come into the market, the inference is, that there is some intrinsic defect in them which has prevented a sale. The securities in this way become *shop-worn*, and must be sold as second hand goods.

We have thus enumerated some of the modes, and some of the difficulties attending the sale of railroad securities in this market. Those who have gone through the *mill* will blame us for stating them on such feeble terms. When a person comes here for money, he must bear in mind that $400,000 or $500,000 is no small sum; that the delivering a capitalist of this is a long and laborious operation, requiring a skilful accoucheur, the fullest evidence in favor of the security, and innumerable formalities. He must remember that money is power, and that the holder can dictate to a great extent his own terms, and above all, he must bear in mind, that he is liable to encounter the opposition of parties he never heard or dreamed of before, and that he will come in contact with those who, for life have made man a study, who, at a glance almost, detect his weak points, and lay their plans accordingly. Life in Wall street is a constant contest, and he who would sustain himself in it must prove himself superior to those he meets in their own way.

Saturday, July 3, 1852
Negotiation of Railroad Securities at Home and Abroad

No person accustomed to read our domestic or English newspapers, for the past few weeks, can have failed to notice that our railroad securities have recently received considerable attention in the London market. The general tone of the English press has been very strongly adverse; many of their journals, the Times in particular, dealing in wholesale denunciations, and pronouncing the great mass of our securities as worthless as were many of the bubbles of 1835, without present basis or prospective value, and cautioning the English public to beware lest they should be caught the second time with worthless American securities, as they were in 1837.

Such is the general tone of the English press. But even these journals find a few bright spots in this general mass of corruption, a few grains of gold in a vast heap of sand, which have been collected from the rubbish, nicely boxed up, and, out of special favor, sent to John Bull. Whereat all these journals are filled with great gratitude, and say grace over the feast to which they are invited, with an unction and fervor in exact inverse ratio to the abundance and variety of the dishes. Thankful for the small favors received, their gratitude knows no bound when they contemplate the danger they have escaped. They have secured the *kernel;* what remains left is nothing but the crust, the shell.

Now John Bull is being a little humbugged in this business of bond-selling, and will very likely be a good deal so, before it is through with. Having made some bad bargains in times past, he has adopted as a general maxim, that the great mass of our securities are good for nothing, and will not take the trouble to inquire into their character, nor inform himself as to their real merits. He consequently remains in almost entire ignorance of what we are doing, of the mode in which our works are constructed, and of their success when brought into operation. The shrewd operator, knowing his frame of mind, goes to him, humors his way of thinking, blows up in the English papers our whole system of doing things, echoes every sentiment and whim of the old fellow, until he has secured a strong hold on his good graces. John Bull begins to think his new acquaintance a mighty fine fellow; and so much like himself, that his opinion can certainly be relied upon. Having got into *position,* the operator tells him that his opinion of our securities is correct, quite correct, entirely correct; that too great caution cannot be used in reference to them, and winds up by gently suggesting that there are some few things that *are good,* one of which he has, out of great regard, brought with him, for Mr. Bull's special use, *"seeing its him."* In this manner the capitalist, who is obstinate through ignorance, and whose timidity is based upon no well reasoned conviction, is induced to buy a security in direct defiance of all properly established business principles; and by violating such rules, will be very likely to make a bad bargain, as he certainly will, if he continues to buy of parties who go to England to peddle out our securities, for no other reason than that they cannot be sold in this market. To the operation of the kind of machinery we have described, is to be attributed the coincidence between the articles in the English papers in reference to our railroads, and the recent sale of certain securities in the English market.

We have labored for years to bring our railroad securities to the favorable notice of foreign capitalists, for the reason that we need their money to assist in developing our resources, and because we have believed the great mass of our securities to be perfectly safe. We wished to attract foreign capital into this country, for the purpose of lessening our rates of interest, which are much too high. We can afford to pay well for money, and we have felt assured, if foreigners would study our condition and resources, inform themselves as to the character of our public works, and their influence in the creation of wealth, they would become very large investors in our securities, to the mutual benefit of all parties.

While all this is true, we have endeavored to pursue such a course as should secure us the greatest amount of capital in the long run. We are exceedingly anxious that nothing should be palmed off upon foreigners that has not a real and intrinsic value, something that would be safe for the purchaser to keep under all circumstances, and conditions of the market, knowing that the amount of future investments would depend entirely upon the confidence felt in our securities, and that this confidence must result from an *experience* of their value.

Now as a condition of safe investment, we would always recommend that they should be made *thro' houses in this country;* we mean, of course, those of the highest respectability. The reason for this is obvious. A person residing in New York, and competent to conduct a banking house, can hardly make a mistake as to the character of a project before the public. He is, or can make himself acquainted with the route of a road, its local resources and the relation it bears to the commerce of the country. He knows, or can easily know, the persons who have charge of the work, their integrity, and capacity to manage its affairs properly and successfully. He can also avail himself of the opinion of others who have, from their position and relation to the work, and the parties connected with it, the best means of forming a correct opinion in reference to it; and lastly, he has all those aids to the forming of a correct opinion which can only be picked up in a thousand different ways, by a person having daily and hourly intercourse with the parties themselves, and moving within the sphere where all public projects are daily discussed, and all their weak points, if they have any, exposed and laid open.

Now our transatlantic friends may rely upon it, that *none* of our securities are taken abroad by *first* hands, that can find a market at fair rates *here.* The only reason why they are taken abroad is that they will not sell at *home.* Our houses who buy on foreign account do not like them. So with the domestic purchasers, "They may be good, but I can do better," is the reply. Shut out from our own market, the holder goes in quest of one abroad, where his project is not so well known, and where his statements cannot be so readily disproved, as at home.

We do not pretend to say that many securities that are carried abroad, and sold directly to the purchaser in England, for instance, are not perfectly sound; but we do say, that merchandise is seldom shipped by the manufacturer to a foreign port, without orders, when there is a good market at home; and that as far as the above rule is concerned, there is no difference between a bale of cotton goods and a railroad bond. We always suspect an invoice of goods sent out at the risk of the foreign manufacturer, well knowing that he would sell them at home, if he could find a purchaser.

Another reason why it is better for foreigners to purchase through an American house is, that he constitutes such house his agents, to apprise him of any change that may threaten in the value of his security, thus giving him an opportunity to dispose of it, should the retaining it involve present or prospective loss.

By adopting and adhering to the plain common sense rules that we have given, foreigners can always keep themselves on the safe side; for we assume that our companies will always pay their debts so long as they have the means to do so. Those investing, therefore, must be careful to buy into roads that *will* pay. Now it may be set down as a safe rule, that where the amount borrowed, or sought to be borrowed, does not exceed the sum paid up as *capital,* such a loan is perfectly safe. The reason is this: the lender has a double security for his money; but a still stronger and more satisfactory one is, that our people will not contribute one half the means necessary to build a road, and pledge this sum for an equal amount, unless they feel perfectly secure that the project is a good one. We are no more fond of wasting our money than the foreigner, and the latter may rest assured, that when we have so much at stake, and involved in the proper management of a road, we shall take good care of it.

In commending railroad securities to public attention, we have, and shall, confine our commendations to such as come within the rule laid down. Where those interested in a road contribute one half of its cost, and make this sum the basis of a loan, it ceases to be a merely speculative project. When the country through which a road runs cannot do this, the construction of a road is not demanded by the business of such section, and will not probably *pay.* The ability of the people to contribute, is the best test of their ability to sustain a railroad. The rule that we have laid down, therefore, is a good one, for it not only secures good management to a road, but furnishes the proper evidence of sufficient business upon its line to sustain it.

We do not mean to say that there are no exceptions to this rule. There are, but these exceptions better remain at home, where the character of the project, and the men managing it, are well understood, and when the value of these securities depend upon causes that cannot be appreciated abroad. We have, too, an abundance of the first class securities, so that there is no necessity for foreigners taking those about which there shall be the least risk.

Such are the grounds upon which we commend our securities to the foreign purchaser, and for the foreign market. We shall recommend none that do not come up to the standard we have set up. It is bad faith to send abroad an unsound security. If *our* people will purchase them, possessing the fullest means of informing themselves, it is their concern, not ours. If we do not think well of a security, this is no reason why *we* should condemn it. Our convictions may be wrong; and where we do not *know,* we are in duty bound to be silent.

A great flourish has been made about the recent loans effected in England for the Illinois Central, and Erie railroads. It is a matter of general congratulation in the streets. We do not so regard it. Upon the Central road, the first blow has hardly been struck. The whole cost of the work is estimated at some $17,000,000. The capital stock of the company is $1,000,000!!! The company, to be sure, have a large body of land; but the value of these is indefinite and uncertain. To obtain them, the company have made a sacrifice of the appropriate routes for their road, and have entirely abandoned the great thoroughfares of travel. The project is a speculation, owned by a few individuals, who are determined that the *public* shall build the road. If anything is to be made, they get it. Should the speculation turn out disastrously, the public are to be the losers. The bonds of the company were sent to Europe, because they could not be sold here where the project is best known. We do not profess to discuss the intrinsic value of the security offered, only to show that it by no means comes up to the standard which we have set up, as the safe one for foreigners to be governed by.

So with the Erie road. Here is a road that has probably cost $27,000,000, represented by $6,000,000 stock and $21,000,000 debt!! We showed in our last, a much larger sum than that represented by the *stock* of the road, to have been lost in construction. Such being the fact, the last bondholders have no security whatever. They guarantee the safety of their own loans. This rests entirely with the success of the work. If the project be a good one, and well managed, they are safe. If not, they must lose. They have nothing to fall back upon. But this does not fairly state the case. The person who now lends to the company, cannot get anything till the two mortgages for $7,000,000 are taken care of. He does not come in for a pro rata share with all the bondholders. The project may be partially successful, and he get nothing. We have always thought, and still think, Wall street to be the proper place where Erie securities should be held; and we are by no means pleased to see new issues going to Europe. Should the company be unable to meet the interest on the new loan, the result would be most disastrous for the credit of all our securities. The reason for our opinion as to the inability of that company to meet the interest upon its *stock*, as well as its more recent debts, are given in full in our last issue.

.   .   .   .

That English capitalists will make some unlucky investments in our credits now offering, is very probable. They are just in that frame of mind to be imposed upon, and led astray. They have, as already stated, adopted as a maxim, that our securities are unsafe, consequently they will not examine into their character. In any negotiations into which they may be pursuaded, they labor under the disadvantage of dealing in a new business, of purchasing a kind of merchandise without experience, or skill as to difference of *quality*. Their only safety consists in purchasing through houses that possess what they lack—the means of forming correct opinions.

The French and German buyers adopt a more sensible course. They follow in the line of safe precedents. All their orders come through responsible American houses. But their precaution is not confined within this limit. They send out to this country competent men, who critically examine all our public works, and study their condition and prospects, until they are enabled to form a correct opinion as to their merits, and the value of the securities upon which they are based. Their prejudices do not preclude investigation, nor warp their judgment. The consequence is, that knowing what they are purchasing, they take our choicest securities, leaving the others to the less fastideous, or less informed buyer. Were an American to take one of our *unknown* securities to Germany, he could not give it away unless it had the endorsement of a responsible American house.

.   .   .   .

b] THE STORY FROM J. F. D. LANIER

I CONTINUED in the management of the Madison Branch Bank and a member of the Board of Control till 1849, when the subject of railroad construction again began to excite general attention and interest. During the twelve years that had elapsed since the great calamity of 1837, the West had increased rapidly in population and wealth, and the necessity for improved highways was felt to be more imperative than ever. The acquisition of California, and the discovery of immense deposits of gold within it, gave to the whole nation an impulse never before felt. Numerous railway enterprises were again proposed in the West, and I felt that the time had at last come when they could be safely undertaken as remunerative investments for capital. Residing at Madison, Indiana, I had been instrumental in the resuscitation of the Madison and Indianapolis Railroad, originally a part of the system of public work which the State had attempted to construct, and had learned from the early success of that road what might be expected of other lines more favorably situated. For the purpose, therefore, of embarking in the construction of railroads on a wider scale, I went to New York in the latter part of 1848, and on the first day of January, 1849, I formed a copartnership with Mr. Richard H. Winslow, the chief object of which was the negotiation of railway securities, although we contemplated, in connection therewith, a general banking business. At that time there were in operation in the West only about 600 miles of line.[1] These roads were chiefly the remains of the old State systems which had been sold out to private companies, and were almost without exception badly located and imperfectly built. They were in all cases laid with the light flat bar, upon longitudinal sills, and were utterly incapable of sustaining heavy trains, high speed, or a large traffic. They had, consequently, involved in heavy loss all who had been engaged in their construction. I felt, however, their want of success to be no argument against lines prop-

[1] On the first day of January, 1849, the following lines of railroad were in operation in the States north and west of the Ohio River:

	Length of Line (in miles)
OHIO—Little Miami	84
Mansfield and Sandusky	56
Mad River	102
INDIANA—Madison and Indianapolis	86
MICHIGAN—Michigan Central	146
Michigan Southern	70
Erie and Kalamazoo	33
Detroit and Pontiac	25
ILLINOIS—Sangamon and Morgan	53
Total	655

FROM J. F. D. Lanier, "Winslow, Lanier and Company," *Sketch Life of J. F. D. Lanier* (New York, 1870), pp. 18–21, 24–29.

erly constructed upon good routes. I undertook to demonstrate this in every way in my power, particularly in newspaper articles and pamphlets, of which I published great numbers in connection with the negotiation of the securities of various companies which we undertook. The result of our efforts soon far exceeded our expectations. Although we began in a very small way, every step we took gave us increased business and strength, and we soon had all the business we could attend to. Commencing with the bonds of the Madison and Indianapolis Railroad, which were the first securities of the kind ever brought out in the New York market, we followed them with the bonds of the Little Miami; Columbus and Xenia; Cleveland, Columbus and Cincinnati; Cleveland, Painesville and Ashtabula; Ohio and Pennsylvania (now a part of the Pittsburg, Fort Wayne and Chicago); Michigan Southern, and other important lines. We not unfrequently negotiated a million of bonds daily. The aggregate for the year was enormous. We were without competitors for a business we had created, and consequently made money very rapidly. The commissions for the negotiation of bonds averaged at first five per cent. With their negotiation we often coupled contracts for the purchase, at a large commission, of rails. Our business soon became so great that it was a question with us, not so much what we would undertake, as what we would reject. We not unfrequently took, on our own account, an entire issue of bonds of important lines.

The negotiation of the securities of companies was followed by arrangements that made our house the agent for the payment of interest accruing on them, as well as transfer agents. Such arrangements naturally led the way to the banking business to which we afterward chiefly confined ourselves. The extent of our business as well as of our success exceeded all expectation. During the period of six years, from 1849 to 1854 inclusive, in which we were actually engaged in the negotiation of railway securities, 10,724 miles of line were constructed, nearly one-half of which were in the Western States. With all the more important lines we were, in one way or another, connected. At one period we paid the interest on fifty different classes of securities. These facts will convey some idea of the magnitude of our business and the vigor and energy with which it was conducted.

The uniform success of the enterprises in behalf of which we acted was something remarkable, and has since been a source of great satisfaction. I feel that investors, as well as the country at large, have been greatly benefited by my labors. The interest on almost all the securities brought out by us has been regularly paid, while in not a few instances there has been an enormous profit upon the prices paid. Our house was the first to bring out county and city securities, issued for the construction of railroads. These securities were instrumental in the construction of an immense extent of line, which, but for them, could not have been built, while they have proved a most excellent investment. In no instance, I believe, have the counties and cities, the bonds of which we negotiated, made default, either in principal or interest.

·   ·   ·   ·   ·   ·   ·   ·   ·   ·   ·   ·

. . . [During the depression following the panic of 1857] many of our most valuable enterprises were forced into bankruptcy, and had to be reorganized by new adjustments of interests, and, in most cases, by large sacrifices on the part of the stock and bondholders. A period of great general depression and discouragement followed one of previous confidence and hope. In this crisis it devolved naturally upon parties who had been instrumental in providing the means for the construction of roads to raise them from their depressed condition, and place them, if possible, in a position in which they could be successfully worked and realize the expectations formed of them. Among the companies that yielded to the financial storm was the Pittsburg, Fort Wayne and Chicago—a company with which I had been early identified, whose securities we had negotiated, and for whose good name and success I was most solicitous. To its restoration I consequently devoted no small portion of my time, till all its embarrassments were happily surmounted, and the road placed in a position of perfect independence, in which it proved itself to be one of the most valuable enterprises of the kind in the United States. Perhaps I cannot better show the difficulties into which this work, in common with many others, had fallen, and of its subsequent recovery, than by copying the following article in reference thereto, from the New York *Times* newspaper, under date of July 21, 1867:

"In 1859 the Pittsburg, Fort Wayne and Chicago Railroad, in common with most other lines, was overwhelmed in the financial revulsion which had swept with resistless force over the whole country. The road had been just opened to Chicago. The line was originally undertaken by three companies, none of which possessed means at all adequate to the construction of their several links. The road when opened was hardly more than half completed. Its earnings, not equaling one-quarter their present amount, were wholly insufficient to meet current expenses and the interest on its funded debt. Default, by necessary consequence, was made on all classes of its securities. Bankruptcy stared the concern full in the face, threatening the loss of nearly the whole amount invested.

In this crisis a meeting of its creditors, chiefly first mortgage bondholders, was called at the office of Winslow, Lanier & Co., to consider what was to be done. This class of creditors, of course, had the precedence. If they insisted upon the letter of the law, they would inevitably cut off all subsequent parties in interest, who represented an amount of capital invested in the road twice greater. After much deliberation it was decided to raise a committee to be invested with full power, and if possible, save the interests of all. This committee consisted of Mr. J. F. D. Lanier, who was appointed by the creditors its chairman; Mr. Samuel J. Tilden,[2] Mr. Louis H. Meyer,[3] Mr. J. Edgar Thomson, President of the Pennsylvania Railroad,

2 [Tilden, a corporation lawyer and Democratic politician, became that party's candidate for the presidency in 1876.]

3 [Meyer was the senior partner in Meyer and Stucken, a German-oriented investment banking firm.]

and Mr. Samuel Hanna [4] of Fort Wayne. To give some idea of the chaos existing in the affairs of the Company, we may state that there were outstanding, at the time, nine different classes of bonds, secured, in one way or another, upon the different portions of the road; two classes secured by real estate belonging to the Company, and several issued in the funding of coupons. Upon all these, interest for several years, amounting to many millions of dollars, was overdue. The principal sums of several of the first mortgages were speedily to mature. The Company also owed more than $2,000,000 of floating debt, portions of it in the form of judgments recovered in the State courts. The road was in extremely bad condition, and required the expenditure of a large sum to enable it to conduct its business with any degree of economy or dispatch.

Such was the condition of affairs when the Committee commenced work. The value of the securities of the Company was merely nominal. Its stock would not sell for five cents on the dollar. Each class of creditors was striving to gain some advantage at the expense of the others. The first step of the Committee, consequently, was to put the property beyond the reach of individuals and in the custody of the courts. An order for this purpose was obtained in the United States District Court for the Northern District of Ohio, on the 17th of January, 1860, and Mr. Wm. B. Ogden [5] was appointed receiver.

The Committee set out with the determination of preserving, if possible, the rights of all the parties in interest—not alone those of the first mortgage bondholders. It was hoped that when the property was put beyond the reach of individual creditors, an arrangement might be effected and the rights of the various parties preserved in the relations they had previously maintained. But such an adjustment required the assent of each creditor and stockholder. This, in the multiplicity and conflict of interests, it was found impossible to obtain. The next, and only remaining course, was to sell the road and property of the Company by an order of Court in behalf of the first mortgagees. Such sale would vest absolutely the title to the road in the hands of the purchasers, who would thus be in position to make such disposition of it as in their view equity and justice might demand. It would also enable them to apply the net earnings to the construction of a good road, without which the investment itself would be of no value.

With this purpose a full plan of reorganization, such as was finally adopted, was prepared and published, and brought, as far as possible, to the attention of every party in interest. Decrees for sale had to be obtained in the Courts of the United States for four different States. The time required for this purpose was occupied by the Committee in incessant efforts in removing one impediment after another thrown in their way by importunate and dissatisfied creditors, who were indifferent to the fate of the concern, provided they could get their pay. All difficulties were at last

4 [Hanna was an active Indiana railroad promoter.]

5 [Ogden, one of Chicago's founding fathers, became a leading real estate and railroad promoter and manager.]

overcome, and on the 24th of October, 1861, the road and property was sold at auction, and purchased by Mr. Lanier, in behalf of himself and his associates, for the sum of $2,000,000. The Courts, we are happy to say, facilitated legal proceedings as far as this could be properly done. They had full confidence in the Committee, and sympathized with the unfortunate creditors of the concern, and not, as at the present day, in our State, with bands of conspirators against the public welfare, who seek the control of great lines with no other purpose but to plunder them. Eight years ago, measured by what has since transpired, was a golden age of judicial purity.

By the sale of the road a most important step was gained. The title to it vested, absolutely, in the purchasers. They could convey it to whom, at what price and upon what terms they pleased. What followed was more a matter of detail, though involving great patience and labor. For the creation of a new Company, according to the original plan of reorganization, legislation had to be obtained in the States of Pennsylvania, Ohio, Indiana and Illinois. Such legislation was at last secured, a new Company formed, to which was conveyed the railroad and everything appertaining thereto, the Committee receiving therefor, first, second and third mortgage bonds, in amounts sufficient to meet the sums due the different classes of creditors in the old Company; and also certificates of stock corresponding in amount to that outstanding in the old. First mortgage bonds, to the amount of $5,200,000, were issued to the first mortgage bondholders of the old Company, and of the several links of which its road was composed, and for accrued interest. The bondholders were also required to fund, for two years, the interest accruing on the new bonds, so as to allow, for such a period, the application of the net earnings to construction. The second mortgage bondholders received, in the same manner, and subject to similar conditions, second mortgage bonds to the amount of $5,250,000. The unsecured creditors were paid off in third mortgage bonds to the amount of $2,000,000. The shareholders received new certificates in exchange for the old. By such means each class of creditors, without the abatement of a dollar, were fully and completely reinstated in the new Company in the order they stood in the old. The proper transfers and exchanges were made, and on the 1st day of May, 1862, two years and six months after the road was placed in the hands of a receiver, and six months after the sale, the trust, so long held and faithfully executed, was brought to a virtual close, to the entire satisfaction of every party in interest in the road.

During the period of reorganization the road was operated, under the general direction of the Committee, by Geo. W. Cass, its former and subsequent President. His well-known abilities as a railroad manager were never more conspicuously displayed than in this service. He had every difficulty to contend with—an impoverished and half completed road, with clamorous creditors at every turn. The Chairman of the Committee was not unfrequently called upon to advance, from his private funds, considerable sums in aid of the operations of the road. Such advances were, of course, repaid, but only with simple interest. The good name and financial strength of Mr. Lanier, joined to his well-known prudence and caution, tended to inspire great confidence in the action of the Committee in which he justly exerted great influence. Mr. Thomson's position as chief of a great and successful enterprise, enabled him to render very great aid to the Committee in the operations of the road. Indeed, it was through his instrumentality that the old Company was enabled to push its line through to Chicago. Mr. Tilden was the chief legal adviser of the Committee and Company throughout. He had charge of the proceedings, not only for the winding up of the old, but for the formation of the new Company, and for the recent transfer of the road to the Pennsylvania Company, and drew up all the documents and guarantees relating to the same. The proper discharge of his duties involved the fate and security of the whole investment. Not a suggestion has been ever raised that they were not ably and faithfully performed. The directors of the Company, pending its reorganization, rendered valuable assistance. Many of them resided upon the line of the road, and were enabled to exert a salutary influence, not only among the creditors of the Company, but in securing the legislation required. But it is, perhaps, invidious to particularize when all worked faithfully and well. Not a dollar was ever paid to secure the legislation required for the formation of the new Company; not a dollar to buy off importunate or unreasonable creditors. The Committee never had a secret which they turned to account at the expense of the stock and bondholders. Their plans were prepared and published in the outset, and scrupulously adhered to.

Soon after the new Company commenced operations it was seen the enterprise had passed its darkest days. For the year ending December 31, 1862, the net earnings of the road equaled nearly $2,000,000, all of which were applied to construction. The Committee was enabled to add largely to its available means by the sale of property purchased with the road, but not needed in its future operations, and which, in fact, they were not, by the terms of the trust, to account for to the new Company. The sums realized from these sources, and paid over to the Company, equaled about $600,000, of which some $400,000 was saved by a compromise which the Committee were enabled to make with European holders of bonds secured by real estate. All the advantages gained by such settlements were given to the new Company.

In 1863 the net earnings equaled nearly $3,000,000. These sums enabled the Company to place its road in first-rate condition."

.   .   .   .

3] The Financier As Speculator and Exploiter

. . . .

THE SERIES of events in the Erie history which culminated in the struggle about to be narrated may be said to have had its origin some seventeen or eighteen years before, when Mr. Daniel Drew first made his appearance in the Board of Directors, where he remained down to the year 1868, generally holding also the office of treasurer of the corporation. Mr. Drew is what is known as a self-made man. Born in the year 1797, as a boy he drove cattle down from his native town of Carmel, in Putnam County, to the market of New York City, and, subsequently, was for years proprietor of the Bull's Head Tavern. Like his contemporary, and ally or opponent,—as the case might be,—Cornelius Vanderbilt, he built up his fortunes in the steamboat interest, and subsequently extended his operations over the rapidly developing railroad system. Shrewd, unscrupulous, and very illiterate,—a strange combination of superstition and faithlessness, of daring and timidity,—often good-natured and sometimes generous,—he ever regarded his fiduciary position of director in a railroad as a means of manipulating its stock for his own advantage. For years he had been the leading bear of Wall Street, and his favorite haunts were the secret recesses of Erie. As treasurer of that corporation, he had, in its frequently recurring hours of need, advanced it sums which it could not have obtained elsewhere, and the obtaining of which was a necessity. He had been at once a good friend of the road and the worst enemy it had as yet known. His management of his favorite stock had been cunning and recondite, and his ways inscrutable. Those who sought to follow him, and those who sought to oppose him, alike found food for sad reflection; until at last he won for himself the expressive *sobriquet* of the Speculative Director. Sometimes, though rarely, he suffered greatly in the complications of Wall Street; more frequently he inflicted severe damage upon others. On the whole, however, his fortunes had greatly prospered, and the outbreak of the Erie war found him the actual possessor of some millions, and the reputed possessor of many more.

In the spring of 1866 Mr. Drew's manipulations of Erie culminated in an operation which was at the time regarded as a masterpiece; subsequent experience has, however, so improved upon it that it is now looked upon as an ordinary and inartistic piece of what is called "railroad financiering," a class of operations formerly known by a more opprobrious name. The stock of the road was then selling at about 95, and the corporation was, as usual, in debt, and in pressing need of money. As usual, also, it resorted to its treasurer. Mr. Drew stood ready to make the desired advances—upon

FROM Charles Francis Adams, Jr., "A Chapter of Erie," *North American Review*, July, 1869, reprinted in Charles Francis Adams, Jr., and Henry Adams, *Chapters of Erie and Other Essays* (New York, 1871), pp. 5–15, 17–19, 29–31, 45–49, 52–59.

security. Some twenty-eight thousand shares of its own authorized stock, which had never been issued, were at the time in the hands of the company, which also claimed, under the statutes of New York, the right of raising money by the issue of bonds, convertible, at the option of the holder, into stock. The twenty-eight thousand unissued shares, and bonds for three millions of dollars, convertible into stock, were placed by the company in the hands of its treasurer, as security for a cash loan of $3,500,000. The negotiation had been quietly effected, and Mr. Drew's campaign now opened. Once more he was short of Erie. While Erie was buoyant,—while it steadily approximated to par,—while speculation was rampant, and that outside public, the delight and the prey of Wall Street, was gradually drawn in by the fascination of amassing wealth without labor,—quietly and stealthily, through his agents and brokers, the grave, desponding operator was daily concluding his contracts for the future delivery of stock at current prices. At last the hour had come. Erie was rising, Erie was scarce, the great bear had many contracts to fulfil, and where was he to find the stock? His victims were not kept long in suspense. Mr. Treasurer Drew laid his hands upon his collateral. In an instant the bonds for three millions were converted into an equivalent amount of capital stock, and fifty-eight thousand shares, dumped, as it were, by the cart-load in Broad Street, made Erie as plenty as even Drew could desire. Before the astonished bulls could rally their faculties, the quotations had fallen from 95 to 50, and they realized that they were hopelessly entrapped.[1]

The whole transaction, of course, was in no respect more creditable than any result, supposed to be one of chance or skill, which, in fact, is made to depend upon the sorting of a pack of cards, the dosing of a race-horse, or the selling out of his powers by a "walkist." But the gambler, the patron of the turf, or the pedestrian represents, as a rule, himself alone, and his

[1] A bull, in the slang of the stock exchange, is one who endeavors to increase the market price of stocks, as a bear endeavors to depress it. The bull is supposed to toss the thing up with his horns, and the bear to drag it down with his claws. The vast majority of stock operations are pure gambling transactions. One man agrees to deliver, at some future time, property which he has not got, to another man who does not care to own it. It is only one way of betting on the price at the time when the delivery should be made; if the price rises in the mean while, the bear pays to the bull the difference between the price agreed upon and the price to which the property has risen; if it falls, he receives the difference from the bull. All operations, as they are termed, of the stock exchange are directed to this depression or elevation of stocks, with a view to the settlement of differences. A "pool" is a mere combination of men contributing money to be used to this end, and a "corner" is a result arrived at when one combination of gamblers, secretly holding the whole or greater part of any stock or species of property, induces another combination to agree to deliver a large further quantity at some future time. When the time arrives, the second combination, if the corner succeeds, suddenly finds itself unable to buy the amount of the stock or property necessary to enable it to fulfil its contracts, and the first combination fixes at its own will the price at which differences must be settled. The corner fails or is broken, when those who agree to deliver succeed in procuring the stock or property, and fulfilling their contracts. The *argot* of the exchange is, however, a language by itself, and very difficult of explanation to the wholly uninitiated. It can only be said that all combinations of interests and manipulations of values are mere weapons in the hands of bulls and bears for elevating or depressing values, with a view to the payment of differences.

character is generally so well understood as to be a warning to all the world. The case of the treasurer of a great corporation is different. He occupies a fiduciary position. He is a trustee,—a guardian. Vast interests are confided to his care; every shareholder of the corporation is his ward; if it is a railroad, the community itself is his *cestui que trust*. But passing events, accumulating more thickly with every year, have thoroughly corrupted the public morals on this subject. A directorship in certain great corporations has come to be regarded as a situation in which to make a fortune, the possession of which is no longer dishonorable. The method of accumulation is both simple and safe. It consists in giving contracts as a trustee to one's self as an individual, or in speculating in the property of one's *cestui que trust,* or in using the funds confided to one's charge, as treasurer or otherwise, to gamble with the real owners of those funds for their own property, and that with cards packed in advance. The wards themselves expect their guardians to throw the dice against them for their own property, and are surprised, as well as gratified, if the dice are not loaded. These proceedings, too, are looked upon as hardly reprehensible, yet they strike at the very foundation of existing society. The theory of representation, whether in politics or in business, is of the essence of modern development. Our whole system rests upon the sanctity of the fiduciary relations. Whoever betrays them, a director of a railroad no less than a member of Congress or the trustee of an orphans' asylum, is the common enemy of every man, woman, and child who lives under representative government. The unscrupulous director is far less entitled to mercy than the ordinary gambler, combining as he does the character of the traitor with the acts of the thief.

No acute moral sensibility on this point, however, has for some years troubled Wall Street, nor, indeed, the country at large. As a result of the transaction of 1866, Mr. Drew was looked upon as having effected a surprisingly clever operation, and he retired from the field hated, feared, wealthy, and admired. This episode of Wall Street history took its place as a brilliant success beside the famous Prairie du Chien and Harlem "corners," and, but for subsequent events, would soon have been forgotten. Its close connection, however, with more important though later incidents of Erie history seems likely to preserve its memory fresh. Great events were impending; a new man was looming up in the railroad world, introducing novel ideas and principles, and it could hardly be that the new and old would not come in conflict. Cornelius Vanderbilt, commonly known as Commodore Vanderbilt, was now developing his theory of the management of railroads.

Born in the year 1794, Vanderbilt was a somewhat older man than Drew. There are several points of resemblance in the early lives of the two men, and many points of curious contrast in their characters. Vanderbilt, like Drew, was born in very humble circumstances in the State of New York, and like him also received little education. He began life by ferrying passengers and produce from Staten Island to New York City. Subsequently, he too laid the foundation of his great fortune in the growing steamboat navigation, and likewise, in due course of time, transferred himself to the

railroad interest. When at last, in 1868, the two came into collision as
representatives of the old system of railroad management and of the new,
they were each threescore and ten years of age, and had both been successful in the accumulation of millions,—Vanderbilt even more so than Drew.
They were probably equally unscrupulous and equally selfish; but, while
the cast of Drew's mind was sombre and bearish, Vanderbilt was gay and
buoyant of temperament, little given to thoughts other than of this world,
a lover of horses and of the good things of life. The first affects prayer-
meetings, and the last is a devotee of whist. Drew, in Wall Street, is by
temperament a bear, while Vanderbilt could hardly be other than a bull.
Vanderbilt must be allowed to be by far the superior man of the two.
Drew is astute and full of resources, and at all times a dangerous opponent;
but Vanderbilt takes larger, more comprehensive views, and his mind has
a vigorous grasp which that of Drew seems to want. While, in short, in a
wider field, the one might have made himself a great and successful despot,
the other would hardly have aspired beyond the control of the jobbing
department of some corrupt government. Accordingly, while in Drew's
connection with the railroad system his operations and manipulations
evince no qualities calculated to excite even a vulgar admiration or respect, it is impossible to regard Vanderbilt's methods or aims without recognizing the magnitude of the man's ideas and conceding his abilities.
He involuntarily excites feelings of admiration for himself and alarm for
the public. His ambition is a great one. It seems to be nothing less than
to make himself master in his own right of the great channels of communication which connect the city of New York with the interior of the
continent, and to control them as his private property. Drew sought to
carry to a mean perfection the old system of operating successfully from the
confidential position of director, neither knowing anything nor caring
anything for the railroad system, except in its connection with the movements of the stock exchange, and he succeeded in his object. Vanderbilt,
on the other hand, as selfish, harder, and more dangerous, though less
subtle, has by instinct, rather than by intellectual effort, seen the full
magnitude of the system, and through it has sought to make himself a
dictator in modern civilization, moving forward to this end step by step
with a sort of pitiless energy which has seemed to have in it an element of
fate. As trade now dominates the world, and railways dominate trade, his
object has been to make himself the virtual master of all by making himself absolute lord of the railways. Had he begun his railroad operations
with this end in view, complete failure would have been almost certainly
his reward. Commencing as he did, however, with a comparatively insignifi-
cant objective point,—the cheap purchase of a bankrupt stock,—and developing his ideas as he advanced, his power and his reputation grew, until
an end which at first it would have seemed madness to entertain became
at last both natural and feasible.

Two great lines of railway traverse the State of New York and connect
it with the West,—the Erie and the New York Central. The latter communicates with the city by a great river and by two railroads. To get these
two roads—the Harlem and the Hudson River—under his own absolute

control, and then, so far as the connection with the Central was concerned, to abolish the river, was Vanderbilt's immediate object. First making himself master of the Harlem road, he there learned his early lessons in railroad management, and picked up a fortune by the way. A few years ago Harlem had no value. As late as 1860 it sold for eight or nine dollars per share; and in January, 1863, when Vanderbilt had got the control, it had risen only to 30. By July of that year it stood at 92, and in August was suddenly raised by a "corner" to 179. The next year witnessed a similar operation. The stock which sold in January at less than 90 was settled for in June in the neighborhood of 285. On one of these occasions Mr. Drew is reported to have contributed a sum approaching half a million to his rival's wealth. More recently the stock had been floated at about 130. It was in the successful conduct of this first experiment that Vanderbilt showed his very manifest superiority over previous railroad managers. The Harlem was, after all, only a competing line, and competition was proverbially the rock ahead in all railroad enterprise. The success of Vanderbilt with the Harlem depended upon his getting rid of the competition of the Hudson River railroad. An ordinary manager would have resorted to contracts, which are never carried out, or to opposition, which is apt to be ruinous. Vanderbilt, on the contrary, put an end to competition by buying up the competing line. This he did at about par, and, in due course of time, the stock was sent up to 180. Thus his plans had developed by another step, while through a judicious course of financiering and watering and dividing, a new fortune had been secured by him. By this time Vanderbilt's reputation as a railroad manager—as one who earned dividends, created stock, and invented wealth—had become very great, and the managers of the Central brought that road to him, and asked him to do with it as he had done with the Harlem and Hudson River. He accepted the proffered charge, and now, probably, the possibilities of his position and the magnitude of the prize within his grasp at last dawned on his mind.

. . . .

From the moment Vanderbilt stepped into the management of the Central, but a single effort seemed necessary to give the new railroad king absolute control over the railroad system, and consequently over the commerce, of New York. By advancing only one step he could securely levy his tolls on the traffic of a continent. Nor could this step have seemed difficult to take. It was but to repeat with the Erie his successful operation with the Hudson River road. Not only was it a step easy to take, but here again, as so many times before, a new fortune seemed ready to drop into his hand. The Erie might well yield a not less golden harvest than the Central, Hudson River, or Harlem. There was indeed but one obstacle in the way,—the plan might not meet the views of the one man who at that time possessed the wealth, cunning, and combination of qualities which could defeat it, that man being the Speculative Director of the Erie,—Mr. Daniel Drew.

The New York Central passed into Vanderbilt's hands in the winter of 1866–67, and he marked the Erie for his own in the succeeding autumn.

As the annual meeting of the corporation approached, three parties were found in the field contending for control of the road. One party was represented by Drew, and might be called the party in possession, that which had long ruled the Erie, and made it what it was,—the Scarlet Woman of Wall Street. Next came Vanderbilt, flushed with success, and bent upon fully gratifying his great instinct for developing imperialism in corporate life. Lastly, a faction made its appearance composed of some shrewd and ambitious Wall Street operators and of certain persons from Boston, who sustained for the occasion the novel character of railroad reformers. This party, it is needless to say, was as unscrupulous, and, as the result proved, as able as either of the others; it represented nothing but a raid made upon the Erie treasury in the interest of a thoroughly bankrupt New England corporation, of which its members had the control. The history of this corporation, known as the Boston, Hartford, & Erie Railroad,—a projected feeder and connection of the Erie,—would be one curious to read, though very difficult to write. Its name was synonymous with bankruptcy, litigation, fraud, and failure. If the Erie was of doubtful repute in Wall Street, the Boston, Hartford, & Erie had long been of worse than doubtful repute in State Street. Of late years, under able and persevering, if not scrupulous management, the bankrupt, moribund company had been slowly struggling into new life, and in the spring of 1867 it had obtained, under certain conditions, from the Commonwealth of Massachusetts, a subsidy in aid of the construction of its road. One of the conditions imposed obliged the corporation to raise a sum from other sources still larger than that granted by the State. Accordingly, those having the line in charge looked abroad for a victim, and fixed their eyes upon the Erie.

As the election day drew near, Erie was of course for sale. A controlling interest of stockholders stood ready to sell their proxies, with entire impartiality, to any of the three contending parties, or to any man who would pay the market price for them. Nay, more, the attorney of one of the contending parties, as it afterwards appeared, after an ineffectual effort to extort black mail, actually sold the proxies of his principal to another of the contestants, and his doing so seemed to excite mirth rather than surprise. Meanwhile the representatives of the Eastern interest played their part to admiration. Taking advantage of some Wall Street complications just then existing between Vanderbilt and Drew, they induced the former to ally himself with them, and the latter saw that his defeat was inevitable. Even at this time the Vanderbilt party contemplated having recourse, if necessary, to the courts, and a petition for an injunction had been prepared, setting forth the details of the "corner" of 1866. On the Sunday preceding the election Drew, in view of his impending defeat, called upon Vanderbilt. That gentleman, thereupon, very amicably read to him the legal documents prepared for his benefit; whereupon the ready treasurer at once turned about, and, having hitherto been hampering the Commodore by his bear operations, he now agreed to join hands with him in giving to the market a strong upward tendency. Meanwhile the other parties to the contest were not idle. At the same house, at a later hour in the day, Vanderbilt explained to the Eastern adventurers his new plan of operations, which included the continuance of Drew in his directorship. These gentlemen were puzzled, not to say confounded, by this sudden change of front. An explanation was demanded, some plain language followed, and the parties separated, leaving everything unsettled; but only to meet again at a later hour at the house of Drew. There Vanderbilt brought the new men to terms by proposing to Drew a bold *coup de main,* calculated to throw them entirely out of the direction. Before the parties separated that night a written agreement had been entered into, providing that, to save appearances, the new board should be elected without Drew, but that immediately thereafter a vacancy should be created, and Drew chosen to fill it. He was therefore to go in as one of two directors in the Vanderbilt interest, that gentleman's nephew, Mr. Work, being the other.[2]

. . . .

. . . The real conflict was now impending. Commodore Vanderbilt stretched out his hand to grasp Erie. Erie was to be isolated and shut up within the limits of New York; it was to be given over, bound hand and foot, to the lord of the Central. To perfect this programme, the representatives of all the competing lines met, and a proposition was submitted to the Erie party looking to a practical consolidation on certain terms of the Pennsylvania Central, the Erie, and the New York Central, and a division among the contracting parties of all the earnings from the New York City travel. A new illustration was thus to be afforded, at the expense of the trade and travel to and from the heart of a continent, of George Stephenson's famous aphorism, that where combination is possible competition is impossible. The Erie party, however, represented that their road earned more than half of the fund of which they were to receive only one third. They remonstrated and proposed modifications, but their opponents were inexorable. The terms were too hard; the conference led to no result; a ruinous competition seemed impending as the alternative to a fierce war of doubtful issue. Both parties now retired to their camps, and mustered their forces in preparation for the first overt act of hostility. They had not long to wait.

Vanderbilt was not accustomed to failure, and in this case the sense of treachery, the bitter consciousness of having been outwitted in the presence of all Wall Street, gave a peculiar sting to the rebuff. A long succession of victories had intensified his natural arrogance, and he was by no means disposed, even apart from the failure of his cherished plans, to sit down and nurse an impotent wrath in presence of an injured prestige. Foiled in intrigue, he must now have recourse to his favorite weapon,—the brute force of his millions. He therefore prepared to go out into Wall Street in his might, and to make himself master of the Erie, as before he had made himself master of the Hudson River road. The task in itself was one of magnitude. The volume of stock was immense; all of it was upon the street, and the necessary expenditure involved many millions of dollars. The peculiar difficulty of the task, however, lay in the fact that it had to

2 [At the same election Jay Gould, still an unknown stockbroker but close associate of the Boston group, became a director.]

be undertaken in the face of antagonists so bold, so subtle, so unscrupulous, so thoroughly acquainted with Erie, as well as so familiar with all the devices and tricks . . . of Wall Street, as were those who now stood ready to take up the gage which the Commodore so arrogantly threw down.

The first open hostilities took place on the 17th of February. For some time Wall Street had been agitated with forebodings of the coming hostilities, but not until that day was recourse had to the courts. Vanderbilt had two ends in view when he sought to avail himself of the processes of law. In the first place, Drew's long connection with Erie, and especially the unsettled transactions arising out of the famous corner of 1866, afforded admirable ground for annoying offensive operations; and, in the second place, these very proceedings, by throwing his opponent on the defensive, afforded an excellent cover for Vanderbilt's own transactions in Wall Street. It was essential to his success to corner Drew, but to corner Drew at all was not easy, and to corner him in Erie was difficult indeed. Very recent experiences, of which Vanderbilt was fully informed, no less than the memories of 1866, had fully warned the public how manifold and ingenious were the expedients through which the cunning treasurer furnished himself with Erie, when the exigencies of his position demanded fresh supplies. It was, therefore, very necessary for Vanderbilt that he should, while buying Erie with one hand in Wall Street, with the other close, so far as he could, that apparently inexhaustible spring from which such generous supplies of new stock were wont to flow. Accordingly, on the 17th of February, Mr. Frank Work, the only remaining representative of the Vanderbilt faction in the Erie direction, accompanied by Mr. Vanderbilt's attorneys, Messrs. Rapallo and Spenser, made his appearance before Judge Barnard, of the Supreme Court of New York, then sitting in chambers, and applied for an injunction against Treasurer Drew and his brother directors, of the Erie Railway, restraining them from the payment of interest or principal of the three and a half millions borrowed of the treasurer in 1866, as well as from releasing Drew from any liability or cause of action the company might have against him, pending an investigation of his accounts as treasurer; on the other hand, Drew was to be enjoined from taking any legal steps towards compelling a settlement. A temporary injunction was granted in accordance with the petition, and a further hearing was assigned for the 21st. Two days later, however,—on the 19th of the month,—without waiting for the result of the first attack, the same attorneys appeared again before Judge Barnard, and now in the name of the people, acting through the Attorney-General, petitioned for the removal from office of Treasurer Drew. The papers in the case set forth some of the difficulties which beset the Commodore, and exposed the existence of a new fountain of Erie stock. It appeared that there was a recently enacted statute of New York which authorized any railroad company to create and issue its own stock in exchange for the stock of any other road under lease to it. The petition then alleged that Mr. Drew and certain of his brother directors, had quietly possessed themselves of a worthless road connecting with the Erie, and called the Buffalo, Bradford, & Pittsburg Railroad, and had then, as occasion and their own exigencies required, proceeded to supply themselves with whatever Erie stock they wanted, by leasing their own road to the road of which they were directors, and then creating stock and issuing it to themselves, in exchange, under the authority vested in them by law.

[Adams next describes Vanderbilt's continuing efforts to tighten the legal noose around Drew while buying up Erie stock. But mere legal proceedings failed to intimidate Drew.]

All was now ready. The Drew party were enjoined in every direction. One magistrate had forbidden them to move, and another magistrate had ordered them not to stand still. If the Erie board held meetings and transacted business, it violated one injunction; if it abstained from doing so, it violated another. By the further conversion of bonds into stock pains and penalties would be incurred at the hands of Judge Barnard; the refusal to convert would be an act of disobedience to Judge Gilbert. Strategically considered, the position could not be improved, and Mr. Drew and his friends were not the men to let the golden moment escape them. At once, before a new injunction could be obtained, even in New York, fifty thousand shares of new Erie stock were flung upon the market. That day Erie was buoyant,—Vanderbilt was purchasing. His agents caught at the new stock as eagerly as at the old, and the whole of it was absorbed before its origin was suspected, and almost without a falter in the price. Then the fresh certificates appeared, and the truth became known. Erie had that day opened at 80 and risen rapidly to 83, while its rise even to par was predicted; suddenly it faltered, fell off, and then dropped suddenly to 71. Wall Street had never been subjected to a greater shock, and the market reeled to and fro like a drunken man between these giants, as they hurled about shares by the tens of thousands, and money by the million. When night put an end to the conflict, Erie stood at 78, the shock of battle was over, and the astonished brokers drew breath as they waited for the events of the morrow. The attempted "corner" was a failure, and Drew was victorious,—no doubt existed on that point. The question now was, could Vanderbilt sustain himself? In spite of all his wealth, must he not go down before his cunning opponent?

The morning of [March] 11th found the Erie leaders still transacting business at the office of the corporation in West Street. It would seem that these gentlemen, in spite of the glaring contempt for the process of the courts of which they had been guilty, had made no arrangements for an orderly retreat beyond the jurisdiction of the tribunals they had set at defiance. They were speedily roused from their real or affected tranquillity by trustworthy intelligence that processes for contempt were already issued against them, and that their only chance of escape from incarceration lay in precipitate flight. At ten o'clock the astonished police saw a throng of panic-stricken railway directors—looking more like a frightened gang of thieves, disturbed in the division of their plunder, than like the wealthy representatives of a great corporation—rush headlong from the doors of the Erie office, and dash off in the direction of the Jersey ferry. In their hands were packages and files of papers, and their pockets were crammed with assets and securities. One individual bore away with him in a hackney-coach bales containing six millions of dollars in greenbacks. Other members of the board followed under cover of the night; some of them, not daring to expose themselves to the publicity of a ferry, attempted to cross in open boats concealed by the darkness and a March fog. Two directors, who lingered, were arrested; but a majority of the Executive Committee collected at the Erie Station in Jersey City, and there, free from any apprehension of Judge Barnard's pursuing wrath, proceeded to the transaction of business.

Meanwhile, on the other side of the river, Vanderbilt was struggling in the toils. As usual in these Wall Street operations, there was a grim humor in the situation. Had Vanderbilt failed to sustain the market, a financial collapse and panic must have ensued which would have sent him to the wall. He had sustained it, and had absorbed a hundred thousand shares of Erie. Thus when Drew retired to Jersey City he carried with him seven millions of his opponent's money, and the Commodore had freely supplied the enemy with the sinews of war. He had grasped at Erie for his own sake, and now his opponents derisively promised to rehabilitate and vivify the old road with the money he had furnished them, so as more effectually to compete with the lines which he already possessed. Nor was this all. Had they done as they loudly claimed they meant to do, Vanderbilt might have hugged himself in the faith that, after all, it was but a question of time, and the prize would come to him in the end. He, however, knew well enough that the most pressing need of the Erie people was money with which to fight him. With this he had now furnished them abundantly, and he must have felt that no scruples would prevent their use of it.

Vanderbilt had, however, little leisure to devote to the enjoyment of the humorous side of his position. The situation was alarming. His opponents had carried with them in their flight seven millions in currency, which were withdrawn from circulation. An artificial stringency was thus created in Wall Street, and, while money rose, stocks fell, and unusual margins were called in. Vanderbilt was carrying a fearful load, and the least want of confidence, the faintest sign of faltering, might well bring on a crash. He already had a hundred thousand shares of Erie, not one of which he could sell. He was liable at any time to be called upon to carry as much more as his opponents, skilled by long practice in the manufacture of the article, might see fit to produce. Opposed to him were men who scrupled at nothing, and who knew every in and out of the money market. With every look and every gesture anxiously scrutinized, a position more trying than his can hardly be conceived. It is not known from what source he drew the vast sums which enabled him to surmount his difficulties with such apparent ease. His nerve, however, stood him in at least as good stead as his financial resources. Like a great general, in the hour of trial he inspired confidence. While fighting for life he could "talk horse" and play whist. The manner in which he then emerged from his troubles, serene and confident, was as extraordinary as the financial resources he commanded.

[Now the contest moved to Albany. Both Vanderbilt and the Erie crowd needed legislative support. Many legislators relished the opportunity to meet these needs. In fact the legislature had already shown a serious interest in the controversy.]

One favorite method of procedure at Albany is through the appointment of committees to investigate the affairs of wealthy corporations. The stock of some great company is manipulated till it fluctuates violently, as was the case with Pacific Mail in 1867. Forthwith some member of the Assembly rises and calls for a committee of investigation. The instant the game is afoot, a rush is made for positions on the committee. The proposer, of course, is a member, probably chairman. The advantages of the position are obvious. The committee constitutes a little temporary outside ring. If a member is corrupt, he has substantial advantages offered him to influence his action in regard to the report. If he is not open to bribery, he is nevertheless in possession of very valuable information, and an innocent little remark, casually let fall, may lead a son, a brother, or a loving cousin to make very judicious purchases of stock. Altogether, the position is one not to be avoided.

The investigation phase was the first which the Erie struggle assumed at Albany. During the early stages of the conflict the legislature had scented the carnage from afar. There was "money in it," and the struggle was watched with breathless interest. As early as the 5th of March the subject had been introduced into the State Senate, and an investigation into the circumstances of the company was called for. A committee of three was ordered, but the next day a senator, by name Mattoon, moved to increase the number to five, which was done, he himself being naturally one of the additional members. This committee had its first sitting on the 10th, at the very crisis of the great explosion. But before the investigation was entered upon, Mr. Mattoon thought it expedient to convince the contending parties of his own perfect impartiality and firm determination to hold in check the corrupt impulses of his associates. With this end in view, upon the 9th or the 10th he hurried down to New York, and visited West Street, where he had an interview with the leading Erie directors. He explained to them the corrupt motives which had led to the appointment of the committee, and how his sole object in obtaining an increase of the number had been to put himself in a position in which he might be able to prevent these evil practices and see fair play. Curiously enough, at the same interview he mentioned that his son was to be appointed an assistant sergeant-at-arms to aid in the investigation, and proved his disinterestedness by mentioning the fact that this son was to serve without pay. The labors of the committee continued until the 31st of March, and during that time Mr. Mattoon, and at least one other senator, pursued a course of private inquiry which involved further visits to Jersey City. Naturally enough, Mr. Drew and his associates took it into their heads that the man wanted to be bought, and even affirmed subsequently that, at one interview, he had in pretty broad terms offered himself for sale. It has not been distinctly stated in evidence by any one that an attempt was made on his purity or on that of his public-spirited son; and it is difficult to believe that one who came to New York so full of high purpose could have been sufficiently corrupted by metropolitan influences to receive bribes from both sides. Whether he did so or not his proceedings were terribly suggestive as regards legislative morality at Albany. Here was a senator, a member of a committee of investigation, rousing gamblers from their beds at early hours of the morning to hold interviews in the faro-bank parlor of the establishment, and to give "points" on which to operate upon the joint account. Even then the wretched creature could not even keep faith with his very "pals"; he wrote to them to "go it heavy" for Drew, and then himself went over to Vanderbilt,—he made agreements to share profits and then submitted to exposure sooner than meet his part of the loss. A man more thoroughly, shamefacedly contemptible and corrupt,—a more perfect specimen of a legislator on sale haggling for his own price, could not well exist. In this case he cheated every one, including himself. Accident threw great opportunities in his way. On the 31st the draft of a proposed report, exonerating in great measure the Drew faction, was read to him by an associate, to which he not only made no objection, but was even understood to assent. On the same day another report was read in his presence, strongly denouncing the Drew faction, sustaining to the fullest extent the charges made against it, and characterizing its conduct as corrupt and disgraceful. Each report was signed by two of his associates, and Mr. Mattoon found himself in the position of holding the balance of power; whichever report he signed would be the report of the committee. He expressed a desire to think the matter over. It is natural to suppose that, in his eagerness to gain information privately, Mr. Mattoon had not confined his unofficial visits to the Drew camp. In any case his mind was in a state of painful suspense. Finally, after arranging in consultation on Tuesday for a report favoring the Drew party, on Wednesday he signed a report strongly denouncing it, and by doing so settled the action of the committee. Mr. Jay Gould must have been acquainted with the circumstances of the case, and evidently supposed that Mr. Mattoon was "fixed," since he subsequently declared he was "astounded" when he heard that Mr. Mattoon had signed this report. The committee, however, with their patriotic sergeant-at-arms, whose services, by the way, cost the State but a hundred dollars, desisted at length from their labors, the result of which was one more point gained by Commodore Vanderbilt.

Indeed, Vanderbilt had thus far as much outgeneraled Drew in the manufacture of public opinion as Drew had outgeneraled Vanderbilt in the manufacture of Erie stock. His whole scheme was one of monopoly, which was opposed to every interest of the city and State of New York, yet into the support of this scheme he had brought all the leading papers of New York City, with a single exception. Now again he seemed to have it all his own way in the legislature, and the tide ran strongly against the exiles of Erie. The report of the investigation committee was signed on April 1st, and may be considered as marking the high-water point of Vanderbilt's success. Hitherto the Albany interests of the exiles had been confided to mere agents, and had not prospered; but, when fairly roused by a sense of danger, the Drew party showed at least as close a familiarity with the tactics of Albany as with those of Wall Street. The moment they felt themselves settled at Jersey City they had gone to work to excite a popular sympathy in their own behalf. The cry of monopoly was a sure card in their hands. They cared no more for the actual welfare of commerce, involved in railroad competition, than they did for the real interests of the Erie Railway; but they judged truly that there was no limit to the extent to which the public might be imposed upon. An active competition with the Vanderbilt roads, by land and water, was inaugurated; fares and freights on the Erie were reduced on an average by one third; sounding proclamations were issued; "interviewers" from the press returned rejoicing from Taylor's Hotel to New York City, and the Jersey shore quaked under the clatter of this Chinese battle. The influence of these tactics made itself felt at once. By the middle of March memorials against monopoly began to flow in at Albany.

While popular sympathy was thus roused by the bribe of active competition, a bill was introduced into the Assembly, in the Erie interest, legalizing the recent issue of new stock, declaring and regulating the power of issuing convertible bonds, providing for a broad-gauge connection with Chicago and the guaranty of the bonds of the Boston, Hartford, & Erie, and finally forbidding, in so far as any legislation could forbid, the consolidation of the Central and the Erie in the hands of Vanderbilt. This bill was referred to the Committee on Railroads on the 13th of March. On the 20th a public hearing was begun, and the committee proceeded to take evidence, aided by a long array of opposing counsel, most of whom had figured in the proceedings in the courts of law. In a few days the bill was adversely reported upon, and the report adopted in the Assembly by the decisive vote of eighty-three to thirty-two. This was upon the 27th of March. The hint was a broad one; the exiles must give closer attention to their interests. So soon as the news of this adverse action reached Jersey City, it was decided that Mr. Jay Gould should brave the terrors of the law, and personally superintend matters at Albany. Neither Mr. Drew nor his associates desired to become permanent residents of Jersey City; nor did they wish to return to New York as criminals on their way to jail. Mr. Gould was to pave the way to a different return by causing the recent issue of convertible bonds to be legalized. That once done, Commodore Vanderbilt was not the man to wage an unavailing war, and a compromise, in which Barnard and his processes of contempt would be thrown in as a makeweight, could easily be effected. A rumor was therefore started that Mr. Gould was to leave for Ohio, supplied with the necessary authority and funds to press vigorously to completion the eighty miles of broad-gauge track between Akron and Toledo, which would open to the Erie the much-coveted connection with Chicago. Having hung out this false light, Mr. Jay Gould went on his mission, the president of the company having some time previously drawn half a million of dollars out of the overflowing Erie treasury.

This mission was by no means unattended by difficulties. In the first place, Judge Barnard's processes for contempt seemed to threaten the liberty of Mr. Gould's person. . . .

[He was, in fact, arrested and brought before Judge Barnard in New York City. Released on bail, Gould immediately returned to Albany.]

The full and true history of this legislative campaign will never be known. If the official reports of investigating committees are to be believed, Mr. Gould at about this time underwent a curious psychological metamorphosis, and suddenly became the veriest simpleton in money matters that ever fell into the hands of happy sharpers. Cunning lobby members had but to pretend to an influence over legislative minds, which every one knew they did not possess, to draw unlimited amounts from this verdant *habitué* of Wall Street. It seemed strange that he could have lived so long and learned so little. He dealt in large sums. He gave to one man, in whom he said "he did not take much stock," the sum of $5,000, "just to smooth him over." This man had just before received $5,000 of Erie money from another agent of the company. It would, therefore, be interesting to know what sums Mr. Gould paid to those individuals in whom he did "take much stock." Another individual is reported to have received $100,000 from one side, "to influence legislation," and to have subsequently received $70,000 from the other side to disappear with the money; which he accordingly did, and thereafter became a gentleman of elegant leisure. One senator was openly charged in the columns of the press with receiving a bribe of $20,000 from one side, and a second bribe of $15,000 from the other; but Mr. Gould's foggy mental condition only enabled him to be "perfectly astounded" at the action of this senator, though he knew nothing of any such transactions. Other senators were blessed with a sudden accession of wealth, but in no case was there any jot or tittle of proof of bribery. Mr. Gould's rooms at the Develin House overflowed with a joyous company, and his checks were numerous and heavy; but why he signed them, or what became of them, he seemed to know less than any man in Albany. This strange and expensive hallucination lasted until about the middle of April, when Mr. Gould was happily restored to his normal condition of a shrewd, acute, energetic man of business; nor is it known that he has since experienced any relapse into financial idiocy.

About the period of Mr. Gould's arrival in Albany the tide turned, and soon began to flow strongly in favor of Erie and against Vanderbilt. How much of this was due to the skilful manipulations of Gould, and how much to the rising popular feeling against the practical consolidation of competing lines, cannot be decided. The popular protests did indeed pour in by scores, but then again the Erie secret-service money poured out like water. Yet Mr. Gould's task was sufficiently difficult. After the adverse report of the Senate committee, and the decisive defeat of the bill introduced into the Assembly, any favorable legislation seemed almost hopeless. Both Houses were committed. Vanderbilt had but to prevent action,—to keep things where they were, and the return of his opponents to New York was impracticable, unless with his consent; he appeared, in fact, to be absolute master of the situation. It seemed almost impossible to introduce a bill in the face of his great influence, and to navigate it through the many stages of legislative action and executive approval, without somewhere giving him an opportunity to defeat it. This was the task Gould had before him, and he accomplished it. On the 13th of April a bill, which met the approval of the Erie party, and which Judge Barnard subsequently compared not inaptly to a bill legalizing counterfeit money, was taken up in the Senate; for some days it was warmly debated, and on the 18th was passed by the decisive vote of seventeen to twelve. Senator Mattoon had not listened to the debate in vain. Perhaps his reason was convinced, or perhaps he had sold out new "points" and was again cheating himself or somebody else; at any rate, that thrifty senator was found voting with the majority. The bill practically legalized the recent issues of bonds, but made it a felony to use the proceeds of the sale of these bonds except for completing, furthering, and operating the road. The guaranty of the bonds of connecting roads was authorized, all contracts for consolidation or division of receipts between the Erie and the Vanderbilt roads were forbidden, and a clumsy provision was enacted that no stockholder, director, or officer in one of the Vanderbilt roads should be an officer or director in the Erie, and *vice versa*. The bill was, in fact, an amended copy of the one voted down so decisively in the Assembly a few days before, and it was in this body that the tug of war was expected to come.

The lobby was now full of animation; fabulous stories were told of the amounts which the contending parties were willing to expend; never before had the market quotations of votes and influence stood so high. The wealth of Vanderbilt seemed pitted against the Erie treasury, and the vultures flocked to Albany from every part of the State. Suddenly, at the very last moment, and even while special trains were bringing up fresh contestants to take part in the fray, a rumor ran through Albany as of some great public disaster, spreading panic and terror through hotel and corridor. The observer was reminded of the dark days of the war, when tidings came of some great defeat, as that on the Chickahominy or at Fredericksburg. In a moment the lobby was smitten with despair, and the cheeks of the legislators were blanched, for it was reported that Vanderbilt had withdrawn his opposition to the bill. The report was true. Either the Commodore had counted the cost and judged it excessive, or he despaired of the result. At any rate, he had yielded in advance. In a few moments the long struggle was over, and that bill which, in an unamended form, had but a few days before been thrown out of the Assembly by a vote of eighty-three to thirty-two, now passed it by a vote of one hundred and one to six, and was sent to the Governor for his signature. Then the wrath of the disappointed members turned on Vanderbilt. Decency was forgotten in a frenzied sense of disappointed avarice. That same night the *pro rata* freight bill, and a bill compelling the sale of through tickets by competing lines, were hurriedly passed, simply because they were thought hurtful to Vanderbilt; and the docket was ransacked in search of other measures, calculated to injure or annoy him. An adjournment, however, brought reflection, and subsequently, on this subject, the legislature stultified itself no more.

The bill had passed the legislature; would it receive the Executive signature? Here was the last stage of danger. For some time doubts were entertained on this point, and the last real conflict between the opposing interests took place in the Executive Chamber at Albany. There, on the afternoon of the 21st of April, Commodore Vanderbilt's counsel appeared before

Governor Fenton, and urged upon him their reasons why the bill should be returned by him to the Senate without his signature. The arguments were patiently listened to, but, when they had closed, the Executive signature placed the seal of success upon Mr. Gould's labors at Albany. Even here the voice of calumny was not silent. As if this remarkable controversy was destined to leave a dark blot of suspicion upon every department of the civil service of New York, there were not wanting those who charged the Executive itself with the crowning act in this history of corruption. The very sum pretended to have been paid was named; the broker of Executive action was pointed out, and the number of minutes was specified which should intervene between the payment of the bribe and the signing of the law.[3]

Practically, the conflict was now over, and the period of negotiation had already begun. The combat in the courts was indeed kept up until far into May, for the angry passions of the lawyers and of the judges required time in which to wear themselves out. Day after day the columns of the press revealed fresh scandals to the astonished public, which at last grew indifferent to such revelations. Beneath all the wrangling of the courts, however, while the popular attention was distracted by the clatter of lawyers' tongues, the leaders in the controversy were quietly approaching a settlement. In the early days of his exile Mr. Drew had been more depressed in spirit, more vacillating in counsel, than his younger and more robust associates. . . . Early in April Mr. Drew took advantage of that blessed immunity from arrest which the Sabbath confers on the hunted of the law, to revisit the familiar scenes across the river. His visit soon resulted in conferences between himself and Vanderbilt, and these conferences naturally led to overtures of peace. Though the tide was turning against the great railroad king, though an uncontrollable popular feeling was fast bearing down his schemes of monopoly, yet he was by no means beaten or subdued. His plans, however, had evidently failed for the present; as he expressed himself, he could easily enough buy up the Erie Railway, but he could not buy up the printing-press. It was now clearly his interest to abandon his late line of attack, and to bide his time patiently, or to possess himself of his prey by some other method. The wishes of all parties, therefore, were fixed on a settlement, and no one was disposed to stand out except in order to obtain better terms. The interests, however, were multifarious. There were four parties to be taken care of, and the depleted treasury of the Erie Railway was doomed to suffer.

The details of this masterpiece of Wall Street diplomacy have never come to light, but Mr. Drew's visits to New York became more frequent and less guarded; by the middle of April he had appeared in Broad Street on a week-day, undisturbed by fears of arrest, and soon rumors began to spread of misunderstandings between himself and his brother exiles. It was said that his continual absences alarmed them, that they distrusted him, that

3 It is but justice to Governor Fenton to say, that, though this charge was boldly advanced by respectable journals of his own party, it cannot be considered as sustained by the evidence. The testimony on the point will be found in the report of Senator Hale's investigating committee. Documents (Senate), 1869, No. 52, pp. 146–148, 151–155.

his terms of settlement were not theirs. It was even asserted that his orders on the treasury were no longer honored, and that he had, in fact, ceased to be a power in Erie. Whatever truth there may have been in these rumors, it was very evident his associates had no inclination to trust themselves within the reach of the New York courts until a definitive treaty, satisfactory to themselves, was signed and sealed. This probably took place about the 25th of April; for on that day the Erie camp at "Fort Taylor," as their uninviting hotel had been dubbed, was broken up, the President and one of the Executive Committee took steamer for Boston, and the other directors appeared before Judge Barnard, prepared to purge themselves of their contempt.

Though the details of negotiation have never been divulged, yet it was clear enough what three of the four parties desired. Commodore Vanderbilt wished to be relieved of the vast amount of stock with which he was loaded, and his friends Work and Schell, in whose names the battle had been fought, must be protected. Mr. Drew desired to settle his entangled accounts as treasurer, and to obtain a release in full, which might be pleaded in future complications. Mr. Eldridge and his Boston friends were sufficiently anxious to be relieved of the elephant they found on their hands, in the Erie Railway of New York, and to be at leisure to devote the spoils of their victim to the development of their New England enterprise. Messrs. Gould and Fisk alone were unprovided for, and they alone presented themselves as obstacles to be overcome by railroad diplomacy.

At last, upon the 2d of July, Mr. Eldridge formally announced to the Board of Directors that the terms of peace had been agreed upon. Commodore Vanderbilt was, in the first place, provided for. He was to be relieved of fifty thousand shares of Erie stock at 70, receiving therefor $2,500,-000 in cash, and $1,250,000 in bonds of the Boston, Hartford, & Erie at 80. He was also to receive a further sum of $1,000,000 outright, as a consideration for the privilege the Erie road thus purchased of calling upon him for his remaining fifty thousand shares at 70 at any time within four months. He was also to have two seats in the Board of Directors, and all suits were to be dismissed and offences condoned. The sum of $429,250 was fixed upon as a proper amount to assuage the sense of wrong from which his two friends Work and Schell had suffered. . . . Why the owners of the Erie Railway should have paid this indemnity of $4,000,000 is not very clear. The operations were apparently outside of the business of a railway company, and no more connected with the stockholders of the Erie than were the butchers' bills of the individual directors.

While Vanderbilt and his friends were thus provided for, Mr. Drew was to be left in undisturbed enjoyment of the fruits of his recent operations, but was to pay into the treasury $540,000 and interest, in full discharge of all claims and causes of action which the Erie Company might have against him. The Boston party, as represented by Mr. Eldridge, was to be relieved of $5,000,000 of their Boston, Hartford, & Erie bonds, for which they were to receive $4,000,000 of Erie acceptances. None of these parties, therefore, had anything to complain of, whatever might be the sensations of the real owners of the railway. A total amount of some $9,000,000 in cash was drawn from the treasury in fulfilment of this *settlement,* as the persons concerned were pleased to term this remarkable disposition of property intrusted to their care.

Messrs. Gould and Fisk still remained to be taken care of, and to them their associates left—the Erie Railway. These gentlemen subsequently maintained that they had vehemently opposed this settlement, and had denounced it in the secret councils as a fraud and a robbery. . . . Probably at this time these gentlemen seriously debated the expediency of resorting again to a war of injunctions, and carefully kept open a way for so doing; however this may have been, they seem finally to have concluded that there was yet plunder left in the poor old hulk, and so, after four stormy interviews, all opposition was at last withdrawn and the definitive treaty was finally signed.

.   .   .   .

4] The Financier As Railroad Reorganizer and System-Builder

J. Pierpont Morgan in Railway Finance, 1879–88

THE YEAR 1879 was a turning point in the career of J. Pierpont Morgan. That year closed the government operations which had been the chief investment occupation of the Morgan houses and of other bankers in the 1870's and possibly since the Civil War. It was clear that in the near future the outstanding investment field would be railroads. For taking on new work, no one was in a better position than Morgan—no other banker in New York had the combination of vigor, good standing and support, and experience that he had.

J. Pierpont Morgan's first large operation in railroad finance was in the sale of New York Central stock in 1879. When William H. Vanderbilt [1] decided to sell a large part of his stock in order to counteract the threat of adverse legislation and heavy taxation, he turned to Morgan. Only a powerful banking firm could possibly handle the sale of so large a block of stock without upsetting the market. It was rumored that Vanderbilt was also interested in making through the Morgans a connection with the Wabash, St. Louis & Pacific.[2]

Morgan arranged for the underwriting of 250,000 shares of New York Central by a syndicate composed of J. S. Morgan & Co., August Belmont

1 [When the Commodore died in 1877, his son William took over the ownership and management of the Central.]

2 *Railway Gazette,* vol. xi, p. 636 (Nov. 28, 1879) and p. 645 (Dec. 5, 1879). It was suggested in the *Com. & Fin. Chron.* (vol. xxix, p. 530, Nov. 22, 1879) that there was to be an exchange of New York Central for Erie and Wabash stock.

FROM N. S. B. Gras and Henrietta M. Larson, "J. Pierpont Morgan," *Casebook in American Business History* (New York, 1939), pp. 552–55, 557–59. Copyright, 1939, F. S. Crofts & Co., Inc. Reprinted by permission of Appleton-Century-Crofts.

& Co., Morton, Bliss & Co., and Jay Gould. The shares were purchased at 120 and were sold in London at 130, all without causing any noticeable disturbance on the market. The affair was regarded as a "grand financial operation"[3] and it gave J. Pierpont Morgan and the Morgan houses a strong position of leadership in railroad finance. Morgan became a director of the road in order to protect his clients' interests, and three men influential in Wabash administration were also put on the Central board. This seems to bear out the *Chronicle's* suggestion that heavy capital was anxious to get control of trunk-line stocks in order to secure harmony and prevent the cutthroat competition that meant the end of profits.[4]

The next big operation of the Morgans was in Northern Pacific stock. That road had been laboriously pulling itself out of its failure in 1873. In 1876 earnings for the first time exceeded expenditures, and the road embarked on a policy of cautious expansion. Settlement began to move westward again, and there was prospect of increasing traffic. By 1880 the Northern Pacific was a substantial property in a condition to attract capital, and it turned to New York for funds for building its line from the Missouri to the Pacific Coast. The result can best be shown by quoting from a statement of Drexel, Morgan & Co. which appeared in the *Commercial & Financial Chronicle* on December 4, 1880:[5]

The largest transaction in railroad bonds ever made in the United States has just been closed by Messrs. Drexel, Morgan & Co., Winslow, Lanier & Co., and August Belmont & Co., they having made a contract with the Northern Pacific Railroad Company for $40,000,000 6 per cent gold bonds having forty years to run. . . .

The three firms named as contractors have associated with them several of the best-known bankers here and in other cities, as well as in Europe, among whom are the following: Messrs. Drexel & Co., Philadelphia; Messrs. J. S. Morgan & Co., London; Messrs. Drexel, Harjes & Co., Paris. In this city the associates are as follows: National Bank of Commerce, Messrs. J. & W. Seligman & Co., Messrs. Kuhn Loeb & Co., Messrs. Woerishoeffer & Co., Third National Bank, Messrs. L. Von Hoffman & Co., Messrs. J. S. Kennedy & Co., Messrs. Speyer & Co. In Boston associated with them are the following: Messrs. Lee, Higginson & Co., Messrs. Brewster, Basset & Co. In Baltimore: Messrs. Johnston Bros. & Co.

. . . .

By terms of the agreement with the company, the contractors are to name two directors in the board, and the persons selected for the positions are Messrs. J. C. Bullitt, of Philadelphia, and John W. Ellis, of Winslow, Lanier & Co., of New York.

The prosperity which began in the late 1870's brought a boom in American railroads, but when the boom was ended there was the bill to pay. *Poor's Manual* in 1884 called attention to the "immense increase of fictitious capital" of the railroads in 1880–83. Though they were overcapitalized, the old roads could support themselves as long as they occupied the field

3 *Com. & Fin. Chron.,* vol. xxix, p. 554 (Nov. 29, 1879).
4 *Ibid.*
5 For further details see J. B. Hedges, *Henry Villard and the Railways of the Northwest* (New Haven, 1930).

alone, but by 1885 there were five trunk lines from New York to Chicago—three tottering on the edge of bankruptcy—and two more were being built. Bitter and destructive war was the result.

On his trip to Europe in the early summer of 1885 Morgan became impressed with the necessity of doing something about trunk-line competition.[6] He was convinced that the points to attack were a road built parallel to the New York Central from New York to Buffalo and another threatening the Pennsylvania from Pittsburgh eastward. The former had been built by promoters who took heavy profits from promotion and construction and then proceeded to threaten the Central with their bankrupt road; the Pennsylvania road was the work of Vanderbilt, backed by Andrew Carnegie and other iron interests that wanted to break the monopoly of the Pennsylvania eastward from Pittsburgh. A further factor in the situation was the Baltimore & Ohio, which was also fighting the Pennsylvania and, like the Reading, was attempting to obtain access to New York by means of the tracks of the Central of New Jersey.

Morgan saw that the two key men in solving the problem were Vanderbilt and President Roberts of the Pennsylvania, who could stop the threat of parallel lines by purchasing the competitors. Vanderbilt was reluctant, however, to give up the South Pennsylvania and was still smarting under the sting of the heavy price he had paid for the Nickel Plate to remove its competition with his Lake Shore road. Roberts was openly committed to enmity with the South Pennsylvania and hated to make concessions to Vanderbilt and Carnegie. But Morgan could use the argument of necessity. Vanderbilt capitulated first, and, after a long conference on Morgan's yacht, Roberts accepted Morgan's proposals.

Drexel, Morgan & Co. managed the transactions necessary to carry out Morgan's proposals. The New York line was purchased at foreclosure by the West Shore Railway Co., which was organized for that purpose. A Morgan partner became its first president, and several men close to Drexel, Morgan & Co. were on its board. The West Shore was then leased to the New York Central, with a guarantee of principal and interest on $50,000,-000 new bonds.[7] It was agreed that the Pennsylvania should buy its enemy at cost, but under the law of the State a direct purchase was impossible. J. Pierpont Morgan, therefore, personally bought a 60 per cent interest in the road from a syndicate consisting chiefly of Vanderbilt and "Rockafellow" interests; he paid for the purchase by means of bonds of another road, which securities were provided and guaranteed by the Pennsylvania.[8]

Morgan's next step was to take the leading hand in reorganizing and refinancing some of the tottering roads. These were the Reading, the Baltimore & Ohio, and the Chesapeake & Ohio.

The reorganization of the Philadelphia & Reading came in 1886–87. That road was suffering from the usual competition and from the terrific capital charges resulting from former President Gowen's policy of expansion.

6 The temper of the English investor is reflected in the detailed discussion of the New York Central-Pennsylvania difficulties in the *Economist* in December, 1885.

7 *Com. & Fin. Chron.*, vol. xli, p. 689 (Dec. 12, 1885); *Poor's Manual*, 1886, p. 491.

8 *Com. & Fin. Chron.*, vol. xli, pp. 445–446 (Oct. 17, 1885).

Morgan organized a syndicate which improved the capital position of the Reading, cutting fixed charges and rentals from about $14,000,000 as of 1885 to about $6,500,000. The Morgan syndicate provided $15,000,000 in cash, of which it received 5 per cent as compensation. Morgan is said to have established peace with the Pennsylvania and arranged with other anthracite lines for limiting production and maintaining prices. A voting trust, headed by Morgan, was formed to control the Reading for five years, and it chose a New York banker to be president of the road.[9]

Morgan next undertook to place the Baltimore & Ohio on a sound financial basis and in 1888 organized a group to furnish the money. In the contract with the company this group stipulated that the statements of the B. & O. should be verified, the management of the road should be placed in competent hands acceptable to the syndicate, and agreements should be made with other roads about the New York traffic.[10] In carrying out these stipulations, Morgan found that the B. & O. and its home community would accept only informal agreements, which virtually meant the continuance of competition. The syndicate did not insist, however, since the road was strengthening its finances under the new president and was trying to improve its operation. But when reform threatened to uncover faults in management under the younger Garrett, the family interests elected their own candidate president and thus blocked Morgan's efforts.[11]

In 1888 Drexel, Morgan & Co. also reorganized the Chesapeake & Ohio. That road was heavily loaded with debt and fixed charges, and it did not have satisfactory connections with the Atlantic Coast or with the Middle West. At Morgan's suggestion a committee, including C. H. Coster who was the Drexel, Morgan expert in this field, was put in charge of reorganization, and voting power for five years was given to J. Pierpont Morgan, John C. Brown, and George Bliss. New securities were issued for buying up the old securities and taking care of floating obligations, for providing working capital and funds for finishing a western extension, and for setting up a reserve. An assessment was levied on the stockholders. Control was gained of the Richmond & Allegheny Railroad, which gave access to Newport News, and the work on the new western division was put under way.[12] Reorganization was followed by the purchase of C. P. Huntington's controlling interest in the road by a syndicate of parties interested in the C. C. C. & St. L. Thus was put together, according to the *Commercial & Financial Chronicle,* a strong system of roads which reached from Chicago to Newport News.[13]

By this time the Morgans were recognized far and wide as conservative forces working for peace and harmony and increased confidence. These early Morgan recapitalizations did not necessarily mean a great scaling-down of the capital or even of the fixed capital charges; they generally

9 Jules I. Bogen, *The Anthracite Railroads* (New York, 1927), pp. 63–66.
10 Stuart Daggett, *Railroad Reorganization* (Boston, 1908), pp. 11–22.
11 *Ibid.,* pp. 13–16.
12 *Com. & Fin. Chron.,* vol. xlvi, p. v (Feb. 11, 1888), and vol. xlvii, p. 199 (Aug. 18, 1888).
13 *Ibid.,* vol. xlix, pp. 97, 113 (July 27, 1889).

simplified the capital structure, however, increased the stock as compared with the bonded obligations, funded the floating obligations, and provided working capital and reserves. Morgan reorganization plans also worked in general for more efficient management and for the establishment of better relations with competitors.

Creating the Morgan Railway Systems, 1888–1900

When in 1890 J. S. Morgan died, he left about a million dollars in money to his son and the nominal headship of the Morgan houses—the actual headship the son had already attained in New York. Though he was a man of unassuming demeanor and of few words, brusque and retiring in manner, J. Pierpont Morgan's movements were, in the words of the *New York Sun,* "watched more carefully than those of any other man in the financial world." [14]

At this time, as always, Morgan was supported by brilliant and hardworking associates. After the death of the elder Morgan, the London house was ably headed by Walter Burns, the husband of J. Pierpont Morgan's sister. Outstanding among Morgan's partners in New York was Charles H. Coster. Wall Street bankers still speak of Coster's terrific drive in studying a railroad—its physical properties, its management, and its financial condition—and his skill in drawing up reorganization plans. Equally outstanding on the legal side somewhat later was Francis Lynde Stetson. Morgan himself, however, was always the one to formulate the policy of the firm.

.   .   .   .

Morgan's opportunity came with the panic of 1893, which precipitated the failure of many railroads inherently weak from the results of bad management and destructive competition. In 1893 alone, according to one authority,[15] 27,000 miles, with an aggregate capitalization of almost two billion dollars, were taken over by the courts, and in 1894–98 foreclosure sales aggregated 40,503 miles. Among the more important roads failing were the Richmond & West Point Terminal, the Reading, the Erie, the Northern Pacific, the Baltimore & Ohio, the Atchison, and the Union Pacific. Morgan had charge of the reorganization of the first four and was concerned in the reorganization of the B. & O. and the Atchison. He had no competitor in this work—even the Harriman-Rockefeller-National City Bank-Kuhn, Loeb group had not yet risen to a point where they could be classed with the Morgans, though Harriman was soon to rise to first rank in the rehabilitation of the Union Pacific.

The Morgan reorganizations followed a general pattern: (1) the finances of the road were put on a sound basis, with lower fixed charges and a capital stock large in relation to bonded indebtedness; (2) the structure of the roads was greatly simplified by consolidation; (3) by means of voting trusts the Morgans retained control for some time after reorganization, and

14 Quoted from the *Sun* of Feb. 29, 1892, by John K. Winkler, *Morgan the Magnificent* (New York, 1930), p. 123.
15 Daggett, *op. cit.,* p. v.

after the voting trusts had expired Morgan representatives were usually found on the boards—when the managers in one instance objected to turning their roads over to the Morgans, Morgan, himself, is said to have retorted, "Your Roads! Your roads belong to my clients;" [16] and (4) with a nucleus of the roads in which he had a powerful influence, Morgan extended cooperation based on community of interest. Since the reorganizations are treated in detail in E. G. Campbell's *The Reorganization of the American Railroad System, 1893–1900*,[17] they will be considered only briefly here.

The first of Morgan's reorganizations at this time led to the organization of the Southern Railway. Morgan reluctantly went into the Richmond Terminal system to prevent a forced sale that would have destroyed the value of many securities. A reorganization committee headed by Coster drew up a plan for both physical and financial rehabilitation of about 6,000 miles of road (excluding the Central of Georgia). Assessments on stockholders—who received in exchange preferred stock—and the sale of stock and bonds furnished means to replace the old securities, to pay floating obligations and the expenses of reorganization, and to improve the road. The result was an immediate reduction in fixed charges from $9,500,000 to $6,789,000, based on the estimated minimum earning capacity of the system. A relatively large common stock was issued. The addition of the Central of Georgia and the placing of the management under Samuel Spencer made the Southern the strongest system in the South. One commentator, whose judgment has weight, stated that the welding of such unpromising railroad material—built to sell rather than to operate—in the most unpromising territory in the country for a railroad was "one of the noteworthy achievements of American railroad history." [18]

Reorganization of the Erie was not so immediately successful. The first plan had to be abandoned because it did not cut deeply enough. Another plan combined under one corporation all the properties involved, reaching from Chicago to New York, and provided for the issue of noncumulative preferred and common stock and bonds at greatly reduced interest. The stock was placed under a Morgan voting trust. The Morgans were to receive cash for all expenses and $500,000, payable in common stock, for organizing a syndicate to take $15,000,000 in bonds and any stock on which assessments were not paid. The *Chronicle* said this plan possessed the special merit characteristic of J. P. Morgan & Co.'s reorganizations "of exceeding frankness in dealing with the different classes of security holders." The London *Economist* (which was constitutionally upset over American railroad securities and management) admitted that, though the reorganization cost meant a perpetual charge of $50,000, the scheme had "the essential qualities of . . . adequacy, justice, and elasticity." [19]

Reorganization of the Reading presented very special problems because of its connections with the anthracite industry. Much-needed funds were

16 *Wall Street Journal,* April 1, 1913.
17 Published in 1938 by the Columbia University Press.
18 For a detailed discussion of this reorganization, see Campbell, *op. cit.,* pp. 149–159.
19 *Ibid.,* pp. 160–172.

provided for improving the road's physical condition and an attempt was made to diversify the traffic,[20] but the fundamental problem was the problem of the anthracite industry and the system of roads which served it. Morgan is said later to have secured, through the purchase of stock, an influence in the Lehigh Valley and the Central of New Jersey. The Delaware & Hudson and the Delaware, Lackawanna & Western were supposed to be under the Vanderbilts, who were in the Morgan sphere of influence. Morgan, as has been observed, was strong in the Erie. By 1901 Morgan had come to be regarded as the most important influence in transportation in the anthracite region.[21]

The next region to be entered by Morgan was the Northwest. He refused an invitation to reorganize the Union Pacific because it involved too much politics; the reorganization was therefore taken over by Harriman (with the backing of Kuhn, Loeb) and he made the road into a remarkably strong system. Morgan took on the reorganization of the Northern Pacific, however, and in doing so won the close coöperation of James J. Hill of the Great Northern. Morgan and Hill first attempted to combine the Great Northern and the Northern Pacific but were blocked by court decisions. The Northern Pacific was, therefore, purchased at foreclosure in 1896 by a reorganization committee, which appointed J. P. Morgan & Co. reorganization managers. The road was rehabilitated in the usual Morgan way.[22]

While participating in these and other less spectacular reorganizations, J. Pierpont Morgan became strongly interested in the New Haven road in New England. He had been elected in 1891 to the road's board, which already had as members such strong representatives of New York interests as Chauncey Depew and William Rockefeller. In the 'nineties, the New Haven began to absorb other New England railroads. It acquired the New York, Providence & Boston Railroad, the Housatonic, the Old Colony, and the New York & New England, and it took over other roads on long leases. An alliance with the Boston & Maine practically eliminated competition in New England.

Morgan's reorganization work in the 'nineties had important results. It strengthened many railroads and improved their securities and their services. It gave J. P. Morgan & Co., during the initial years, a considerable control through voting trusts, and it usually established them as bankers to the railroad properties in question. The work, of course, yielded handsome fees to the Morgans. To Morgan himself success meant unquestioned leadership in American finance, a leadership that was backed by strong support among the other New York bankers. Only the Harriman-Rockefeller-Kuhn, Loeb group had sufficient resources and following to undertake completely independent operations of like nature.

20 *Ibid.*, pp. 172–187.

21 *Ibid.*, pp. 188–189; *Report of the Industrial Commission*, vol. xix, pp. 461–463. Note that the Industrial Commission is cautious in its statements about the details of the Morgans' relations with those roads, though it concludes that the "total [anthracite] output more or less directly controlled by Morgan interests is probably from two-thirds to three-fourths of the entire shipments."

22 For details on the Northern Pacific see Campbell, *op. cit.*, pp. 196–205.

PART III
The First Modern
Corporate Management

INTRODUCTION

❨ PROBLEMS of administration followed those of finance. On the new large roads of the 1850's and the great reorganized systems of the 1880's, the problems of administration were unprecedented in American business. Like those of finance, they resulted essentially from the size of the new corporate enterprises, but they also reflected the complex needs of safe and efficient operation. No existing business required so many, so varied, and so intricate short-term operating decisions, and none called for such difficult long-term decisions as to pricing and allocation of resources. Thus, even before financiers and speculators grasped the possibilities of the corporation as an engine of exploitation and manipulation, railroad managers were devising ways to transform it into the basic institution for the management of modern large-scale business enterprise.

The trunk lines and the other new large roads of the 1850's were as costly to operate as they were to build. The expense of running one of America's largest industrial enterprises in the 1850's, the three integrated textile mills of the Pepperell Manufacturing Company at Biddeford, Maine, went over $300,000 only one year during the decade of the 1850's. Compare this figure to the $2,861,875 (a drop of $544,000 from the previous year) that it cost to run the New York and Erie Railroad in 1855 and to the $2,149,918 listed as the operating cost of the Pennsylvania for that same year. And these figures would

be much larger, of course, if transposed into present day dollars. By 1862 the Pennsylvania's operating expenses stood at $5,431,072 and in 1869, before its major expansion, at $12,203,268. Even the largest canals had running costs much lower than railroads, lower too than the textile mills, since the canals, like the turnpikes, did not own and operate the carriers using their facilities. Steamboat lines cost little more to run. Their average annual expenses remained well below those of a medium-sized textile corporation.

Large railroads also required many more workers than other contemporary business enterprises. The Pepperell mills in the 1850's employed an average of about eight hundred hands. The Erie had hired by the mid-fifties more than four thousand employees. By the late 1880's the Pennsylvania had come to employ close to fifty thousand on its vast system.

Size was only one dimension of the unique challenges facing managers of the new, large railroads in the 1850's. Their day-to-day operations required decisions that were far more numerous and far more complicated than those for the working of a mill, a canal, or a steamship line. Unlike a textile company, whose group of mills could be viewed within half an hour, a railroad was spread over hundreds of miles and included a wide variety of activities and facilities—such as shops, terminals, stations, warehouses, office buildings, bridges, telegraph lines, and so forth. Unlike a canal, which might have the same geographical spread, the railroad ran, maintained, and repaired the equipment it used in the transporting of goods and passengers. Weeks would be required to view all its men and equipment. So every day, railroad managers had to make decisions controlling the activities of many men to whom they rarely talked or even ever saw.

Moreover, these operational decisions had to be made much more quickly and involved more crucial responsibilities than did most decisions made in the management of a textile factory, canal, or river steamboat. The condition of freight and the safety and, indeed, the very lives of passengers depended on continuous, effective decision-making. Equally important for efficient operations were the continuing decisions as to the number of cars to be sent on scheduled runs in order to meet the constantly changing demands for freight space at the different stations. Each day stations loaded different amounts of freight, and each day there was a change in the variety of traffic. Cargoes, which were often unpredictable in quantity, had to be directed over several hundreds of miles of track to several different destinations. The long-range decisions on the setting and adjustments of rates and the determination of costs, profits, and losses were also endlessly complicated. Therefore both the short-term operating decisions of coordination and appraisal and the long-term policy decisions—involving expansion by construction or purchase of tracks, equipment, terminal, and other facilities and the methods used to finance such expansion—were unprecedented in their intricacies.

For these reasons, the trunk lines completed in the early 1850's were literally forced to pioneer in the new ways of corporate management. With the possible exception of the Western in Massachusetts and the Reading in Pennsylvania no other roads had enough volume or mileage to raise complex administrative problems before that decade. So the Baltimore and Ohio, the Erie, and the Pennsylvania all made notable contributions to the science of modern management. Among them they fashioned the earliest large-scale administrative structures in American business.

Senior officers of the Baltimore and Ohio were the first to separate the management of financial and accounting activities from those of moving trains and traffic. They created an accounting or a controller's office that supervised and carefully accounted for the financial transactions carried on within the corporation. These transactions were far more numerous than those in a textile mill or on a canal because so many more employees—conductors, freight agents, station agents, and others—handled money. The accounting section worked closely with the treasurer's office, which watched over funds raised by the sale of securities to investors and speculators and helped allocate these, as well as the profits made from operations, for new construction and for maintenance and repair. The activities of these two new offices, which in time came under the control of a vice-president in charge of finance, remained quite distinct from the operating or transportation department.

The Erie and then the Pennsylvania made their contributions in the organization of the transportation department. Daniel C. McCallum, the general superintendent of the New York and Erie, was the first to define clearly the duties and responsibilities of the several executive or administrative officers on a large railroad and to spell out the lines of authority and communication between them. He also devised a detailed system of information to flow through these lines. McCallum's achievements assured effective and continuous control over and coordination of the multifarious operations of a large railroad. J. Edgar Thomson, president of the Pennsylvania, refined many of McCallum's policies and procedures. For example, he transformed McCallum's concept of the delegation of authority into the divisional type of structure that came to be generally used by American railroads. In the new type of organization, which made line and staff distinctions, the local division superintendent became the line officer responsible for all orders concerning movement of freight and passengers. Other local officers were staff executives who carried out the division superintendent's orders on matters of transportation. These staff executives reported, however, to their seniors in the central office on methods and timing of the maintenance and repair of motive power, rolling stock, tracks, bridges, and telegraph, as well as the purchasing and installing of new equipment.

In the 1860's, as traffic and mileage increased, the Pennsylvania also pioneered in the creation of a third great functional department—the traffic department—which became responsible for obtaining and processing, but not moving, freight and passengers. The Pennsylvania also formed one of the first central offices manned by executives who concentrated on the broader problems of cost determination, competitive rate-making, and strategic expansion rather than on the more routine operating activities.

The change in the railroad world's concerns from those of expansion to those of competition during the 1870's brought a new emphasis to the tasks of administration. Cost analysis or cost accounting became critically important in the determination of cost, and therefore, in the determination of profits and rate-making. Such analyses also came to be used as effective ways to evaluate the performance of operating executives. The most articulate innovator of these new costing techniques was Albert Fink, a German-born engineer and bridge-builder who received his railroad training on the Baltimore and Ohio and who in 1865 became general superintendent of the Louisville and Nashville Railroad and in 1869 its president. The type of cost data developed by Fink, together with the informational flows first set up by McCallum, made possible the "control through statistics" that has become an essential hallmark of modern corporate administration.

The competition of the 1870's brought administrative challenges in another and more indirect way. As is indicated in Part V, fierce competition led to federation and, when that failed, consolidation. Many of the large railroads of the 1850's and 1860's became the huge systems of the 1880's and 1890's either by purchases and mergers or by new construction. The sudden growth of a railroad from five hundred to five thousand miles greatly magnified all the problems of handling traffic, of moving trains, of maintaining and repairing equipment, of recruiting and training men, of determining cost, and of allocating the corporation's resources to meet present and future needs. The duties of the executives in the great functional departments and in the enlarged central office had again to be carefully defined. Operating and cost analyses had to be further refined.

Indeed the complexity of administering such vast businesses led some managers of the more progressive roads to develop a decentralized type of administrative structure. They divided their system into regional units, each the size of an ordinary large railroad. The general manager of each unit was given wide authority and responsibility for its operation and profits. At the top a small group of general executives coordinated and appraised the activities of the several autonomous operating divisions and planned and allocated the resources of the system as a whole. In the twentieth century, after system-building was completed and after the federal government began to play an increasing part in rate-making, the need for a general office to concentrate on strategic decisions lessened. At the same time operating decisions became increasingly routinized. When this happened, nearly all roads returned to a centralized, functionally departmentalized structure. Nevertheless, the type of decentralized organization created by the Pennsylvania, the Burlington, and other railroads was a significant response to the problems of managing huge business enterprises. It has many similarities to the comparable structure devised by General Motors and other industrial corporations after World War I. (The General Motors' innovations are covered in another volume in this series, *Giant Enterprise: Ford, General Motors, and the Automobile Industry* [1964].)

The readings in this section provide an inside look at the basic developments in the management of the nation's first big business. All three selections were written by the pioneers in modern corporate management at the time they were making their institutional innovations. In the first, Daniel C. McCallum tells the president of the Erie in a report of March, 1856, of the administrative challenges he faced as the road's general superintendent and of the organizational structure he devised to meet them. The widely read report, which had a significant effect on the development of modern business administration, provides an interesting parallel to a later chapter in the Erie's history. The second selection comes from Albert Fink's famous exposition on cost accounting, which was written in 1874 as part of his annual report of the Louisville and Nashville Railroad. Called the "foundation stone of American railway economics," it received even more attention than McCallum's earlier statement. The final document, taken from the papers of Charles E. Perkins, the president of the Chicago, Burlington and Quincy Railroad, is an unpublished memorandum written in 1885. Perkins based his comments on his experience in reorganizing the administrative structure of the Burlington system. Like the Pennsylvania, the Burlington had a divisional structure and clear-cut line and staff distinctions. Yet because of Perkins' concern for decentralization, it did not have a separate traffic department. Instead its traffic executives worked within its several autonomous operating units. No better analysis exists of the organization of a large railroad system and the needs that brought it into being.

THE READINGS

1] Creating an Early Management Structure

Superintendent's Report

OFFICE GENERAL SUP'T N. Y. & ERIE R. R.
NEW YORK, March 25, 1856

HOMER RAMSDELL, ESQ.
PRESIDENT OF THE NEW YORK AND ERIE RAILROAD COMPANY:

SIR:

The magnitude of the business of this road, its numerous and important connections, and the large number of employés engaged in operating it, have led many, whose opinions are entitled to respect, to the conclusion, that a proper regard to details, which enter so largely into the elements of success in the management of all railroads, cannot possibly be attained by any plan that contemplates its organization as a whole; and in proof of this position, the experience of shorter roads is referred to, the business operations of which have been conducted much more economically.

Theoretically, other things being equal, a long road should be operated for a less cost per mile than a short one. This position is so clearly evident and so generally admitted, that its truth may be assumed without offering any arguments in support of it; and, notwithstanding the reverse, so far as *practical* results are considered, has generally been the case, we must look to other causes than the mere difference in length of roads for a solution of the difficulty.

A Superintendent of a road fifty miles in length can give its business his personal attention, and may be almost constantly upon the line engaged in the direction of its details; each employé is familiarly known to him, and all questions in relation to its business are at once presented and acted upon; and any system, however imperfect, may under such circumstances prove comparatively successful.

In the government of a road five hundred miles in length a very different state of things exists. Any system which might be applicable to the business and extent of a short road, would be found entirely inadequate to the wants of a long one; and I am fully convinced, that in the want of a system perfect in its details, properly adapted and vigilantly enforced, lies the true secret of their failure; and that this disparity of cost per mile in operating long and short roads, is not produced by *a difference in length,* but is in proportion to the perfection of the system adopted.

FROM Daniel C. McCallum, "Superintendent's Report," March 25, 1856, in *Annual Report of the New York and Erie Railroad Company for 1855* (New York, 1856), pp. 33–37, 39–41, 50–54, 57–59.

Entertaining these views, I had the honor, more than a year since, to submit for your consideration and approval, a plan for the more effective organization of this department. The system then proposed, has to some extent been introduced, and experience, so far, affords the strongest assurances that when fully carried out, the most satisfactory results will be obtained.

In my opinion a system of operations, to be efficient and successful, should be such as to give to the principal and responsible head of the running department a complete daily history of details in all their minutiae. Without such supervision, the procurement of a satisfactory annual statement must be regarded as extremely problematical. The fact that dividends are earned without such control, does not disprove the position, as in many cases the extraordinarily remunerative nature of an enterprise may ensure satisfactory returns under the most loose and inefficient management.

It may be proper here to remark, that in consequence of that want of adaptation before alluded to, we cannot avail ourselves to any great extent of the plan of organization of shorter lines in framing one for this, nor have we any precedent or experience upon which we can fully rely in doing so. Under these circumstances, it will scarcely be expected that we can at once adopt any plan of operations which will not require amendment and a reasonable time to prove its worth. A few general principles, however, may be regarded as settled and necessary in its formation, amongst which are:

1. A proper division of responsibilities.

2. Sufficient power conferred to enable the same to be fully carried out, that such responsibilities may be real in their character.

3. The means of knowing whether such responsibilities are faithfully executed.

4. Great promptness in the report of all derelictions of duty, that evils may be at once corrected.

5. Such information, to be obtained through a system of daily reports and checks that will not embarrass principal officers, nor lessen their influence with their subordinates.

6. The adoption of a system, as a whole, which will not only enable the General Superintendent to detect errors immediately, but will also point out the delinquent.

Organization

The following comprises a list of the principal officers acting directly under the General Superintendent, with powers and duties arranged with reference to obtaining the results proposed.

1. Division and Branch Superintendents.
2. Masters of Engine and Car Repairs.
3. Car Inspectors.
4. General Freight Agent.
5. General Ticket Agent.
6. General Wood Agent.
7. Superintendent of Telegraph.
8. Foreman of Bridge Repairs.

For the more convenient working of the road it is now separated into Divisions, as follows:

The EASTERN DIVISION and UNION RAILROAD extending from Jersey City, to Port Jervis in the county of Orange,—88 miles.

The DELAWARE DIVISION extending from the Port Jervis Station, to Susquehanna Station in the county of Susquehanna, Penn.,—104 miles.

The SUSQUEHANNA DIVISION extending from the Susquehanna Station, to Hornellsville in the county of Steuben,—139 miles.

The WESTERN DIVISION extending from Hornellsville, to Dunkirk on Lake Erie,—128 miles.

NEWBURGH BRANCH extending from Newburgh, westward, to the intersection with the main line near Chester, in the county of Orange,—19 miles.

PIERMONT BRANCH extending from Piermont to Sufferns,—18 miles.

The several Divisions and Branches are in charge of Superintendents, who are held responsible for the successful working of their respective Divisions, and for the maintenance of proper discipline and conduct of all persons employed thereon, except such as are in the employment of other officers acting under directions from this office, as hereinafter stated. They possess all the powers delegated by the organization to the General Superintendent, except in matters pertaining to the duties of General Ticket Agent, General Freight Agent, General Wood Agent, Telegraph management, and Engine and Car Repairs.

They have authority to change, by telegraph or otherwise, the movement of trains from the times specified in the tables.

Masters of Engine Repairs are held responsible for the good condition of the engines and machinery in shops, and the cost of their repairs. It is their duty to make frequent and thorough inspection of the engines so as to guard them from accidents and injuries which may result from the want of seasonable and trifling renewals; also to see that the engines are otherwise in efficient condition for use. They are also required to report to the Division Superintendents all cases they may discover of abuse or maltreatment of locomotives by engineers or dispatchers.

There are eight Engine Repair Shops on the line. . . .

[McCallum identifies the shops and the personnel in charge of them and then outlines the duties of the Car Inspectors.]

THE GENERAL FREIGHT AGENT has the supervision of the Freight Charges. His duties are, with the approval of the President or General Superintendent, to make and regulate prices for the transportation of freight; to negotiate contracts and arrangements with individuals and other Companies, and to see that such contracts are fairly and equitably complied with. Also, to investigate and examine all claims for damages and losses of freight or baggage, and certify such of them as are found valid, to the General Superintendent for approval.

THE GENERAL TICKET AGENT is required, with the approval of the President or General Superintendent, to regulate the prices for transportation of Passengers; to negotiate ticket arrangements with other Companies, and to supervise all matters connected with the sale of tickets.

[McCallum next describes the duties of the General Wood Agent, the Superintendent of Telegraph, and the Foreman of Bridge Repairs.]

The above will serve to show the division of the administrative duties upon the line, and the general organization of this department. Each officer possesses all the power necessary to render his position efficient, and has authority, with the approval of the President and General Superintendent, to appoint all persons for whose acts he is held responsible, and may dismiss any subordinate when in his judgment the interests of the Company will be promoted thereby.

The enforcement of a rigid system of discipline in the government of works of great magnitude is indispensable to success. All subordinates should be accountable to, and *be directed by their immediate superiors only;* as obedience cannot be enforced where the foreman in immediate charge is interfered with by a superior officer giving orders directly to his subordinates.

It is very important, however, that principal officers should be in possession of all the information necessary to enable them to judge correctly as to the industry and efficiency of subordinates of every grade.

To acquaint themselves in this particular, and remedy imperfections without weakening the influence of subordinate officers, should be the aim of officers of the higher grades.

.   .   .   .

It would occupy too much space to allude to all the practical purposes to which the telegraph is applied in working the road; and it may suffice to say, that without it, the business could not be conducted with anything like the same degree of economy, safety, regularity, or dispatch. The constantly increasing amount of business to be performed by it, has rendered it necessary to put up an additional wire over the Delaware Division, for through messages; and I have no doubt the increase of traffic will soon compel its extension over every portion of the road.

The minimum amount of service consistent with the largest net revenue, is also an important subject for consideration, the proper regulation of which must mainly depend upon data derived from the actual expenses and earnings of each train, as nearly as can be ascertained.

In the economical management of a freight traffic are involved:

First. The most effective use of motive power.

Second. The regulation and reduction of speed to the lowest standard consistent with the exigencies of business.

Third. The means of controlling the movement of rolling stock, that the greatest amount of service may be derived therefrom.

Fourth. The reduction of dead weight,[1] and a corresponding increase of useful load [2] hauled.

Fifth. The reduction of friction, by which the cost of repairs of rolling

1 Weight of *cars.*
2 Weight of *freight.*

stock is diminished, and the facilities for economical transportation are proportionably increased.

By the introduction of a system of reports, and the use of the telegraph, much has been accomplished in obtaining these and other desirable results; and when the telegraphic system shall have become fully matured and carried out, I have the best of reasons for believing that its efficacy will justify the most sanguine expectations.

It would be tasking your patience too much to force the consideration of its details on you at the present time, but as the results of the last year's operations have shown a gratifying reduction in the expenses of the road, and believing as I do, that it is mainly attributable to this cause, I should be doing injustice to my own feelings were I to omit furnishing at least a faint sketch of it.

The powers and duties of the principal officers on the line have been given, and are such as to harmonise in all branches of duty. It will be seen that their subordinates cannot communicate with higher officers, but through them, and can only be communicated with through the same means. There are, however, some exceptions to this rule, as Conductors and Station Agents report, daily, their operations directly to the General Superintendent; and it is in a great measure through these means that the business—so far as relates to the movement of trains, the amount of freight carried, and its prompt transmission—is controlled.

System of Reports and Checks

Hourly reports are received by telegraph, giving the position of all the passenger and the principal freight trains. In all cases where passenger trains are more than ten minutes, or freight trains more than half-an-hour behind time, on their arrival at a station the conductors are required to report the cause to the operator, who transmits the same by telegraph to the General Superintendent; and the information being entered as fast as received, on a convenient tabular form, shows, at a glance, the position and progress of trains, in both directions, on every Division of the Road.

The importance of ascertaining the particulars connected with delays cannot be over-estimated, as they are frequently the result of mismanagement, are often the primary cause of accidents, and in their history is developed a class of facts and delinquencies which could not be so easily detected in any other way. By these means, the prevailing causes of delays are made known, and an opportunity is given to apply the corrective, where the nature of the case will permit.

The daily reports of *passenger* conductors give the designating numbers of the engines and cars, the names of the persons employed on the trains, the time of arrival at and departure from the several stations, the particulars in regard to delays, and such other matters of interest as occur on the trip.

The daily reports of *freight* conductors, in addition to the above, give a general description of the load contained in each car, the place whence taken, where left, and destination as per waybills.

The station agents' daily reports give the time of the arrival and departure of all freight trains at their respective stations; the name of the conductor and number of the engine; the numbers of the cars taken and left, with the tonnage of freight in each; the numbers and kinds of cars remaining at their station, and whether the same be loaded or empty; how many are required for the business of the station, and the nature of that business; and whether any conductor has refused to take cars or freight waybilled to other stations; also, a statement of freight over or short of bills, or damaged or wrongly directed; delays of freight and causes thereof; damaged cars at stations, with particulars as to cause thereof; an accurate daily report of all baggage received and forwarded; from whom received and to whom given; a list of unclaimed baggage remaining on hand at the close of the report; and any other information of interest pertaining to the business of their respective stations.

The Division Superintendents report monthly the number of miles run, the expense of engineers and firemen, and the quantity and cost of oil, waste, and tallow for each engine on their respective Divisions.

The Masters of Engine Repairs report monthly the amount expended for repairs on each engine.

The General Wood Agent reports monthly the number of cords of wood used by each engine, and the cost of the same.

The information thus obtained is embodied in the statistical accounts kept in this office, and from it we deduce the following:

The speed of the train between the several stations.
The average load carried in each car.
The tonnage of useful load carried.
The tonnage of cars in which it was transported.
The tonnage of empty returned cars.
The position or location of the cars.

Each of the above items is given for the different trains over the several Divisions.

As relates to engines, we obtain for each:

The number of miles run.
The cost per mile run for engineer and fireman.
The gallons of oil used.
The miles run to one pint.
The pounds of waste used.
The pounds of tallow used.
The cost for oil, waste, and tallow.
The cost per mile run for oil, waste, and tallow.
The cost for repairs.
The cost per mile run for repairs.
The cords of fuel used.
The cost of fuel.
The cost per mile run for fuel.
The total cost for all of the above items, and
The cost per ton per mile for the same.

The above reports, with others not now enumerated, furnish to the officer at the head of this department, a fund of information, the judicious use of which materially assists in directing the business of the road to the best advantage; but interesting as this information is, in instituting comparisons between the business performed by the several engines and trains and the cost thereof, it is only in its practical application in pointing out the neglect and mismanagement which prevail, thus enabling us to remedy the defect, that its real value consists.

.   .   .   .

[An] experiment referred to in another portion of this report has furnished data for determining the effects of the ruling grades and curvature on each Division, and from this data a tabular statement giving the amount of load each engine is capable of moving over the several Divisions has been prepared, and we shall be enabled hereafter to observe whether they work up to their capacity. Proper attention to this subject I have no doubt will effect the necessary reform.

The experiment to which I have alluded, furnishes data for determining what ought to be the relative cost of transporting freight over the several Divisions, having reference to their grades, allignment and condition; and it is proposed, as soon as the necessary arrangements can be made, to keep *Division accounts,* with the view of ascertaining how far the actual results agree. This comparison will show the officers who conduct their business with the greatest economy, and will indicate, in a manner not to be mistaken, the relative ability and fitness of each for the position he occupies. It will be valuable in pointing out the particulars of excess in the cost of management of one Division over another, by a comparison of details; will direct attention to those matters in which sufficient economy is not practised; and it is believed, will have the effect of exciting an honorable spirit of emulation to excel.

It will be seen that to some extent the operations on the road are conducted under the directions of officers wholly independent of each other; and it may be thought difficult, under such an organization, to preserve that harmony, in all the branches of duty, which is so essential to success. Subject as they all are to one principal officer, who, as the head of the department, prescribes rules for each, no difficulty need be entertained on this subject; and as a precautionary measure, it is provided that, should any difficulty or misunderstanding arise between Division or Branch Superintendents, General Freight Agent, General Ticket Agent, Masters of Engine Repairs, General Wood Agent, Car Inspectors, Superintendent of Telegraph, or either of them, as to the performance of their respective duties, or the relative powers of each, or in reference to the acts of any subordinate of either, copies of all correspondence in relation thereto shall be furnished to the General Superintendent, in order that all matters in discussion may be at once adjusted.

The foregoing will probably be sufficient to point out the general features of our Organization, without descending to the particulars as affecting the officers of lower grades, where the same rigid discipline is maintained, and whose duties are all systematically arranged with the view of enforcing *personal accountability*. To enter fully into all the details would extend this communication to too great a length. I trust what has been said will be sufficient to show that, under its operations, provision has been made for carrying out those leading principles which are of such vital importance in conducting great and important works.

It seems to have been generally conceded, that railroad companies have not the same means of controlling the various items of earnings and expenditures, as are within the reach of persons managing the same business but acting in an individual capacity; and whilst it is a humiliating circumstance that railroad companies have not, in many particulars, conducted their business with the same economy as would have been done by private enterprise, it by no means proves that they have not the power to do so.

All that is required to render the efforts of railroad companies in every respect equal to that of individuals, is a rigid system of personal accountability through every grade of service.

. . . .

2] Developing Modern Cost Accounting

Classification of Operating Expenses

BEFORE leaving this subject attention is called to the classification of accounts in table [1]. It will be observed that the accounts are divided into three classes:

Maintenance of road, buildings, and general expense, from account 1 to 29.
Station expenses, from account 30 to 40.
Movement expenses, from account 41 to 74.

The expenditures of each class bear a distinct character, to which I will now refer more particularly.

Those in *the first class* are not affected by the amount of business transacted, within certain limits to be referred to hereafter. The roadway must be kept in good order. Cross-ties when decayed must be renewed, bridges kept in repair, and a certain organization of officers and men must be kept up, whether one or more trains are to pass over the road.

This class of expenditure per mile of road will vary on different roads according to the permanency of construction, the number of bridges to be kept in repair, the nature of the soil, the climate, and many other local conditions. They will also vary with the amount of business, but only to the extent to which an increase of business requires more extensive accommodation, such as depot-buildings, side-tracks, etc., which have to be kept

FROM Albert Fink, "Classification of Operating Expenses," in *Annual Report of the Louisville & Nashville Railroad Company for the Year Ending June 30, 1874* (Louisville, Ky., 1874), pp. 37–47, 63–64.

in repair. On a road with an established business, and having suitable accommodation for the same, considerable variation in business may take
place without affecting this class of expenditures.

The *second class* of expenditures are incurred at stations in keeping up
an organized force of agents, laborers, etc., for the purpose of receiving and
delivering freight, the selling of tickets, etc.

One portion of these expenditures does not vary with the amount of
business; another portion does. A certain number of agents have to be
employed, whether there is more or less work to be done; but the number
of persons employed to handle freight may be varied in proportion to the
number of tons of freight to be handled. This whole class of expenditures,
however, is entirely uninfluenced by the length that either freight or passengers are hauled, or, in other words, by the work of transportation performed. Freight or passengers may be hauled five or two hundred miles,
the station expenses incurred on their account being the same.

In the *third class* of expenditures have been collected all those that vary
with the number of trains run.

On roads on which there is sufficient freight business to fill all trains that
are run from one terminus of the road the amount of freight transported
will be nearly in proportion to the number of freight train-miles; and hence
on such roads this third class of expenditures will be nearly in proportion
to the amount of business. It is this class of expenditures alone which possesses that characteristic.

On roads, however, upon which freight-trains have to be run at stated
times, whether fully loaded or not, this class of expenditures does not vary
with the business, but very nearly with the number of trains run. The
expenditures and amount of freight transported in this case are irrelative,
the cost of transporting freight being dependent entirely upon the loads
as accidentally offered for transportation.

To the three classes of expenditures just named, and which have been
shown separately and in detail in [table 1], must be added a fourth, not
shown in [this table], but which forms a large proportion of the total operating expenses of railroads—viz., the interest on the capital invested.

This class is mainly uninfluenced by the amount of work done. Only
so far as an increase of business involves the necessity of additional investments for its accommodation is it influenced by the amount of business.

In the consideration of the subject of the cost of railroad transportation
it is of the greatest importance to discriminate between the expenditures
which vary with the amount of work performed and those which are entirely
independent thereof. The latter form so large a proportion of the total
operating expenses of railroads that it becomes impossible to make the
amount of work performed a criterion or measure of the cost.

The fixed or inevitable expenses which attach to the operation of railroads, and which are the same whether one or many trains are run over a
road, have to be ascertained separately in each individual case. These expenditures are in the nature of a tax upon the business of the road; the
smaller the business the larger the tax. What the tax may or should be per

ton of freight or per passenger carried in any one case can not be predetermined by any general rule or law, but can only be ascertained after the two elements on which it depends—(1) the fixed expenditures, and (2) the amount of work done—are actually known. These elements vary on all roads; it would be a singular accident to find them alike on any two.

The disregard of these facts in estimating the cost and the value of railroad transportation with a view of judging of the reasonableness of railroad tariffs has led to many erroneous conclusions, which appear to be now fixed in the public mind. It is of great importance to the owners of railroad property at this present time—more so perhaps than heretofore—to possess correct information upon the subject of the cost of railroad transportation. It may therefore not be considered out of place here to show how the cost of transportation varies upon the various roads operated by the Louisville & Nashville Railroad, and the reasons therefor.

The following table (A) shows the percentage of the four classes of ex-

TABLE A

	M. S.	M. L.	N. & D.	K. B.	B. B.	R. B.	G. B.
Movement expenses	41.367	38.589	38.594	22.428	19.490	17.634	28.761
Station expenses	18.161	12.924	12.259	4.367	6.209	5.832	5.007
Maintenance of road	14.453	17.179	17.554	17.964	22.505	17.295	9.361
Interest on investment	26.019	31.308	31.593	55.241	51.796	59.239	56.871
Total	100.000	100.000	100.000	100.000	100.000	100.000	100.000

penditure above referred to, of the total operating expenses on the seven roads operated by the Louisville & Nashville Railroad Company.

From this table will be seen the great diversity existing in the relative proportions of each class of expenditures.

The movement expenses, the cost of conveying freight from one place to another after it is loaded in the cars—the transportation expenses proper —are 41.3 per cent on the Main Stem, and only 17.6 on the Richmond Branch, of the total operating expenses. We have therefore in one case 58.7, in the other 82.4 per cent of the total operating expenses, which are entirely uninfluenced by the amount of work performed as measured by weight and distance, or ton-miles.

The station expenses vary from 4.3 per cent on the Knoxville Branch to 18.1 per cent on the Main Stem of the total operating expenses.

The cost of maintenance of road is 9.3 per cent on the Glasgow Branch, and 22.5 on the Bardstown Branch.

The interest account is 26 per cent on the Main Stem, and 59.2 per cent on the Richmond Branch.

With such great variations in the constituting elements of the cost of transportation uniformity in the final results can not be expected.

Causes of Difference in Cost of Transportation

I will now compare the expenditure of each class per ton-mile on the seven roads, and show more particularly the reasons for the great difference in cost.

The following table (B) shows each class of operating expenses per ton-mile on the seven roads operated by the L. & N. R. R. Co.

TABLE B

COST PER TON-MILE (IN CENTS)	M. S.	M. L.	N. & D.	K. B.	B. B.	R. B.	G. B.
Movement expenses	.7365	.8102	.9787	.9364	1.5039	1.6934	5.4928
Station expenses	.3233	.2714	.3109	.1823	.4791	.5601	.9563
Maintenance of road	.2573	.3607	.4451	.7499	1.7366	1.6608	1.7877
Total operating expenses	1.3171	1.4423	1.7347	1.8686	3.7196	3.9143	8.2368
Interest	.4633	.6574	.8011	2.3061	3.9968	5.6887	10.8615
Total oper'g exp. and interest	1.7804	2.0997	2.5358	4.1747	7.7164	9.6030	19.0983

Movement expenses (comprised of items 41–73 [table 1]). It appears that on the first four roads this class of expenditures varies from .73 cents to .97 cents per ton-mile; on the last three named from 1.50 cents to 5.49 cents per ton-mile. The first four roads belong to that class on which fully loaded freight-trains can be started from one terminus of the road; on the last three named trains are started at regular times, regardless of the amount of load that is to be carried. Hence we find greater agreement in the cost of moving one ton one mile on the first four roads than on the latter, on which the cost depends altogether upon accidental causes.

If on the first four roads the grades, curves, and the cost of labor and material were the same, and also the character of the business, then the cost per ton-mile should be the same; but as these elements of cost differ, uniformity in the cost even in the movement expenses can not be expected.

The character of the business of a road has a great influence upon the cost of transportation.

We find the average train-loads carried on the first four roads, and the movement expenses per ton-mile, as follows:

	M. S.	M. L.	N. & D.	K. B.
Average train-loads (in tons)	135	113	96	77
Movement expenses per ton (in cents)	0.73	0.81	0.97	0.93

On the Main Stem the average net load carried per train is nearly twice as much as on the Knoxville Branch.

On the first-named road a large amount of freight is carried over its whole length; while on the latter, which is a mere local road, it only passes over a portion of its whole length. The capacity of the locomotive and train can not therefore be as fully utilized on the latter as on the former road.

On the Main Stem the tonnage in one direction is 73 per cent of the tonnage in the other direction, while on the Knoxville Branch it is only 21 per cent; hence more empty cars have to be run on the latter than on the former road.

The result is that an average of 135 tons of freight is being carried per train on the Main Stem, while only 77 tons can be carried on the Knoxville

Branch; yet the same attention is paid on both roads to secure maximum loads to each train.

It is the character of the business peculiar to each road that brings about this great difference, which of course influences the cost of transportation.

On roads on which there is not sufficient business to secure full loads to the trains from one or the other of the terminal stations the difference in the movement expenses per ton is found still greater.

The following table shows the average loads carried in the trains of the three branch roads, and the cost per ton-mile for moving the freight:

	B. B.	R. B.	G. B.
Average number of tons freight carried on one train	18.2	24.0	4.9
Movement expenses per ton-mile (in cents)	1.5	1.7	5.5

It is on account of the small loads carried on the Glasgow Branch per train (4.9 tons) that the movement expenses are so much larger than on the other branches, on which the trains carry from 18.2 to 24 tons.

Station expenses (items 30–40 [table 1]). The elements controlling the cost per ton-mile for station expenses are—

a. The cost of handling one ton of freight—for loading, unloading, clerking, agents' salaries, depot expenses, switching, etc.

b. The length of haul.

Supposing that the cost of handling freight per ton were the same on all roads and at all stations of a road, then the cost per ton-mile of freight would vary according to the length of haul. For each particular length of haul there would be a different cost per ton-mile for this service.

. . . The average cost of station expenses per ton of freight handled on the Main Stem of the road is 23 cents per ton. For freight that passes over the whole length of the line, say between Louisville and Memphis, the cost per ton-mile would be $2 \times 23/377 = 0.12$ cents, and for freight carried only five miles it would be $2 \times 23/5 = 9.2$ cents. We have therefore a difference between the cost per ton-mile from 0.12 to 9.2 cents, although the actual cost of performing the work was the same in both cases; thus showing that the ton-mile is not a proper unit of measure of cost of this service.

But there is even considerable variation in the cost of handling one ton of freight at various stations. . . .

. . . Dividing the number of tons into the number of ton-miles gives the average haul, and dividing this into the cost per ton for handling gives the average cost per ton-mile for handling freight.

For example, take Brooks Station. Number of tons of freight received and forwarded . . . 654; freight to and from Brooks Station was carried 14,335 miles . . . therefore the average haul $14,335/654 = 21.8$ miles; station expenses per ton at Brooks Station . . . 71 cents; cost per ton-mile $71/21.8 = 3.26$ cents. To this has to be added the expenses at the station from or to which the freight was forwarded.

If both stations are known, the cost per ton-mile for station expenses can be readily ascertained. . . . For example, for freight shipped between Louisville and Brooks Station, distance 9.2 miles:

IN CENTS

Station expenses at Brooks Station per ton	71.0
Station expenses at Louisville per ton	24.3
Total cost per ton	95.3

Length of haul, 9.2 miles; cost per ton-mile, 10.4 cents.

This example sufficiently illustrates the great variety in cost, and the impossibility of making the ton-mile the measure of cost of or compensation for this service. The ton handled would be a more correct measure, although there is necessarily much variety even in this cost, as we have seen. . . .

It must therefore be evident that it is impossible to predetermine the cost per ton-mile of freight for handling without taking into consideration the length of the haul and the conditions under which the station service has to be performed.

Maintenance of roadway and general expense (items 1–29). The two elements that determine the cost per ton-mile for this service are—

1. The cost of maintaining one mile of road, etc., during a given time.
2. The number of tons of freight passed over it during the same time.

The former differs on each road, and so does the latter; hence uniformity in cost per ton-mile is impossible.

The following table shows the cost of maintenance of roadway and general expense per mile of road on the seven roads operated by the Louisville & Nashville Railroad Company during the last year, and the average number of tons of freight passed over one mile of each road; also the cost per ton-mile:

	M. S.	M. L.	N. & D.	K. B.	B. B.	R. B.	G. B.
Cost of maintenance of road per mile per year (Table [1] item 29)	$1,857.87	$1,142.25	$1,243.49	906.76	436.69	436.61	262.73
Tons of freight passed over one mile of road	433,662	152,273	143,378	72,456	11,538	16,656	6,137
Cost per ton-mile (in cents)	0.26	0.36	0.44	0.75	1.74	1.66	1.78

Part of the cost of maintenance of roadway and buildings is chargeable to the passenger traffic. The division of charges between the two classes of traffic has been made in proportion to train-miles. It follows from this that the cost per ton-mile of freight is in a measure affected by the relative use made of a road by the passenger and freight traffic.

From this statement will be noticed the great difference in cost of maintaining one mile of road, buildings, etc. On the Main Stem this cost is $1,857.87, on the Glasgow Branch $262.73 per mile.

An examination of the items from 1 to 28 . . . will show in what particulars these differences occur. A few may be mentioned here. The cost per mile on the Main Stem and Glasgow Branch is as follows:

	M. S.	G. B.
Renewal of ties	368.89	32.96
Bridge superstructure	250.26	25.14
Ditching	69.23	26.06
General expense	346.14	—
Salaries, insurance, and taxes	100.40	—
Total	$1,134.92	$84.16

The difference in cost in these five items on the Main Stem and Glasgow Branch is $1,050.76 per mile of road. Part of this great difference is caused from the fact that on one road greater expenditures were made during this year than was due to the year's business; on the other road less. It will be remembered that the yearly depreciation of cross-ties on the Main Stem was found to be for 16½ years at the rate of $257.11 per mile, while during the past year there was expended $368.89 on the Main Stem, and on the Glasgow Branch only $32.96 per mile; the first sum more, the latter considerably less than is required to make good a year's depreciation.

There are great differences in other expenses, such as repairs of bridges, on the two roads. On the Main Stem, as has been mentioned before, the cost of bridge repairs during the last year was unusually heavy, while on the Glasgow Branch, with only one small bridge, the cost is very small. The general expenses of administration on the Main Stem are not incurred on the Glasgow Branch, which is also exempt from taxation. Hence the great difference in cost of maintenance of road and buildings and general superintendence between the two roads.

When we examine into the differences existing in regard to the amount of business transacted in one year over one mile of road—the other element named which enters into the cost of one ton per mile—we find the variation still greater. On the Main Stem 433,662 tons, on the Glasgow Branch only 6,137 tons, pass over one mile of road per year. We can therefore not be surprised that the cost on the Main Stem for maintenance of road is only one fourth of a cent per ton-mile and on the Glasgow Branch 1.8 cents.

Interest account. The original cost of the road and the rate of interest form one element and the amount of business transacted the other which determines the cost per ton-mile.

The cost of roads per mile and the business transacted over the same vary so much that the cost per ton-mile for interest can not be expected to be the same in any two cases.

It is impossible to predetermine what is a proper charge for interest on any particular road until these elements—viz., the cost of road and the amount of business—are known.

On the Main Stem of the Louisville & Nashville Railroad, dividing the number of ton-miles of freight carried into the interest chargeable to the freight business, the cost per ton-mile is 0.46, while on the Richmond Branch it is 10.86 cents, over twenty times as much. On the five other roads the interest charge varies from 0.65 to 5.7 cents per ton-mile. (For further particulars refer to Table B, page 111.)

We have now considered the variation in each class of expenditures and the causes therefor per ton-mile. When we find so much variation in the elements which make up the cost of transportation we can not expect to find uniformity in the total cost.

From Table B it appears that the variation in the total cost per ton-mile is from 1.78 cents on the Main Stem to 19.09 cents on the Glasgow Branch. The work performed—viz., the movement of one ton of freight one mile— is the same on all roads, yet the cost of performing is ten times more on one road than on the other.

Great as this variation is on the seven roads under the same management, the variation of the cost per ton-mile is still greater even on the same road, depending as it does upon the different conditions under which the service has to be performed. It would lead here too far to thoroughly analyze the cost of railroad transportation in all its details, and I will only state that a careful investigation shows that under the ordinary conditions under which transportation service is generally performed the cost per ton-mile in some instances may not exceed one seventh of a cent and in others will be as high as 73 cents per ton-mile on the same road. The lower cost applies to freight carried in cars that otherwise would return empty; the higher cost to freight in small quantities carried short distances.

It is impossible to predetermine the cost of carrying freight on any one road unless the conditions under which it is to be carried, as far as they affect the cost of transportation, be previously known.

In order to estimate the cost of transportation under the various conditions that occur it is necessary to classify the expenditures, and to separate those that increase with the amount of work done from those that are fixed and independent of it; and to ascertain the ratio of increase of cost with the increase of work. Without such an analysis of the cost it is impossible to solve the question of cost of transportation that arises in the daily practice of railroad operation. A mere knowledge of the average cost per ton-mile of all the expenditures during a whole year's operation is of no value whatever in determining the cost of transporting any particular class of freight, as no freight is ever transported under the average condition under which the whole year's business is transacted. We can therefore not make the average cost per ton-mile the basis for a tariff, if it is to be based upon cost; but we must classify the freight according to the conditions affecting cost of transportation, and ascertain the cost of each class separately.

TABLE 1. HEADING OF ACCOUNTS

MAINTENANCE OF ROADWAY AND GENERAL SUPERINTENDENCE

Road Repairs per Mile of Road—
1. Adjustment of track.
2. Ballast.
3. Ditching.
4. Culverts and cattle-guards.
5. Extraordinary repairs—slides, etc.
6. Repairs of hand and dump-cars.
7. Repairs of road tools.
8. Road watchmen.
9. General expense of road department.
10. Total.
11. Cross-ties replaced—value.
12. Cross-ties, labor replacing.
13. Cross-ties, train expenses hauling.
14. Total cost of cross-ties per mile of road.
15. Bridge superstructure repairs.
16. Bridge watchmen.
17. Shop-building repairs.
18. Water-station repairs.
19. Section-house repairs.
20. Total cost of bridge and building repairs per mile of road.

21. General superintendence and general expense of operating department.
22. Advertising and soliciting passengers and freight.
23. Insurance and taxes.
24. Rent account.
25. Total per mile of road.
26. Salaries of general officers.
27. Insurance and taxes and general expense.
28. Total per mile of road.
29. *Total cost per mile of road for maintenance of roadway and buildings.*
29½ *Total cost per train mile for maintenance of roadway and buildings.*

STATION EXPENSES PER TRAIN MILE
30. Labor loading and unloading freight.
31. Agents and clerks.
32. Gen'l expense of stations—lights, fuel, etc.
33. Watchmen and switchmen.
34. *Expense of Switching—* Engine repairs.
Engineers and firemen's wages.
Expense in engine-house.

Supervision and general expense.
Oil and waste.
Water supply.
Fuel.
35. Total per train mile.
36. Stationery and printing.
37. Telegraph expenses.
38. Depot repairs.
39. Total per train mile.
40. *Total station expenses per train mile.*

MOVEMENT EXPENSES PER TRAIN MILE
41. Adjustment of track.
42. Cost of renewal of rails—value.
43. Labor replacing rails.
44. Train expenses hauling rails.
45. Joint Fastenings.
46. Switches.
47. Total cost of adjustment of track and replacing rails per train mile.
48. Locomotive repairs.
49. Oil and waste used on locomotives.
50. Watching and cleaning.
51. Fuel used in engine-house.

52. Supervision and general expense in engine-house.
53. Engineers and firemen's wages.
54. Total engine expenses per train mile.
55. Conductors and brakemen.
56. Passenger-car repairs.
57. Sleeping-car repairs.
58. Freight-car repairs.
59. Oil and waste used by cars.
60. Labor oiling and inspecting cars.
61. Train expenses.
62. Total car expenses per train mile.
63. Fuel used by locomotives.
64. Water supply.
65. Total fuel and water expense per train mile.
66. Damage to freight, and lost baggage.
67. Damage to stock.
68. Wrecking account.
69. Damage to persons.
70. Gratuity to employees.
71. Fencing burned.
72. Law expenses.
73. Total per train mile.
74. *Total movement expenses per train mile.*
75. GRAND TOTAL for maintenance and movement per train mile.

FORMULA FOR ASCERTAINING THE COST OF RAILROAD TRANSPORTATION PER TON-MILE

$$\text{Movement expenses per ton-mile} = \frac{\text{Movement expenses per train mile (items 41 to 74)}}{\text{average number of tons of freight in each train}} = a$$

$$\text{Station expenses per ton-mile} = \frac{\text{Cost of handling freight (items 30 to 40) at forwarding station} + \text{at delivery station}}{\text{length of haul}} = b$$

$$\text{Maintenance of road per ton-mile} = \frac{\begin{array}{c}\text{Cost of maintenance} \\ \text{of road per mile} \\ \text{per year (items 1 to 29)}\end{array} \times \dfrac{\text{total miles run by freight-trains per year}}{\begin{array}{c}\text{total revenue trains,} \\ \text{pass. and fr't, pr. yr.}\end{array}}}{\begin{array}{c}\text{average number of tons of freight trans-} \\ \text{ported over one mile of road per year}\end{array}} = c$$

$$\text{Interest per ton-mile} = \frac{\begin{array}{c}\text{Cost of road} \\ \text{per mile}\end{array} \times \dfrac{\begin{array}{c}\text{rate of interest} \\ \text{per annum}\end{array}}{100} \times \dfrac{\begin{array}{c}\text{number of freight-train} \\ \text{miles per year}\end{array}}{\begin{array}{c}\text{number of revenue-train miles,} \\ \text{fr't and pass., per year}\end{array}}}{\begin{array}{c}\text{average number of tons of freight transported} \\ \text{over one mile of road per year}\end{array}} = d$$

$$\text{Total cost per ton-mile} = a + b + c + d.$$

In order to make use of this formula it is necessary to know . . . fifty-eight items of expense [above], all of which vary on different roads, and enter into different combinations with each other. Some of the items of movement expenses (41 to 74) change with the weight of trains, and have to be ascertained in each individual case. The average cost for the year can be made the basis of the estimate. Besides the items shown [above], the following other items enter into the calculation: the average number of tons of freight in train per mile of the round trip of the train, the average length of haul, the number of miles run over the road with freight and passenger-trains per annum, the cost of the road, the rate of interest, and the total number of tons of freight carried during a year over one mile of road. Without these data it is impossible to make a correct estimate of the cost of transportation on railroads.

3] Administering a Great Railroad System

III

IN DECIDING the question of organization it will be necessary to consider two stages, so to speak, of railroad development. The first stage where the volume of traffic is not sufficient to make necessary or to warrant the highest degree of physical efficiency; and the second stage where the volume of traffic is so great as not only to warrant the expenditure, but also to make it economical to maintain the physical efficiency at the highest point.

Ordinarily the second stage will come only with increased mileage and while there are exceptional cases where roads of small fixed mileage acquire a large business by reason of their forming a link in a through line, or being in direct competition with one or more other roads between two commercial centers, they are so rare that it is best in considering the general question of organization to assume that a road in the second stage will be one of 500 miles or more in length. On the other hand a road of even larger mileage may belong to the first stage.

IV

The responsible head of the operations of a road in the first stage is usually the general superintendent, a general manager only becoming necessary when the road has grown and business has so increased as to make it desirable to confine the general superintendent to the care of the machine alone. In the first stage he can and will himself look closely after his track and rolling stock as well as the traffic. In the second stage with the increase of traffic he will find his time and mind largely occupied with business questions, and also that he can draw the straight line of perfection to work to, and can safely trust to educated experts most of the questions relating to the efficient maintenance of the machine. The proper economical maintenance of a road in the first stage is not an exact science, while that of a road in the second stage is, and scientific methods which would be unnecessary and extravagant on the one may become necessary and economical on the other.

V

An organization for the management of a road in the first stage is comparatively simple. The duties of the president will be to advise the chief financial and accounting officer and the chief operating officer and also the purchasing and supply agents, to supervise and execute all important contracts, to conduct the most important negotiations, to specifically approve all expenditures chargeable to capital account before they are incurred, to supervise and direct the more important purchases of material and

FROM a memorandum of Charles E. Perkins, "Organization of Railroads," written in 1885, from the personal papers of Charles E. Perkins, president of the Chicago, Burlington and Quincy Railroad, 1881–1901. © 1965 by Richard C. Overton. Printed by permission.

equipment, and to watch closely the results by means of reports from the heads of the two great departments of accounts and operations.

One officer as secretary and treasurer will have charge of accounts, finances, archives, titles, etc., or perhaps if the road be a large one it may be necessary to have an auditor also.

Such a road will ordinarily not have miles enough or business enough to require both a general manager and a general superintendent, and if so the general superintendent will take care of the business matters as well as of the track and the equipment. He will need to be a man of ability and energy, and he will attend to all important details himself, including questions of engineering if he has been educated as an engineer. His general freight and passenger agent or agents, if one should be required for each of these two departments, will consult him frequently,—and especially as to all departures from established rates or rules. His track master and his train master, or if the road embraces miles enough to be put into divisions, his superintendents of divisions will come to him daily as will also the master mechanic.

He will himself see his road every few days and will decide all questions as to quality and quantity of material—and on all questions of wages, down to individuals, he will himself be the judge. If receipts are falling off he will cut down expenses.

Business being light, he can often safely delay making renewals of track and equipment, because having personal knowledge of the whole situation, and being able to watch it, he can personally judge just how far it is safe to go.

The business questions which he will have to decide will be mostly local and in direct connection with his own road. And his time will not therefore be largely taken up in meeting the managers of other roads to arrange rates, pools, time schedules, etc., but can be devoted closely to his home affairs as above.

VI

An organization for the management of a large road in the second stage is on the other hand more complex. Here the duties of the president will be the same as in the first stage of development, but the amount of expenditure, the number of contracts, negotiations, reports, interviews, new schemes, etc., will have so largely increased that the president may require the aid of one vice president to assist him generally and possibly two or three personal assistants with fixed duties besides.

The departments of accounts and finances will also have grown so that a second vice president may be needed to look after the treasurer, the auditor and the secretary, three offices which in the first stage would be so combined as to be held by one, or at the most two, persons.

So of the departments of operation and construction. If the mileage is large it will be found expedient probably to put a third vice president at the head of this great department, which controls so largely the income and outgo. Under him again will be a general manager in direct charge of the daily details and taking the position occupied by the general super-

intendent in the first stage. The purchasing agent will act under the 3rd
vice president and also especially in making large purchases of rails, rolling
stock etc. directly under the president.

VII

The purchasing agent should buy or regulate the buying of all supplies,
acting under the president and 3rd vice president.

The purchasing agent would buy all supplies for operating the road
upon order from the general superintendent or others properly authorized
by the president or 3rd vice president. All materials and supplies should
be turned over *as bought* to the general superintendent or to an officer
acting under him and on his staff, called supply agent.

The duty of inspecting and testing supplies and materials would thus
be thrown upon the general superintendent as a check upon the purchasing agent.

The supply agent may be authorized by the purchasing agent to make
certain purchases of a local character.

VIII

In the second stage the business questions will be numerous and difficult
and the physical questions in many respects different from those arising
in the first stage; and if, as is often the case, such a road embraces large
mileage, the general manager in command of its operations will find his
time so fully occupied with general matters as to make systematic attention
to details impossible. So that it will be necessary that he should have under
him men of ability, education and experience at the heads of the four
chief branches of the service conducted by him, namely:—

First. The general superintendent managing the road itself and the rolling stock as a machine.

Second. The chief engineer.

Third. The general freight agent in charge of the freight traffic.

Fourth. The general passenger agent in charge of the passenger traffic.

IX

The general superintendent should have as his staff an engineer of track,
bridges and buildings, a superintendent of motive power and cars, a supply
agent and an agent in charge of the daily distribution of cars. This office
is distinct from that of the car accountant, who belongs to the audit department, although the two offices may sometimes be held by one man.

The engineer of track, bridges and buildings will act as an inspector of
work and supervisor of plans and methods and will also have charge of
such other engineering matters as the general superintendent may direct.

The superintendent of motive power and cars will regulate the power
in use upon the different divisions, will overlook the assistant superintendents of motive power and cars, and will distribute the motive power
as directed by the general superintendent.

Under the general superintendent will be the superintendents of divisions.

The supply agent will have charge of all supplies as soon as purchased, will regulate their inspection and distribution and may purchase certain local supplies like coal, ties, etc., being authorized to do so by the purchasing agent.

X

The duties of the chief engineer on the staff of the general manager will be of an advisory rather than of an executive character, except as regards the construction of new roads.

He will supervise plans and standards and will advise the general manager, as well as the general superintendent and the superintendents of divisions, the engineer of track, bridges and buildings and the assistant engineer of each division. He should be a man thoroughly educated in the science of engineering rather than in managing men. The direct management of all new work, except the construction of new roads, as well as of maintenance and repairs should be in the hands of the superintendents of divisions. The general manager may deem it expedient in special cases to charge the chief engineer, rather than the general superintendent, with the execution of certain work—but as a rule it is not expedient to do so. The location and construction of new roads or branches to be included in any unit of management would be in charge of the chief engineer acting under the general manager until ready for business when they would be turned over to a general superintendent.

XI

The duties of the general freight agent and the general passenger agent will be the same here as in the first stage, but the field being larger they will need a number of assistants not only in the general office but also in the different divisions of the road.

The supply agent on the staff of the general superintendent will keep himself and the purchasing agent advised as to the requirements of the service. All requisitions for supplies on the road will go to and be filled by him in accordance with such rules as the general superintendent shall establish.

XII

The property in the second stage will perhaps consist of a main line belonging clearly to the second stage while many short branches running to and feeding it will belong more properly to the first stage. But as they make a part of the homogeneous whole their management cannot be separated from that of the main stem, the whole making what may be called a unit of management all under one general manager. This unit, under the organization described and operated as one property with the results merged so far as accounts are concerned, should nevertheless be managed with the fact clearly in view that its main line is a road of one kind while its branches are roads of another kind.

XIII

Remembering this it will be expedient wherever a branch is 100 miles or more in length to make a division or a sub-division of it depending upon circumstances, more especially its geographical relation to other parts of the property, and put over it a division or an assistant superintendent as the case may be, capable of looking after both the track and trains in detail subject to the general superintendent if it is a division, or to a division superintendent, if it is a sub-division.

The traffic of the branch being light it will not be economical to spend money enough upon it to get scientific accuracy in every detail.

The main line with such branches as are too short to be made into separate divisions will then be cut into divisions, each in charge of a superintendent responsible to the general superintendent. Local circumstances will to a certain extent determine the size of a division. It should not exceed 500 miles. The division will again be divided into sub-divisions of from 100 to 200 miles in length depending upon the proportion of main line and other circumstances.

XIV

The superintendent of a division if it is a large one, should have attached to his staff a division engineer of track, bridges and buildings, and a division superintendent of motive power and cars, a division car distributor and a division supply agent. The division engineer of track, bridges and buildings would be the maker of plans and methods and an inspector of work. He would be more an executive officer than the engineer of track, bridges and buildings because nearer to the details on a division there would be more or less new work of such a character as to be carried on by orders direct from the superintendent of division through the division engineer of track, bridges and buildings, and he would also in fact be the division superintendent of track repairs acting under the superintendent of division.

There should also be attached to each larger division a representative of the freight and passenger departments acting under the heads of those departments, but also responsible to the superintendent of division who would be the ranking officer on the spot.

XV

On the main line when the traffic is heavy it will be found economical to insist upon having the track maintained at the highest point of scientific accuracy. To accomplish this there should be an assistant engineer in charge of each 100 miles of main line track with nothing else to look after, and directly responsible to the assistant superintendent of the sub-division, as well as to the engineer, or division engineer, of tracks, bridges and buildings. This assistant engineer should be a man of scientific education as an engineer and of practical experience as well, and with orders to make and keep a perfect track he can and will do it, and while it will cost what may at first seem a large amount of money the expenditure will pay in the end.

The amount of main line track to be so placed under one man should not exceed 100 miles, because it is important that the assistant engineer should see his road frequently by walking over it. Under him should be two roadmasters one for each 50 miles of road who would have the immediate direction of the section men, the field of each roadmaster being sub-divided into sections of about five miles length. . . .

XVI

Obviously there is a limit to the proper growth of any single unit of management under one general manager. Where the proper limit is will depend upon circumstances.

A road 500 miles long as to its main stem may have 1,500 miles of branches, and the whole may be of such a character as to make it almost necessarily one unit for the purpose of operation. Anywhere from 250 to 2,000 miles may be operated successfully as one unit under a general manager if in the second stage or a general superintendent if in the first.

An important question in the management of a large railroad system is how to get local responsibility on the part of those engaged in operating different arms of the system.

It is obvious that to hold a manager responsible for results it is necessary to give him pretty full power over the property which he must use to produce those results, both as to income and outgo. It is also clear that to get this kind of responsibility it is desirable that the unit of management, so to speak shall not be too large, and that it shall be homogeneous. That is to say one manager with his necessary staff having control of the every day details of business must not have too large a field or too many roads differing in character. On the other hand it is desirable and economical to have uniformity in many things and not to cut the system up into too small pieces locally independent of one another. The unit of management being determined the officer in command should in order to keep himself and his men up to their work be able to know at all times what his road is earning and what he is spending—and he should have the responsibility for a loss of business as well as for an excess of expenditure.

Experience shows that where branches or side lines are operated under the same local management as that for the through, or main line, the inevitable tendency is to do things on the branches in the same way as on the main line, which is often a more expensive way than is really necessary for a branch.

Also as regards wages: on a through line with a large and unsteady volume of business where 1,000 men are employed one month and 800 the next wages are fixed at an average point high enough to attract the best *class* of men to be had under the circumstances for the work to be done. Whereas on small roads where few men are employed and the work is steady and less wearing, and they can be selected by the superintendent himself and are drawn mostly from the fixed population along the line of the road the few required can generally be obtained at lower wages than the average paid by a big road.

It is always difficult however to pay one rate of wages on the main line, and another rate on a branch line, where one management operates both.

Theoretically it can be, and sometimes is done to some extent, but the drift is always strong in the direction of pushing up the branch wages to the same level as the main line, when the two are operated as one road. With short branches which are run merely as feeders to the main stem, this evil can hardly be overcome.

A branch too short for a superintendent of its own, is put in charge of the force operating the part of the main line contiguous to it, and men are almost of necessity changed about from the branch to the main line and vice versa, either because trains run through sometimes over the branch and part of the main line, or for other reasons. But when it is practicable to group a sufficiently large mileage of second class or "branch" road to justify it, it is clearly desirable to separate the local management from that of the main line, even if it can be conveniently done, to the extent of making a distinct unit of management.

XVII

A railroad system owned by one company may therefore embrace one or more units of management, each under a general manager responsible directly to the president and the 3rd vice president and one or more smaller units of management embracing roads in the first stage, each under a general superintendent also responsible directly to the president and the 3rd vice president. Each unit may also if thought expedient have its own accounting office at the head of which would be a local auditor, and its own money office with a local treasurer in charge, and both of these officers would through the auditor and the treasurer respectively be responsible to the 2nd vice president.

By thus operating the property each unit can receive the kind of management most economical under the circumstances, and details will receive an amount of attention from the respective general managers or general superintendents which could not be given if one management were put over the whole and the different heads of departments on the general manager's staff made responsible over so wide a field.

XVIII

The general idea of the plan of management suggested, is that whatever the size of the unit and however many units may be owned by one company, the general organization would not be changed.

The president assisted by the three vice presidents could take care of an indefinite number of units if they keep clearly before them the necessity of local self government.

By local self government is meant the possession of very full powers by each general manager or general superintendent as the case may be.

The accounts of two or more units may with proper system be kept in one place and under one general auditor, but if that is done, they should be kept distinct so that each general manager or general superintendent, may be held responsible for his results independently.

The importance of not letting the unit of management become either too large or too heterogeneous is so great that it may sometimes be found expedient in acquiring a new road to continue to operate it under its own corporate organization.

When the consolidation of railroads began it was supposed and argued that one of the things to be gained by it would be the saving of the necessary cost of maintaining separate corporations and general offices—

This was true within limits—two roads each 100 miles long and each maintaining its corporate organization and staff could with economy in the general offices be put together under one set of officers throughout. But this is not true in the same degree of two roads each 1,000 miles long.

And when one general manager, responsible to those over him for the general results, has been charged with the daily supervision of 2,000 miles of railroad he has reached about the limit of physical ability. The amount of necessary attention to details is enormous. It would generally produce better results to limit one man to about 1,000 miles,—but with the growth of the large systems and the complications of the business management it has been found in some cases difficult if not impracticable to do this. No line however should be rigidly drawn, as it well can be in almost all cases, at about 2,000 miles, and as much less than that down to 1,000 as the circumstances will admit of.

It is sometimes urged against this division of one great property into units of management, that there constantly arise general questions affecting the whole property—that the different operating units will clash and money will be lost to the company owning the whole by reason of efforts on the part of one general manager to get some advantage over another—that the use of red tape will become too much extended—that car mileage offices and other offices will be unnecessarily multiplied, etc. But the simple answer to all this is that the gain by reason of the more efficient attention to details on the part of the man responsible for results will be far greater than any possible loss by the unnecessary use of red tape etc.

As to general questions about which the general managers cannot agree among themselves, they are easily referred to the president or to his representative the third vice president, or in matters of accounts to the second vice president—and as to the objection that offices are multiplied it needs only to be said that very few more men are employed than if they were all under one general manager, but being directly responsible to some one near at hand they do more work and do it better. Not the least among the advantages to be derived from the division into units of management is the fact that the local population in the country and towns through which the road passes can more readily know and more often see in person the general manager. This is a consideration of importance and is alone a good reason for not making a unit too large. Personal acquaintance promotes good understanding and the people like to see those in authority. Again the president and the vice presidents can under this system bring to bear their judgment upon important local questions affecting any unit more effectively through the one local head than through the heads of a number of different departments far removed often from the scene of action.

. . . .

PART IV

The Beginnings of Modern Labor Relations

INTRODUCTION

❡ IF THE railroads pioneered in the ways of modern management, they also were leaders in developing patterns of modern labor relations. Railroad employees were the first to work in large numbers for the big impersonal corporation. Moreover, locomotive engineers, firemen, brakemen, and switchmen were trained men whose skills were hard to replace and who were daily responsible for the operation and maintenance of valuable and expensive equipment. Such skills and responsibilities gave these railroad workers a potentially stronger bargaining power than most nineteenth-century workers enjoyed. Such a potential soon came to be realized through organization. As the railroad workers were among the first to form local unions and then to build a national federation of their locals, their brotherhoods quickly became the most powerful and effective unions developed in the United States before the twentieth century.

At first the brotherhoods were essentially fraternal and mutual-aid societies. Their members helped to protect themselves from the vicissitudes of an industrial society by providing life, sickness, and, in time, unemployment insurance. But when American railroads moved from their period of growth to that of competition, and when severe economic depression brought lay-offs and wage cuts, the engineers, firemen, and others began to use their organizations as instruments of economic power through which to gain some control over their immediate economic situation.

Union officials began to bargain with representatives of corporate management over hours, wages, and conditions of work. And bargaining was effectively backed up by the threat of the strike. Beyond the bread-and-butter issues lay a more fundamental conflict. The unions were always anxious to be formally recognized by management as the only bargaining agent for their type of worker on any one road. The professional managers and the bankers who financed them preferred to deal with the individual employee, but where they could not avoid bargaining through the union, they tried to deal only with the specific points of hours and wages then at issue. These managers saw the brotherhoods as outsiders trying to obtain control over their laboring force. "We should show at once that the row is not a question of money," wrote one railroad executive, "but as to who shall manage the road." Others insisted that the men must not "dictate" to their employers.

Because they were among the first to organize on national lines and because they had skills that were hard to replace, the railroad brotherhoods pioneered in the modern methods of collective bargaining, grievance procedures, and union organization. But they also did so because they were the first to deal with professional corporate managers. Most of the earlier pre-Civil War unions had been local in scope and were usually made up of journeymen seeking better conditions from their master workmen, a situation that had few parallels in the later industrial economy. The more stable local unions of skilled craftsmen began to build lasting national organizations at about the same time as did the railroad unions. In 1886 these national organizations came together to form the American Federation of Labor. However, nearly all the early craft unions had grown up in industries consisting of small shops or family businesses. They were successful in the construction and building trades, in small machine shops, and in cigar-making, glass-blowing, and printing establishments. But the AF of L never became strong in the factory-dominated industries where modern corporation management first appeared in American manufacturing. The AF of L unions therefore, learned to deal primarily with the owners of small firms and not, as did railroad brotherhoods, with the salaried managers of large enterprises.

During the 1870's and the 1880's, when the brotherhoods and craft unions were becoming established, another type of labor organization was becoming extremely popular with American workingmen. The Knights of Labor opened its locals to nearly everyone, regardless of craft, skill, creed, or color. The Knights' purpose was not to improve wages, hours, and the conditions of work but to replace the wage system by cooperative enterprises. As Terence V. Powderly, the Grand Master of the Order, stressed: "The aim of the Knights of Labor—properly understood —is to make each man his own employer." While such an aim had a powerful appeal to workers who only recently had left the farm, it hardly encouraged the development of modern collective bargaining between labor and management. The Knights' failure to develop effective organization and bargaining procedures to wring concessions from employers led to their sharp decline in membership in the 1890's and then to their final demise.

In the 1880's a number of American labor leaders began to advocate a union that was not as exclusive as the craft unions and not as unwieldy and unrealistic as the Knights. Eugene V. Debs, long an officer in the Brotherhood of Firemen and a founder of the brakemen's national union, had become convinced that the only effective way to assure workers, other than the highly skilled ones, of some control over the conditions of their work was to form a union that included all the workers in a single industry. This type of industrial unionism had its initial start in the United States in railroading. It failed quickly, and its failure helped delay for many years any widespread establishment of the industrial union in this country.

When Debs formed the American Railway Union in June, 1893, he opened it to all "persons employed in railway service." He welcomed mechanics and day laborers in locomotive, car-making, and car-repair shops and factories even if such industrial establishments were not under the control of a railroad company. But before it was more than a year old, the ARU had been disastrously defeated in its first major campaign—the Pullman and the Chicago railroad strikes of 1894.

The Pullman strike had its roots in the severe economic depression that struck the country in 1893. In the winter and spring of 1894, Pullman's Palace Car Company began to lay off men at its main shops in South Chicago and to reduce the wages of those still on the job. Pullman workers, who had been enthusiastically joining an ARU local, decided to strike. They then asked the national union to back them. Debs was fully aware of the difficult position in which the request placed the new union. It had not had time to acquire either the organization or the funds so necessary to win an extended boycott or strike. Nevertheless, if it failed to support a local in one of the first requests for aid, it would seriously damage its prestige and chances for future growth. In any case, delegates from several hundred locals then meeting in Chicago took the decision out of Debs' hand. They voted to support the Pullman strikers by refusing to handle Pullman cars on any road entering Chicago.

The boycott began on June 26, 1894. When the railroads immediately refused to allow Pullman cars to be detached, the union struck the railroads. The strike never had a chance. If Debs' union had neither the organization nor the money to wage industrial warfare, the railroads most certainly did. From its headquarters in Chicago, their General Managers Association recruited strikebreakers, brought legal action against the strikers and their unions, and kept in close communication with civil and military authorities as to the movement of police, marshals, and troops.

Moreover, the railroads had the backing of much of the public and also of the federal government. Many middle-class Americans were disturbed by the railroads' economic power and by the discriminatory practices in rates and services (see Part VI, below). But in the early 1890's they were even more concerned by the growing political and economic protests of the farmers and the workers that seemed to threaten the very fabric of their society. In 1894 the Populist cause with its demands for national ownership of utilities and railroads and for inflation through the free

and unlimited coinage of silver had reached the height of its popularity among the Southern and Western farmers. In 1892 industrial warfare had flared with harsh violence at the great Homestead steel works outside of Pittsburgh and in the silver mines of the Coeur d'Alene region of Idaho. Then, only a few weeks before the Pullman strike, an army of unemployed led by Populist Jacob S. Coxey had attempted a march on Washington. So when violence broke out early in the Chicago railroad strike, many Americans welcomed federal intervention.

The federal government began to take part in the strike on July 2, when a district judge issued a sweeping injunction against the union leaders that for all practical purposes prohibited them from continuing the strike. When Debs and his lieutenants failed to comply, they were arrested and jailed. The injunction, issued under the Sherman Antitrust Act, was upheld by the Supreme Court not on the grounds of violation of the Sherman Act but rather on the Constitution's commerce clause. At the same time, under authority of an obscure law passed during the Reconstruction period, President Grover Cleveland sent federal troops to Chicago over the protest of the Illinois Governor, John P. Altgeld. While the troops were not used directly as strikebreakers, their presence made it easier for the railroads to keep the trains moving. Thus, besides retarding the development of industrial unionism, the Pullman strike set a precedent for government intervention on the side of owners and managers in later strikes and industrial conflicts.

The Chicago railroad strike had another result, which pointed to a more neutral and more lasting role for the government. The commission set up by President Cleveland to investigate the strike recommended that a governmental body be appointed to mediate similar industrial conflicts. The suggestion was embodied in the Erdman Act, passed in 1898, which provided for mediation by the chairman of the Interstate Commerce Commission and the commissioner of the Bureau of Labor. Although little used until the Theodore Roosevelt administration, sixty-one railroad labor disputes were settled under its terms between 1906 and 1913. In this way then the railroads had developed collective-bargaining procedures including government mediation a generation before such patterns appeared in most of American industry.

The readings that follow were selected to show when, why, and how the railroad labor unions pioneered in the building of modern craft unionism and to illustrate the procedures used by these unions in bargaining collectively with their employers. The readings also indicate the swift rise and fall of the industrial union and suggest the changing role of government in labor disputes. The first two selections are from the pen of C. H. Salmons, an active leader in the Brotherhood of Locomotive Engineers local of the Chicago, Burlington and Quincy Railroad, who wrote a book on the Burlington strike of 1888. In the first of these, this engineer tells why he and his fellows felt the need for organization and then he describes the coming of the first brotherhoods. While accepting the wage system and the class structure that accompanies it, the skilled worker still cherished economic mobility. Salmons points with pride to the locomotive engineers

who had left their trade and their union to rise high in the ranks of management.

The second selection from Salmons' book reveals the methods of collective bargaining developed by 1886. Here a local union in bargaining with the road's vice-president in charge of operations was supported in the negotiations by Peter M. Arthur, the Grand Chief Engineer of the Brotherhood. Arthur and the local union officers obtained their aims by the explicit threat of the strike weapon. Both the specific and the underlying issues are clear. The engineers wanted more uniform pay and pay for time spent on the job during delays for which they were not responsible. They also asked for protection from arbitrary discharge. Most importantly, they hoped for recognition of the union. Their adversaries were less disturbed by demands for increasing pay than by signing a contract that seemed to suggest that the union had dictated to management.

The final selection comes from the careful, objective report of the President's commission to study the Chicago railway strike of 1894. It describes and analyzes as well as any later account the rise of the American Railroad Union, the coming of the Pullman strike, and the resulting boycott and railroad strike, and so focuses more on the background of the strike and on the make-up of the two antagonists than on the details of the battle itself. Finally, the readings indicate the recommendations for government mediation that Congress was to act upon later in the decade.

THE READINGS

1] The Brotherhoods

Why Do Laboring Men Organize?

.   .   .   .

BUT WHY do the employes of railroads organize?
Let us enumerate some of the reasons:

1. It is the unquestioned usage of legislatures and of congress to grant to railroad corporations almost unlimited franchises, and in perpetuity, without any personal responsibility. On the other hand, no enactment of any importance is on any statute book to protect railroad men, whose work upon trains imperils their lives with almost every duty they perform. It is not unreasonable that trainmen should be disaffected wherever they are paid less than men are usually paid for similar work on other roads, and wherever they are held to a company by an arrangement that compels them to stay where they are, or else be prevented from railroad work anywhere else.

2. It is to be remembered also, that the life of a railroad is a perpetuity; that with time its expenses will lessen and its business will increase. In view of future incomes men will take present risks. Capital can always do this, but labor cannot. Labor represents women and children; it implies food, clothing, shelter and education; the day's work if well done should meet these demands at par. The two millions, or more, now nearly three millions, of persons in the families of railway employes have the first lien on the products of their work. When, therefore, the railway laborer demands reasonable pay, he has behind him a regiment of arguments to enforce his right. The most of the work to be done is so difficult as to require experienced, or skilled labor; it is largely of a kind to impair health and to shorten life, and it exposes the laborer to great irregularities of work, and to a frightful percentage of fatal accidents. When losses occur to a company from mismanagement they should not be made up by abatement of the wages of laborers. If the business of a year proves dull, the stockholder's dividends should not be kept up by cutting down the wages of the men. One man alone counts nothing before a powerful company; one day's work bears a poor proportion to the thousands of millions of capital invested in railroads. Unless labor combines it cannot be heard at all. It has no resort, no appeal for justice if it cannot organize a moral force that will stand between the laborer and the relentless power of gold.

FROM C. H. Salmons, "Why Do Laboring Men Organize?" "Mutual Obligations," "Brotherhood of Locomotive Engineers," "Brotherhood of Locomotive Firemen," and "Switchmen's Mutual Aid Association," *The Burlington Strike* (Aurora, Ill., 1889), pp. 12–18, 22–25, 27–30.

3. The conditions of the trainman's life are hard. If he develops into a man of business, or if he becomes manager of great enterprises, it is in defiance of his surroundings. He usually enters in early life upon his occupation in which there is a premium on strength, alertness and endurance, and in which there is much of both physical weariness and mental dissipation. He is commonly exposed to allurements that tend downwards. Along the line there are drinking places; if not in the station itself, then within a door or two. It is a rare thing that he finds a reading room for railway men, or a resting place away from tempting odors and sights and companions. It does not seem to be recognized at headquarters that what makes a better man makes a better workman. If there are anywhere in depots, reading rooms, and places of quiet rest for the much jolted men, it is very recent, and exceedingly rare, and even where there is considerable work of this kind it is rarely traceable to a railroad company. But almost all roads in this country have, in a very effective way, testified to the capability and the character of the railroad employe. Almost everywhere men are filling the highest positions in railroad management who have come up from the lowest round. This is very noticeable in the Pennsylvania system. President Roberts, and A. J. Cassatt, formerly vice-president, began as rodmen in the engineers' corps. Second vice-president Thompson was a machinist of Altoona; general manager Pugh began as a brakeman; general passenger agent Carpenter, and James McCrea, general manager west of Pittsburg, both began as messenger boys. A. M. Tucker, division superintendent on the Erie, was a track laborer. C. W. Bradley, general superintendent of the West Shore, was a brakeman, then conductor, on the same road. President Caldwell of the Nickel Plate was a clerk on the Pennsylvania. The engineers and firemen have been very prolific in this direction. One Division, No. 34, of Columbus, Ohio, has on its roll of honor two railroad presidents, three master mechanics, and four roundhouse foremen. There can be no doubt that everywhere similar talent abounds among men in subordinate positions along all our great railway lines. That so many reach distinction in spite of great disadvantage is an inspiring argument in favor of organization for mutual improvement and protection. It encourages honest emulation and true pride. Its result must be to make the men sober, industrious, frugal, faithful, and self-helpful.

4. The capital invested in banks and that employed in insurance companies, though in large amounts, is yet comparatively harmless as regards labor. But when capital is pitted against labor; when the issue is Money vs. Men; when the returns upon the invested capital are in proportion to the pressure upon the laborer, then as capital is heartless, the rights of the man must go under. The greatest danger is reached when capital succeeds in holding the laborer in one hand, and grasping legislation with the other. The money invested in railroad stocks, with the addition of the amount of all the funded debts of the railway companies in this country, will soon reach the enormous amount of ten thousand millions of dollars ($10,000,-000,000). A very small percentage of this sum will support a lobby, the third house, in every state capital, as well as at Washington. An assessment of one-fourth of one cent on each dollar of this vast sum would produce

a revenue of twenty-five millions. At present rates of increase we shall soon have in this country one million of railway laborers. A reduction of five cents per day upon that number of men would produce the sum of eighteen millions of dollars ($18,250,000). We do not say that any one has proposed this, but we do say that similar things have been done. Wages have been cut down to replenish a foolishly exhausted treasury. How easy a thing it would be for capital to declare war on labor and then assess upon labor the expense of it. How easy to keep up dividends to stockholders by cutting down wages; or to cover the ruinous expense of an unwise policy in the management by issuing a lower rate of payments.

Capital, controlling lobbies and newspapers, constitutes a trio for evil, before which, if it is left unchecked, the rights of the American laborer will be of as little value to him as to the toilers of Russia, or of Algiers. In Europe, when contests are on between money and labor, the appeal is to the bayonet; but in this country the appeal is to argument, to righteousness, and to the ballot. Our method of protection is not by violence, but by the peaceable combination of the endangered men, so as to make themselves felt by their moral force, their intelligence. and by their numbers.

Mutual Obligations

. . . .

We believe that there are certain great principles in equity in which both capital and labor ought heartily to agree, and beyond which the demands of either would be both unreasonable and unrighteous. There is really but one universal and unerring rule, viz: As ye would that men should do to you, do ye also to them.

Most men, given to one kind of work, become skilled in it, and unfit themselves for other employments, but at the same time increase the value of their labor to their employer. To be discharged implies the loss of the time used in acquiring the skill, and also the waste of time and money in seeking a new place. It may require a removal of hundreds of miles at great expense. If permanent employment is uncertain, it will prevent the laborer from embellishing, or even from making a home, and it tends to make of him an improvident, hand-to-mouth hanger-on upon a temporary occupation, and the education of his children becomes a most unlikely thing. He cannot identify himself with permanent interests of the community, and he sinks into a characterless wage-earner. It would not be strange if some times the fear of removal would lead men to try to keep their places by unbecoming and wrongful methods, or they may do a poor service knowing they are liable to dismissal for any cause, or for none.

Now, a corporation might arbitrarily reduce the wages, or compulsorily increase the hours of labor, or frequently require additional hours of work for the pay of ten, or compel the employe to assume the risk of damage to property, or say to the men unfairly burdened, "If you do not like our administration, go elsewhere; you are at liberty." All these methods have, here or there, been resorted to. It is obvious that they deteriorate the character of the laborer, so as not only to lessen the value of the labor, but also to abate the worth of the man as a member of the community. Certainly no corporation has a moral right to do this, for it unfits the employe for honorable and skilled work.

.   .   .   .

Brotherhood of Locomotive Engineers

On the 17th of April, 1863, at Marshall, Michigan, Messrs. E. Nichols, F. Avery, D. Wheeler, John Kennedy, F. Wartsmouth, H. Higgins, B. Northrup, Geo. Q. Adams, and W. D. Robinson, believing that many evils might be remedied, and much good accomplished, by an organization of practical locomotive engineers, met and instituted a society named the Brotherhood of the Foot Board. The 17th and the 18th of the following August was agreed upon by them as the time for holding the first annual convention at Detroit, Michigan, at which convention W. D. Robinson, of Detroit, was duly elected to fill, for the first time in its existence, the very important office of Grand Chief Engineer, and O. T. Johnson, of LaFayette, Indiana, was chosen first Grand Assistant Engineer. By a provision of the original constitution, locomotive firemen and machinists were admitted to equal membership. A short deliberation, and experience, convinced the incorporators that engineers should act separately in the matter of self protection. Hence it became necessary to call a special session of the convention, which assembled on the 22nd of February, 1864, at Detroit, at which time and place this objectionable clause was changed and the locomotive engineers were possessed of an organization exclusively their own.

At the second annual convention, which was held at Indianapolis, Indiana, on August 17th, 1864, Charles Wilson, of Rochester, New York, and Robert Laughlin, of Hornellsville, New York, were chosen to fill the two highest offices of the organization, and the title originally chosen was substituted by the title which is still borne by the order, viz: The Brotherhood of Locomotive Engineers.

That a good thing was done in the organization of the order is evident from its rapid growth. This convention at Indianapolis was held at the end of its first year, when sixty-seven of its subordinate divisions had been established, with a membership of over sixteen hundred. To-day the order extends through every part of the United States, and has a footing also in Canada and Mexico. The number of divisions has reached four hundred and twenty, and the membership exceeds twenty-five thousand.

There is a Mutual Insurance Association connected with the Order and an outgrowth of it, originating in 1867. The business and the reports cover now a period of twenty-one years of the work of insurance with the most satisfactory results. There were paid out, during the year previous to November, 1888, one hundred claims of three thousand dollars each, making a total of three hundred and twenty-seven thousand dollars ($327,000). The entire amount paid to widows, orphans and to disabled members, since 1867, is $2,572,169.61.

During the year ending with November, 1888, the Chief Engineer was called to interpose and to adjust between men and officers on twelve different roads, and in each instance he effected an honorable and amicable adjustment. The contest between the men and the officers of the Burlington System was the only one that has occurred in eleven years that has not yielded to satisfactory adjustment by friendly interposition. The history of the Order is made up of happy results upon individual character, inspiring men with emulation, and virtuous pride in their calling. By its refining and elevating influence upon the character of its members it adds to the efficiency and to the actual wealth of every company whose engines are run by members of the Brotherhood.

. . . .

Brotherhood of Locomotive Firemen

The locomotive firemen effected an organization, a Brotherhood, for mutual benefit, on December 1, 1873, at Port Jervis, New York. Eleven men met to devise means of mutual helpfulness, social, moral and intellectual, to protect the interests of firemen and to promote their general welfare. It has, in these sixteen years, permeated every part of the United States, extending also into Mexico and Canada. The Order receives reports from three hundred and ninety lodges, aggregating over nineteen thousand members. Its object at first was not beyond the mutual advantages that come from close affiliation of men of similar pursuits; but in 1885 the Order extended its purposes and became distinctly a labor organization without losing its benevolent characteristics. The method of adjusting differences between the Order and the authorities of a road, is to appeal directly to the highest authority of the company complained of, and if that is not successful, then to insist upon arbitration. The organization tends to good order, to mutual beneficial influences, and it is a concentration of power which may, at almost any time, be called upon for mutual protection, or in some way in the defense of the interests of labor. There is no antagonism between the firemen and any other society of railway laborers; on the contrary, the Order works for the advantage of the laborer in the interests of fair work for fair pay.

. . . .

Switchmen's Mutual Aid Association

The switchmen at Chicago organized a Union, for mutual aid, intended for only local purposes, on August 18, 1877. The society had but little progress until 1884, when it took in new blood, and various cities began to organize similar societies. A meeting of delegates, for the object of forming a national organization, was held at Chicago, February 22, 1886. The convention deliberated eight days over a constitution, which was adopted at last with enthusiastic unanimity. The object of the Mutual Aid Society, as declared in the preamble to the Constitution, is as follows:

First. To unite and promote the general welfare, and advance the interests—social, moral, and intellectual—of its members.

Second. To endeavor to establish mutual confidence, and create and maintain harmonious relations between employer and employe.

The forms of benevolence undertaken were, "to relieve the distress of disabled brothers, to care for their widows and orphans, and to see to the decent burial of deceased members."

The first annual meeting was held in Kansas City, Monday, September 20, 1886, having delegates from twenty-five lodges.

The first Grand Master was James L. Monaghan, whose ill-health had driven him from the law business to the outdoor work of the switchman. He became a member of the Illinois legislature in 1888. From that time on, the Society has been fortunate in having for officers, good and efficient men. In 1888, Mr. George S. Bailey was made Grand Organizer and Instructor, who also left the law for outdoor railroading work. In 1886 he became a member of the lower house of the Illinois legislature, and carried through a bill for a State Board of Arbitration, but not in time to have the action of the Senate. The Order is a vigorous one, watching carefully the interests of labor.

[Salmons then describes the formation of the Brotherhood of Railroad Brakemen in 1883. He points out that "the Order was greatly indebted to Eugene V. Debs, a good man, who was eminent among the Brotherhood of Firemen."]

2] Collective Bargaining

The Treaty of Peace of 1886

AFTER meeting with the committee and advising moderation, Mr. Arthur and the chairman went to Mr. Potter's office, to arrange for a meeting, which was appointed for 2:30 P.M. On the arrival of the committee at the Burlington offices, Mr. Arthur and the chairman again went into Mr. Potter's office. Whether Mr. Potter [1] had changed his mind, or had adopted a new role was not known, but he had concluded not to see the committee, saying it would do no good. However, he finally consented when the schedule was presented by Mr. Arthur, with the classification left out by the advice of the Grand Chief Engineer. This left only a uniform schedule of pay, and laws to govern subordinate officers. Still, with all the concessions that had been made by the committee, they seemed no nearer a settlement than at the first meeting. Mr. Potter said he would not adopt a uniform schedule, when Mr. Arthur said: "As you will do nothing, it is left with the men to say what they will do. As grand chief, I cannot make them strike, but when my consent is given, it carries with it the consent of the Brotherhood of Locomotive Engineers of the whole United States, Canada and Mexico." Mr. Potter said: "Then they will strike if you give your consent?" Mr. Arthur answered: "Mr. Potter, you have had your own way so long, you think you must have it always. Now I will sanction a strike, and if

---

1 [Thomas J. Potter, third vice-president of the Burlington, resigned in 1887 to become a vice-president of the Union Pacific Railroad.]

FROM C. H. Salmons, "The Treaty of Peace of 1886," *The Burlington Strike* (Aurora, Ill., 1889), pp. 73–79.

you can hire men to run your engines you can do so, but the Brotherhood of Locomotive Engineers can pay as much to hire them not to run them." Mr. Potter evidently did not like this picture, and said he would submit a proposition, but he would want ten days. Mr. Arthur asked each one of the committee if he would grant the time, and each answered "No." It was evident to the committee that negotiations had come to an end, and all, including Mr. Potter, arose, taking their hats, when Mr. Potter said: "I have talked with the stockholders, and they say we cannot accept your schedule, because it would allow labor to dictate to capital." Then said Mr. Arthur, "I will give you forty-eight hours to make a proposition to us, and if reasonable we will accept it. That will give you a ladder on which you can come down from your autocratic position." Mr. Potter said he could not do it in that time. He would have to call in all the officers, as he did not know enough about each run to make a schedule himself. Mr. Arthur said: "If you had any proposition to make you could have made it long ago. You have kept these men waiting around here for twenty days, without any good reason, but to be fair with you we will give you until Friday." Mr. Potter said he could be ready on Thursday, at 2:30 P.M. He had made his point of not accepting any proposed change as dictated by labor, but to prevent financial disasters, which he knew would be the inevitable result of a strike, he had allowed his autocratic position to become badly undermined and had consented to have changes made in both rules and pay, and had signed them. Immediately after the close of this meeting, orders were sent in every direction for the superintendents and the master mechanics of all divisions, to come to Chicago for this conference. On their arrival, Mr. Potter set them at work, fixing up a proposition to present to the committee of engineers.

At the appointed time, on Thursday, March 25, the committee was notified that Mr. Potter was ready to see them. The committeemen again wended their way to the manager's office, with patience and a strong determination to follow the usual conservative course of the Brotherhood. Yet they were resolved, if possible, to secure some kind of an agreement signed by the general manager, as it would carry with it a recognition of the right of the laborer to be a voluntary party to any contract for work. Such an agreement would also be an official recognition of the Brotherhood.

On arriving at the Burlington offices, the committee was invited into Mr. Potter's private office on the ground floor, and presented with the result of the local official deliberation. It had nothing in it to commend itself to the committee, and it was promptly rejected by them. In Mr. Potter's trip over the system, he found that 95 per cent of the enginemen belonged to the two Orders,[2] and he was anxious to prevent an issue with them. In pursuit of this policy, he asked if they would meet the local officers of their respective divisions, and take up each run and condition and see if they could not arrive at some conclusion. Mr. Potter said he was astonished at the lack of ability of some of his local officers, and was

2 [Both the Brotherhood of Locomotive Engineers and the Brotherhood of Locomotive Firemen.]

satisfied they could not make a schedule. The committee consented to this and adjourned to meet them the next morning.

On Friday, March 26, the committee took the elevator at the Burlington headquarters and landed at the room which had been previously used as a meeting room, and met their respective officials. After the usual recognitions they proceeded to business. There were two officers to each grievance committeeman, and they divided off in squads of three, and took up the home work. They went over each run, and increased the pay very materially on many of the runs for both engineers and firemen, discussing delays and other evil conditions. The consent of the local officials was given very reluctantly to these changes, and they should not, by any means, be credited to their liberality. Mr. Potter knew it was concessions or a strike, and the officials were brought in for the purpose of making them. The chief men delegated to their inferiors the work of making the changes, but reserved the credit of being magnanimous. The committee work not being done at noon, the meeting adjourned until 2:30 P.M., when time would suffice for all the runs to be considered. The rules were taken up and an agreement was finally reached. The meeting adjourned until Saturday at 11 o'clock, to receive the schedules and rules which were being prepared by the Company, and which would then be signed by its officers. We append here a note from Mr. Potter, accompanying the revised rules, to which were added signatures of the highest authority. The committeemen who had been away from their homes over forty days, made their preparations to return with pleasant anticipations.

CHICAGO, March 25th, 1886

J. C. PORTER, ESQ.
CHAIRMAN COMMITTEE OF ENGINEERS, CHICAGO

DEAR SIR:

I hand you herewith changes in rate schedule and rules governing the pay of engineers and firemen, on the Chicago, Burlington & Quincy; Burlington & Missouri, in Neb.; Hannibal & St. Joseph; Kansas City, St. Joseph & Council Bluffs; Chicago & Iowa; St. Louis, Kansas & North-West; and Council Bluffs & Kansas City roads.

The officers of these roads have gone over the rates of pay, and recommend that these changes be made, and I approve of their recommendation.

Yours Truly,
(Signed,) T. J. POTTER

CHANGE IN RATE SCHEDULE AND RULES GOVERNING THE PAY OF ENGINEERS AND FIREMEN, TAKING EFFECT APRIL 1, 1886

Article I

No engineer will be dismissed or suspended from the service of this Company without just cause.

Every engineer will be entitled to a full and impartial hearing and investigation by the Superintendent and Master Mechanic.

It is understood that in ordinary cases superintendents and master mechanics will not suspend engineers until such cases have had full investigation.

Article II

Engineers delayed two (2) hours or over, in starting from or arriving at terminals, will be paid at work train rates per hour, for the full delay less one hour.

The same rule will apply in case engineers have been called, and afterward, on account of wreck, are notified they are not wanted.

When delays of over two (2) hours occur at any one point during a trip, on account of no orders to go on, engineers will be paid at work train rates per hour for the full delay, less one hour; but if the delay is occasioned by a wreck, washout, or other physical cause, then engineers will be paid at one-half (½) work train rates per hour for the full delay, less one hour.

Article III

Should engineers be obliged to double hills on account of having more than established rates, they will receive pay for one hour's time, at work train rates.

Article IV

If one or more engines are coupled in with snow plow engines for bucking snow, the engineer of each engine will be paid at one and one-half work train rates; but in no case will the amount paid be less than regular freight rates for the distance run.

In case an engineer called to buck snow is held under orders, such engineer will receive pay at work train rates for all time he is so held.

Article V

Engineers will be called a reasonable time before leaving time. The caller will have a book in which engineers must register their names and hour when called.

Article VI

Right to regular runs when merit and ability are equal will be governed by seniority. Engineers having had regular runs prior to the date of this circular will not be affected by this article.

Article VII

No more extra engineers will be assigned than is necessary to move the traffic with promptness and dispatch, and should any engineer feel himself aggrieved by the assignment of extra engineers he can proceed as in Article I, but will receive no pay for loss of time.

Article VIII

Engineers dead-heading on Company business, will be paid at the same rate as on passenger runs.

Article IX

No fines will be assessed against engineers.

Article X

Fireman's pay will be adjusted in proportion to the engineers.

Article XI

All officers will be provided with copies of this circular, which will be kept posted in the several engine houses.

HENRY B. STONE,   G. W. RHODES,   J. D. BESLER,
    General Manager   Supt. Motive Power   General Superintendent

3] Industrial Unionism and the Role of Government: The Chicago Strike of 1894

The American Railway Union

THIS is an association of about 150,000 railroad employés, as alleged, organized at Chicago on the 20th of June, 1893, for the purpose of including railway employés born of white parents in one great brotherhood.

The theory underlying this movement is that the organization of different classes of railroad employés (to the number of about 140,000) upon the trades-union idea has ceased to be useful or adequate; that pride of organization, petty jealousies, and the conflict of views into which men are trained in separate organizations under different leaders, tend to defeat the common object of all, and enable railroads to use such organizations against each other in contentions over wages, etc.; that the rapid concentration of railroad capital and management demands a like union of their employés for the purpose of mutual protection; that the interests of each of the 850,000 and over railroad employés of the United States as to wages, treatment, hours of labor, legislation, insurance, mutual aid, etc., are common to all, and hence all ought to belong to one organization that shall assert its united strength in the protection of the rights of every member.

The American Federation of Labor, composed of affiliated unions, with a membership of over 500,000, also tends in the direction of broader union for labor. The order of the Knights of Labor, with an estimated membership of from 150,000 to 175,000, has always advocated the solidarity of labor.

In the American Railway Union there are departments of literature and education, legislation, cooperation, mediation, insurance, etc. The organization consists of a general union and of local unions. The general union is formed by representatives of local unions, who elect a board of nine

FROM "The American Railway Union," "The Pullman Strike: Its Causes and Events," and "Railroad Strike," *Report on the Chicago Strike of June–July, 1894, by the United States Strike Commission* (Washington, D.C., 1894), pp. 19–24, 28–29, 33, 51–53.

directors quadrennially. This board has authority to "issue such orders and adopt such measures as may be required to carry out the objects of the order." Any ten white persons employed in railway service, except superintendents, etc., can organize a local union. Each local union has its board of mediation, and the chairmen of the various local boards upon a system of railroads constitute a general board of mediation for that system.

The constitution provides that—

All complaints and adjustments must be first taken up by the local union; if accepted by a majority vote it shall be referred to the local board of mediation for adjustment, and, if failing, the case shall be submitted to the chairman of the general board of mediation, failing in which, they shall notify the president of the general union, who shall authorize the most available member of the board of directors to visit and meet with the general chairman of the board of mediation and issue such instructions as will be promulgated by the directors.

Under these provisions it is claimed that no strike can be declared except by order of a majority of the men involved. This is a commendable feature of the union. So long as strikes are resorted to, the power to order them should never be vested anywhere except in a majority of the employés concerned. If a two-thirds or three-quarters vote were required it would be still better. After a strike is ordered the board of directors of the general union practically directs its conduct.

In its profession of principles and purposes in its general and local constitutions the American Railway Union proposes to protect and promote the interests of its members as wage earners through organization and legitimate cooperation. Its constitution reads:

First. The protection of all members in all matters relating to wages and their rights as employés is the principal purpose of the organization. Railway employés are entitled to a voice in fixing wages and in determining conditions of employment. Fair wages and proper treatment must be the return for efficient service, faithfully performed. Such a policy insures harmonious relations and satisfactory results. The order, while pledged to conservative methods, will protect the humblest of its members in every right he can justly claim; but while the rights of members will be sacredly guarded, no intemperate demand or unreasonable propositions will be entertained. Corporations will not be permitted to treat the organization better than the organization will treat them. A high sense of honor must be the animating spirit, and evenhanded justice the end sought to be obtained. Thoroughly organized in every department, with a due regard for the right wherever found, it is confidently believed that all differences may be satisfactorily adjusted, that harmonious relations may be established and maintained, that the service may be incalculably improved, and that the necessity for strike and lockout, boycott and blacklist, alike disastrous to employer and employé and a perpetual menace to the welfare of the public, will forever disappear.

.   .   .   .

In March, 1894, the employés of Pullman's Palace Car Company, being dissatisfied with their wages, rents, and shop treatment for the first time in the history of the town, sought organization, and joined the American

Railway Union in large numbers. Their meetings were held outside of Pullman, because the town has no facilities for such purposes.

The Pullman company is hostile to the idea of conferring with organized labor in the settlement of differences arising between it and its employés. The position of the company in this respect is clearly stated in the testimony of Mr. Wickes, its second vice-president, which is here cited:

Q. 223. Has the company had any policy with reference to labor unions among its help?—A. No; we have never objected to unions except in one instance. I presume that there are quite a number of unions in our shops now.

Q. 224. What are they?—A. I couldn't tell you, but I have heard of some of them. I suppose the cabinetmakers have a union, and I suppose the car builders have a union, and the carvers, and the painters, and other classes of men. We do not inquire into that at all.

Q. 225. That is, unions among themselves in the works.—A. Members of the craft—belonging to other unions—that is, the cabinet union might have its headquarters in Chicago and our men would be members of it, but we did not object to anything of that kind.

Q. 226. The only objection you ever made was to the American Railway Union, wasn't it?—A. Yes, sir.

Q. 227. What is the basis of your objection to that union?—A. Our objection to that was that we would not treat with our men as members of the American Railway Union, and we would not treat with them as members of any union. We treat with them as individuals and as men.

Q. 228. That is, each man as an individual, do you mean by that?—A. Yes, sir.

Q. 229. Don't you think, Mr. Wickes, that it would give the corporation a very great advantage over those men if it could take them up one at a time and discuss the question with them? With the ability that you have got, for instance, where do you think the man would stand in such a discussion?—A. The man has got probably more ability than I have.

Q. 230. You think that it would be fair to your men for each one of them to come before you and take up the question of his grievance and attempt to maintain his end of the discussion, do you?—A. I think so; yes. If he is not able to do that, that is his misfortune.

Q. 231. Don't you think that the fact that you represent a vast concentration of capital and are selected because of your ability to represent it, entitles him, if he pleases, to unite with all of the men of his craft and select the ablest one they have got to represent the cause?—A. As a union?

Q. 232. As a union?—A. They have the right; yes, sir. We have the right to say whether we shall receive them or not.

Q. 233. Do you think you have any right to refuse to recognize that right in treating with the men?—A. Yes, sir; if we chose to.

Q. 234. If you chose to. Is it your policy to do that?—A. Yes, sir.

Q. 235. Then you think that you have the right to refuse to recognize a union of the men designed for the purpose of presenting through the ablest of their members, to your company, the grievances which all complain of or which any complain of?—A. That is the policy of the company; yes, sir. If we were to receive these men as representatives of the unions they could probably force us to pay any wages which they saw fit, and get the Pullman company in the same shape that some of the railroads are, by making concessions which ought not to be made.

Q. 236. Don't you think that the opposite policy, to wit, that all your dealings are to be with the men as individuals, in case you were one who sought to abuse your power, might enable you to pay to the men on the other hand just what you saw fit?—A. Well, of course; a man in an official position, if he is arbitrary and unfair, could work a great deal of injustice to the men, no doubt about that; but then it is a man's privilege to go to work somewhere else.

Q. 237. Don't you recognize as to many men, after they have become settled in a place at work of that kind, that really that privilege does not amount to much?—A. We find that the best men usually come to the front; the best of our men don't give us any trouble with unions or anything else. It is only the inferior men—that is, the least competent—that give us the trouble, as a general thing.

Since the strike, withdrawal from the American Railway Union is required from those seeking work. The company does not recognize that labor organizations have any place or necessity in Pullman, where the company fixes wages and rents, and refuses to treat with labor organizations. The laborer can work or quit on the terms offered; that is the limit of his rights. To join a labor organization in order to secure the protection of union against wrongs, real or imaginary, is overstepping the limit and arouses hostility. This position secures all the advantage of the concentration of capital, ability, power, and control for the company in its labor dealings, and deprives the employés of any such advantage or protection as a labor union might afford. In this respect the Pullman company is behind the age.

To admit the Pullman shop employés, however, into the American Railway Union as "persons employed in railway service" was not wise or expedient. The constitution can not fairly be construed to include as eligible members those who build cars and run them in and out over private switches. Such loose construction of a labor constitution is certain to involve any organization in such an infinite variety of conflicting positions and to force it into so many contests demanding different and perhaps apparently inconsistent treatment at the same time as to curtail its usefulness and threaten its existence. To reach out and take in those so alien to its natural membership as the Pullman employés, was, in the inception of the organization at least, a mistake. This mistake led the union into a strike purely sympathetic and aided to bring upon it a crushing and demoralizing defeat.

It is undoubtedly true that the officers and directors of the American Railway union did not want a strike at Pullman, and that they advised against it, but the exaggerated idea of the power of the union, which induced the workmen at Pullman to join the order, led to their striking against this advice. Having struck, the union could do nothing less, upon the theory at its base, than support them.

The union was as yet young; its membership was not as extensive as it hoped to obtain; its workings had the roughness of incipient effort in a new direction; it had recently attained some success in a strike upon the "Great Northern," and had thus aroused extravagant expectations among its members generally; great business depression prevailed; large numbers were idle and stood ready to accept almost any offer of work. For these reasons the officers and directors of the union knew that the times were inopportune for striking and did not advocate it.

A union embracing all railroad employés, even, is as yet a doubtful experiment. Such a union will have great difficulty in molding itself to the complex character, nationalities, habits, employments, and requirements of its vast and varied membership.

The trade unionists argue that their strength lies largely in their comparative freedom from these objections; and they insist that the basis of the membership of a successful labor organization must be substantial similarity in interests among the members. Trades unions have a record of success both here and abroad, especially in England, which largely sustains their position. They have promoted conciliation, arbitration, conservatism, and responsibility in labor contentions and agreements.

.   .   .   .

The Pullman Strike: Its Causes and Events

Pullman's Palace Car Company is in the market at all times to obtain all possible contracts to build cars. Its relations with railroads, its large capital and surplus, its complete and well-located plant and efficient management enable it at all times to meet all competitors on at least equal terms. Prior to the business depression of 1893, the company was unusually active in building new cars for itself and for railroads to meet the expanded demands of general business, and for the expected requirements of the Columbian Exposition traffic. Its repair department was also full of work. An average number of 4,497 workmen, during the year ending July 1, 1893, earned $2,760,548.99, or an average of $613.86 each. The wages paid were about the same as paid elsewhere in the business, Mr. Wickes thinks possibly a little higher.

The depression of 1893 naturally affected the business at once, and to a greater extent in some departments than in others. Matters grew worse until, in the fall of 1893, the company closed its Detroit shops, employing about 800, and concentrated its contract and repair business at Pullman. The company and the railroads had a surplus of cars for the decreased traffic obtainable, and hence pending orders were cancelled and car building stopped, except as occasional straggling contracts were obtained at prices which averaged less than shop cost, exclusive of interest upon capital or any charge for depreciation of plant or machinery.

Wages

From September 18, 1893, until May 1, 1894, the company did contract work at the price of $1,421,205.75, which was $52,069.03, or 3.663 per cent below shop cost for labor and materials. Against this the loss to labor by the reduction of wages paid on this work was over $60,000, making the wages of June, 1893, the basis of comparison. It also had $1,354,276.06 of unaccepted bids, upon which its similar loss would have been $18,303.56, or 1.35 per cent. Assuming that the analysis submitted as to the cost of several lots of cars affords a fair basis for averaging the whole of the contracts, it appears that the average percentage of cost of material in this contract work was about 75 per cent. Hence while the amount of loss was nearly equally divided, it seems that the percentage of loss borne by labor in the reduction of wages was much greater than that sustained by the company upon material. Three-quarters of the loss for the company and the balance for labor would have more fairly equalized the division of loss on these contracts.

Some justification for the determination of the company as to the division of loss is claimed from the fact that in addition to its loss the company received no interest upon its capital, etc. On the other hand, it is an economic principle generally recognized that the shutting down of such a plant and the scattering of its forces usually result in a greater loss than that exhibited here by the continuance of business. The Pullman Company could hardly shut down for seven and a half months at a cost and loss of less than 1 per cent upon its capital and surplus. To continue running was for its obvious and unfair advantage so long as it could divide losses equally with its labor.

The cut in wages during this period averaged about 25 per cent. . . .

[The report describes other grievances, particularly the high rents in the Company town of Pullman that ran 20 to 25 per cent more than in Chicago and the alleged "arbitrary and oppressive" treatment by foremen.]

The Strike

The reductions at Pullman after September, 1893, were the result of conferences among the managers; the employés for the first time knew of them when they took effect. No explanations or conferences took place until May 7 and 9 in regard thereto between the employés and the officers of the company. For the reasons stated the employés at Pullman were during the winter in a state of chronic discontent. Upon May 7 and 9 a committee of 46 from all the departments waited upon the management and urged the restoration of wages to the basis of June, 1893. The company refused this, and offered no concession as to wages whatever, maintaining and explaining that business conditions did not justify any change. The company based its entire contention as to every department upon the facts in reference to car building to which we have alluded, and offered to show its books and figures as to the cost and selling prices of cars. This offer, on account of the strike intervening, was not acted upon. Had it been, it would have resulted in the figures we have noted as to car-building contracts. The purpose of the management was obviously to rest the whole matter upon cost, etc., in its most seriously crippled department, excluding from consideration the facts as to wages in the repair department, to which we have alluded.

The demand of the employés for the wages of June, 1893, was clearly unjustifiable. The business in May, 1894, could not pay the wages of June, 1893. Reduction was carried to excess, but the company was hardly more at fault therein than were the employés in insisting upon the wages of June, 1893. There was little discussion as to rents, the company maintaining that its rents had nothing to do with its wages and that its revenue from its tenements was no greater than it ought to receive. Miss Curtis testified as to this as follows:

A. We stated our grievances to Mr. Wickes and told him we wanted our wages raised; he said it was impossible to raise them as the company was losing money on its contracts, and it could not possibly raise our wages a cent; we then asked if they did not think they could lower rents a little; he said, no, it was utterly impossible to lower the rents one penny, as they were only receiving about 3 per cent on their investment now, and were losing money on contracts just to enable their men to have work. Mr. Wickes then appointed another interview with us the following Wednesday, and we went down again and saw Mr. Pullman; he said he could not raise our wages nor lower our rents.

The company had a legal right to take this position, but as between man and man the demand for some rent reduction was fair and reasonable under all the circumstances. Some slight concession in this regard would probably have averted the strike, provided the promise not to discharge men who served upon the committee had been more strictly regarded.

The next day, May 10, three of the committee were laid off by foremen for alleged lack of work, not an unusual proceeding. Those who made the promise had nothing to do with this action and deny knowledge of it at the time. The foremen who did it are suspected by the employés of concluding that some laying off of committeemen just at that crisis would have a good effect and would accord with the policy and general views of the company. The foremen, however, deny this. This incident was inopportune and unfortunate, to say the least, and ought to have been more carefully guarded against by the company. An explanation of this occurrence was not asked for by the employés, as it ought to have been, before striking.

On the evening of May 10 the local unions met and voted to strike at once. The strike occurred on May 11, and from that time until the soldiers went to Pullman, about July 4, three hundred strikers were placed about the company's property, professedly to guard it from destruction or interference. This guarding of property in strikes is, as a rule, a mere pretence. Too often the real object of guards is to prevent newcomers from taking strikers' places, by persuasion, often to be followed, if ineffectual, by intimidation and violence. The Pullman company claims this was the real object of these guards. The strikers at Pullman are entitled to be believed to the contrary in this matter, because of their conduct and forbearance after May 11. It is in evidence, and uncontradicted, that no violence or destruction of property by strikers or sympathizers took place at Pullman, and that until July 3 no extraordinary protection was had from the police or military against even anticipated disorder.

Such dignified, manly, and conservative conduct in the midst of excitement and threatened starvation is worthy of the highest type of American citizenship, and with like prudence in all other directions will result in due time in the lawful and orderly redress of labor wrongs. To deny this is to forswear patriotism and to declare this government and its people a failure.

As soon as the strike was declared the company laid off its 600 employés who did not join the strike, and kept its shops closed until August 2. During this period the Civic Federation of Chicago, composed of eminent citizens in all kinds of business and from all grades of respectable society, called upon the company twice to urge conciliation and arbitration. The company reiterated the statement of its position, and maintained that there was nothing to arbitrate; that the questions at issue were matters of fact and not proper subjects of arbitration. The Civic Federation suggested that competition should be regarded in rents as well as in wages. The company denied this. Wages and rents were to it separate matters; the principles applicable to one had no relation to the other. Later it gave the same answer to a committee of its employés. Upon June 15 and 22 it declined to receive any communication from committees of the American Railway Union, one proposition of that body being that the company select two arbitrators, the court two, and these four a fifth, to determine whether there was anything to arbitrate. The company also refused to consider any arbitration at the solicitation of the common council of Chicago, and repeated its stereotyped answer that there was nothing to arbitrate when appealed to by Mayor Pingree, of Detroit, himself a large manufacturer, whom Mayor Hopkins accompanied to Pullman. At that interview Mayor Pingree claimed to have telegrams from the mayors of over fifty of the largest cities, urging that there should be arbitration.

Railroad Strike

Between June 9 and June 26 a regular convention of the American Railway Union was held with open doors at Chicago, representing 465 local unions and about 150,000 members, as claimed. The Pullman matter was publicly discussed at these meetings before and after its committees above mentioned reported their interviews with the Pullman company. On June 21 the delegates, under instructions from their local unions, unanimously voted that the members of the union should stop handling Pullman cars on June 26 unless the Pullman company would consent to arbitration. On June 26 the boycott and strike began. The strike on the part of the railroad employés was a sympathetic one. No grievances against the railroads had been presented by their employés, nor did the American Railway Union declare any such grievances to be any cause whatever of the strike. To simply boycott Pullman cars would have been an incongruous step for the remedy of complaints of railroad employés. Throughout the strike the strife was simply over handling Pullman cars, the men being ready to do their duty otherwise. The contracts between the railroads and the Pullman company as to Pullman cars created such close relations between them as to increase the natural sympathy of organization between the members of the American Railway Union upon railroads and their brothers at Pullman. It is also apparent that the readiness to strike sympathetically was promoted by the disturbed and apprehensive condition of railroad employés resulting from wage reductions on different lines, blacklisting, etc., and from the recent growth and development of the General Managers' Association, which seemed to them a menace. Hence the railroad employés were ripe to espouse the cause of the Pullman strikers. In some instances

they struck in disregard of existing contracts between their different organizations and the railroads, notably upon the Illinois Central. They
evaded the responsibility of their organizations for this conduct by claim-
ing to act as individuals. They justified themselves under the idea of
balancing wrongs.

After June 26 the officers and agents of the union managed and urged
on the strike at every available point upon the railroads centering at Chicago until it reached proportions far in excess of their original anticipations, and led to disorders beyond even their control. Urgent solicitations
and appeals to strike and to stand firm continued in the many public
meetings held each day in and about Chicago, and appear in the telegrams
sent about the country.

On July 7 the principal officers of the American Railway Union were
indicted, arrested, and held under $10,000 bail. Upon July 13 they were
attached for contempt of the United States court in disobeying an injunction issued on July 2 and served on the 3d and 4th, enjoining them, among
other things, from compelling, or inducing by threats, intimidation, persuasion, force, or violence, railroad employés to refuse or fail to perform
their duties. It is seriously questioned, and with much force, whether courts
have jurisdiction to enjoin citizens from "persuading" each other in industrial or other matters of common interest. However, it is generally recognized among good citizens that a mandate of a court is to be obeyed until
it is modified and corrected by the court that issued it.

Action of Federated Unions

Upon July 12, at the request of the American Railway Union, about 25
of the executive officers of national and international labor unions affiliated
with the American Federation of Labor met at Chicago. The situation was
laid before them. The conference concluded that the strike was then lost;
that a general sympathetic strike throughout the country would be unwise
and inexpedient, and, at the time, against the best interests of labor. This
conference issued a strong and temperate address to members, expressing
sympathy with the purposes of the American Railway Union, advising those
on strike to return to work, and urging that labor organize more generally,
combine more closely, and seek the correction of industrial evils at the
ballot box. To some extent the trade unions of Chicago had struck in
sympathy, but this movement was checked by the action of the conference
of the 12th and extended no further. This action indicates clearer views
by labor as to its responsibilities, the futility of strikes, and the appropriate
remedies in this country for labor wrongs.

Upon July 13 the American Railway Union, through the mayor of Chicago, sent a communication to the General Managers' Association offering
to declare the strike off, provided the men should be restored to their
former positions without prejudice, except in cases where they had been
convicted of crime. The General Managers' Association in advance ad-
vertised that it would receive no communication whatever from the American Railway Union, and when received returned it unanswered. With

reference to this, John M. Egan, strike manager of the General Managers' Association, testified as follows:

A few days later I was out of the office for awhile, and on my return I found the mayor and Alderman McGillen talking to Mr. St. John.[1] I went into the room, and Mr. St. John told me the mayor had come there with a letter signed by the officers of the American Railway Union. I told the mayor I thought he should not have permitted himself to be a messenger boy for those parties, and that I further considered that the General Managers' Association should not receive any such document. The document was left there, and during the afternoon I was requested to take the document back to the mayor. I endeavored to find him, but found he had gone to Kensington. I endeavored to reach him by telephone, but as it was growing late and I could not locate him I took the document back to the city hall and gave it to the chief of police, with the request that he place it on the mayor's desk so he would receive it early the next morning. I wrote a letter in which I stated to the mayor that the General Managers' Association did not consider they should receive any such document. On my return to the office I was able to locate the mayor at Kensington, but they told me he had retired for the night; but I telegraphed the contents of the letter, with a request to the party who received it that he deliver it to the mayor that night. That is all I know about any overtures.

Questions by Commissioner WORTHINGTON:

18. Was there anything in the document itself that was offensive or insulting to you?—A. The document was printed in the papers that afternoon and the next morning, and I think it speaks for itself.

19. Did you consider it offensive or insulting?—A. I considered that any party who attacked railway companies as the American Railway Union had done, and were whipped, as I considered they were, it was displaying considerable cheek to dictate the terms of their surrender.

20. You do not answer my question. I asked you if there was anything in the document itself that was offensive or insulting to you?—A. I don't know as I would be the judge of that.

21. What is your opinion about it?—A. I have not the authority to say whether it was insulting to the general managers, or anything of that kind.

22. Did you return it on that account—because the terms of the document were offensive or insulting to you or to the managers?—A. Well, the managers requested it to be returned.

23. Was that the reason you returned it?—A. That was the reason I returned it; yes, sir.

24. Is it not a fact that, instead of being offensive in its character so far as the composition was concerned, it was a document courteously composed and looking toward the settlement of a great and destructive strike that was then in progress?—A. Well, as I said, the document speaks for itself. I considered that the matter was settled then, practically.

In reply to this Mayor Hopkins testified:

I want to say in this connection that the papers quote Mr. Egan as saying in his testimony that he told the mayor he should not be a messenger boy for those men.

1 [Everett St. John was chairman of the General Managers' Association.]

I want to say emphatically that Mr. Egan never said that to me; I don't think I would have allowed him to say it.

At this date, July 13, and for some days previous, the strikers had been virtually beaten. The action of the courts deprived the American Railway Union of leadership, enabled the General Managers' Association to disintegrate its forces, and to make inroads into its ranks. The mobs had worn out their fury, or had succumbed to the combined forces of the police, the United States troops and marshals, and the state militia. The railroads were gradually repairing damages and resuming traffic with the aid of new men and with some of those strikers who had not been offensively active or whose action was laid to intimidation and fear. At this juncture the refusal of the General Managers' Association to treat with the American Railway Union was certainly not conciliatory; it was not unnatural, however, because the Association charged the American Railway Union with having inaugurated an unjustifiable strike, laid at its door the responsibility for all the disorder and destruction that had occurred, and, as the victor in the fight, desired that the lesson taught to labor by its defeat should be well learned.

The policy of both the Pullman company and the Railway Managers' Association in reference to applications to arbitrate closed the door to all attempts at conciliation and settlement of differences. The commission is impressed with the belief, by the evidence and by the attendant circumstances as disclosed, that a different policy would have prevented the loss of life and great loss of property and wages occasioned by the strike.

Action of General Managers' Association

On June 22 an officer of the Pullman company met the general managers by invitation, and the general managers, among other things, resolved:

That we hereby declare it to be the lawful right and duty of the said railway companies to protest against said proposed boycott; to resist the same in the interest of their existing contracts and for the benefit of the traveling public, and that we will act unitedly to that end.

From June 22 until the practical end of the strike the General Managers' Association directed and controlled the contest on the part of the railroads, using the combined resources of all the roads to support the contentions and insure the protection of each. On June 26 we find in the proceedings of the association the following statement:

A general discussion of the situation followed. It was suggested that some common plan of action ought to be adopted in case employés refused to do switching of passenger trains with Pullman cars, but were willing to continue all of their other work, and it was the general expression that in case any man refused to do his duty he would be discharged.

Headquarters were established; agencies for hiring men opened; as the men arrived they were cared for and assigned to duty upon the different lines; a bureau was started to furnish information to the press; the lawyers of the different roads were called into conference and combination in legal and criminal proceedings; the general managers met daily to hear reports and to direct proceedings; constant communication was kept up with the civil and military authorities as to the movements and assignments of police, marshals, and troops. Each road did what it could with its operating forces, but all the leadership, direction, and concentration of power, resources, and influence on the part of the railroads were centered in the General Managers' Association. That association stood for each and all of its 24 combined members, and all that they could command, in fighting and crushing the strike.

.   .   .   .

Conclusions and Recommendations

.   .   .   .

As authorized by statute, the commission has decided upon certain recommendations and certain suggestions, growing out of its study of the Chicago strike and boycott. These recommendations and suggestions are upon three lines: First, for Congressional action; second, for state action; and third, for the action of corporations and labor organizations. It readily sees the impropriety to a certain extent of making any recommendation for state action, yet feels it a duty, as a result of its investigations, to make such suggestions as will enable citizens interested in state legislation to benefit by its experience, and also to make such suggestions to corporations and labor organizations as shall tend to harmonize some of the existing difficulties. The commission therefore recommends:

I

1. That there be a permanent United States strike commission of three members, with duties and powers of investigation and recommendation as to disputes between railroads and their employés similar to those vested in the Interstate Commerce Commission as to rates, etc.

a. That, as in the interstate commerce act, power be given to the United States courts to compel railroads to obey the decisions of the commission, after summary hearing unattended by technicalities, and that no delays in obeying the decisions of the commission be allowed pending appeals.

b. That, whenever the parties to a controversy in a matter within the jurisdiction of the commission are one or more railroads upon one side and one or more national trade unions, incorporated under chapter 567 of the United States Statutes of 1885–'86, or under state statutes, upon the other, each side shall have the right to select a representative, who shall be appointed by the President to serve as a temporary member of the commission in hearing, adjusting, and determining that particular controversy.

(This provision would make it for the interest of labor organizations to incorporate under the law and to make the commission a practical board of conciliation. It would also tend to create confidence in the commission, and to give to that body in every hearing the benefit of practical knowledge of the situation upon both sides.)

c. That, during the pendency of a proceeding before the commission inaugurated by national trade unions, or by an incorporation of employés, it shall not be lawful for the railroads to discharge employés belonging thereto except for inefficiency, violation of law, or neglect of duty; nor for such unions or incorporation during such pendency to order, unite in, aid, or abet strikes or boycotts against the railroads complained of; nor, for a period of six months after a decision, for such railroads to discharge any such employés in whose places others shall be employed, except for the causes aforesaid; nor for any such employés, during a like period, to quit the service without giving thirty days' written notice of intention to do so, nor for any such union or incorporation to order, counsel, or advise otherwise.

2. That chapter 567 of the United States Statutes of 1885–'86 be amended so as to require national trades unions to provide in their articles of incorporation, and in their constitutions, rules, and by-laws that a member shall cease to be such and forfeit all rights and privileges conferred on him by law as such by participating in or by instigating force or violence against persons or property during strikes or boycotts, or by seeking to prevent others from working through violence, threats, or intimidations; also, that members shall be no more personally liable for corporate acts than are stockholders in corporations.

3. The commission does not feel warranted, with the study it has been able to give to the subject, to recommend positively the establishment of a license system by which all the higher employés or others of railroads engaged in interstate commerce should be licensed after due and proper examination, but it would recommend, and most urgently, that this subject be carefully and fully considered by the proper committee of Congress. Many railroad employés and some railroad officials examined and many others who have filed their suggestions in writing with the commission are in favor of some such system. It involves too many complications, however, for the commission to decide upon the exact plan, if any, which should be adopted.

II

1. The commission would suggest the consideration by the states of the adoption of some system of conciliation and arbitration like that, for instance, in use in the commonwealth of Massachusetts. That system might be reenforced by additional provisions giving the board of arbitration more power to investigate all strikes, whether requested so to do or not, and the question might be considered as to giving labor organizations a standing before the law, as heretofore suggested for national trade unions.

2. Contracts requiring men to agree not to join labor organizations or to leave them, as conditions of employment, should be made illegal, as is already done in some of our states.

III

1. The commission urges employers to recognize labor organizations; that such organizations be dealt with through representatives, with special reference to conciliation and arbitration when difficulties are threatened or arise. It is satisfied that employers should come in closer touch with labor and should recognize that, while the interests of labor and capital are not identical, they are reciprocal.

2. The commission is satisfied that if employers everywhere will endeavor to act in concert with labor; that if when wages can be raised under economic conditions they be raised voluntarily, and that if when there are reductions reasons be given for the reduction, much friction can be avoided. It is also satisfied that if employers will consider employés as thoroughly essential to industrial success as capital, and thus take labor into consultation at proper times, much of the severity of strikes can be tempered and their number reduced.

PART V
New Ways of Competition

INTRODUCTION

⟨ UNPRECEDENTED size created as novel patterns in competition as it did in finance, management, and labor relations. The massive amount of capital investment and equipment required to build the large railroads meant that they were saddled with much higher constant charges (that is, costs which did not fluctuate with the volume of traffic) than any other contemporary business. Such evercontinuing costs created an inexorable pressure to attract traffic. Moreover, in obtaining this business a railroad rarely competed with more than a handful of other corporations. Often a road had no competition at all, particularly for local traffic.

It was thus that the railroads had much more flexibility in setting prices than had the farmers, merchants, small manufacturers, and other businessmen of the day who still sold their products in a relatively impersonal market. The railroads were the first American business to be able to set prices with some relation to costs rather than merely to impersonal market demands. Similar ability to administer prices did not come in other sectors of the economy until the end of the century, when manufacturers in many industries began to combine and consolidate factory production, build large marketing organizations, and do their own purchasing and even production of raw and semifinished materials. The resulting great integrated enterprises that came to dominate many industries quickly developed patterns of pricing and competition that were comparable to those first worked out on American railroads. Once the manufacturers obtained such control, the public began to demand a regulation of industry similar to that which it had urged for the railroads a generation earlier.

The decisions of railroad managers in setting or administering their prices reflected two basic conditions—the pressure of constant costs and the existence of unused capacity. Both conditions became especially critical with the coming of the depression of the 1870's. The costs that did not vary with volume have been described by Albert Fink in his 1874 report (see pp. 108–17). In this period such costs often amounted to two-thirds of the total costs of running a railroad. Managers tried to set and adjust rates so as to encourage the fullest use of their expensive equipment. They specified lower rates on bulk freight such as lumber, coal, and ore than on foodstuffs or general merchandise. Without these lower rates the cost of moving bulk products from distant mines or forests would have simply been too expensive to have made their production profitable. Because traffic on many roads tended to flow in one direction, executives also set much lower rates on business moving on the return route. Since empty cars were returning anyway, traffic at almost any price was profitable. Also, since the moving of a full car was as expensive as that of a partially filled one, traffic managers gave lower rates

on car-load lots than on smaller shipments. Finally, railroad men were the
first to realize that a reduction in price
could increase profit by expanding
trade. In fact, as long as the new business engendered by a rate cut used existing capacity, prices that were above the
cost of putting on an extra car on a
scheduled run or even putting on a new
run helped pay the fixed charges. In
this way, rate-making based on the need
to attract traffic led to discrimination
between persons, places, and types of
traffic even when a railroad route was
unaffected by competition.

Throughout the nineteenth century
price remained the railroad's primary
competitive weapon, and since speed of
movement and efficiency of service were
less important to most shippers than the
lowering of transportation costs, prices
on competitive through traffic quickly
dropped below those on local noncom-
petitive business. Moreover, as nearly
all lines had excess capacity after 1873,
the through traffic obtained by one line
through the cutting of rates usually
meant it had been taken from another
road. As a result, the depression of
the seventies brought a series of increasingly severe rate wars.

Normally the roads with longest and
hence slowest routes or with highest
bonded debts initiated rate cuts in order
to get the traffic needed to meet the
interest on their debt. The strong
roads, to regain the lost business, followed with a comparable cut. Often the
resulting loss of traffic then forced the
weak road into bankruptcy. Once in
receivership and no longer saddled with
the legal responsibility of meeting interest charges, the bankrupt road could
again cut prices. To most railroad executives and analysts the logic of such uncontrolled competition threatened bankruptcy for everybody.

From the first, competing roads co-

operated to prevent such "ruinous competition." At regularly scheduled meetings their managers determined classification and rates on through traffic for
different geographic areas. They also
decided what share of the through rate
would go to the different roads along
the route and worked out methods for
ticketing and billing so that these arrangements might be carried out. These
rate and traffic agreements were in fact
alliances between competing and connecting roads in a single region. From
the 1850's on, major companies
strengthened their alliances with connecting roads by assisting in financing
initial construction and later expansion.
Thus the annual report of the Pennsylvania Railroad printed in January,
1858, emphasized that in pursuing "the
policy of this Company to aid in the
construction of Western Railways designed to facilitate trade to and from
its road," the Company had already invested over $1,600,000.

The pressure of high fixed costs and
excess capacity made these alliances,
even those cemented by cash, extremely
fragile. Rate-cutting continued, but in
secret rather than in the open. The
shipper granted a rate cut would pay
the published one and then the company would secretly rebate him the difference. Once the secret cuts became
known, roads often abandoned their
agreements and turned to open competitive warfare. As Albert Fink pointed
out, the difficulty "has not been so much
in agreeing upon the proper tariffs, but
in carrying them into practical effect."
Fink's answer was the creation of a
more formal regional federation of
roads to control competition.

The primary task of the regional association or federation was to pool traffic
or profits in order to remove the incen-
tive for secret rate-cutting. In a traffic
pool each road carried a prearranged

share of the traffic, the allocation being carried out by the association's administrative office and staff. In a money pool the traffic could go as the shipper directed, but profits were forwarded to the association's office and then divided up according to an earlier agreement. Under the first arrangement a rate cut could not increase the traffic, and under the second it could not increase a road's income.

The determination and enforcement of the allocation of traffic or profits required extensive formal organization. Albert Fink, more than any other man, was responsible for the formation and operation of the American regional railroad federation. He was a founding father of the first of these federations, the Southern Railway and Steamship Association, formed in 1875, and then became its first commissioner. In 1877 the presidents of the great east-west trunk lines, after a particularly severe rate war, called Fink north to set up and then manage an Eastern Trunk Line Association. By 1879 the new federation included nearly all the major roads operating between the Mississippi River and the Eastern seaboard. Almost immediately the railroads west of the Mississippi began to form similar associations.

For all their enthusiastic support and their careful organization, the federations failed to control competition. Weaker roads like the Grand Trunk and the Erie often refused to abide by the rulings of the commissioners and to accept enforcement by their staffs. Nor were speculators like Jay Gould and Russell Sage influenced by the hopes and actions of the associations. Little concerned for stability, they continued to find rate-cutting and -raising useful in the manipulation of the securities of the different roads they bought and sold. As early as 1880, Fink and

many of the more responsible railroad presidents had decided that the associations could be effective only if their rulings could be enforced in the federal courts. Their efforts to legalize pooling met strong resistance from shippers and from the general public, who equated pooling with monopoly. As a result, when the Interstate Commerce Act was passed in 1887, it not only failed to legalize pooling but, indeed, explicitly prohibited it.

Even before the passage of that act, however, most railroad men agreed that the federations had become ineffective. They now turned, as Fink had predicted, to combination and consolidation. Their final answer was, in the words of Charles E. Perkins, to build a "self-sustaining system" that had its own lines into the major commercial centers of any one large region. In the East the drive for self-sufficiency was accomplished through purchases, leases, and mergers. In the West these great systems were created mainly by new construction. Thus the Atchison, Topeka & Santa Fe in 1884 decided to build its own line to the Pacific Coast, then it purchased a connection to the Gulf. Finally in 1887, unhappy with its reliance on the several existing roads from Kansas City to Chicago, it built its own line into the Windy City. By 1890 the Santa Fe was one of the largest roads in the country, operating over nine thousand miles of track. By 1893 it was bankrupt. The later expansion of the American railway network resulted then from competitive construction, from the desire of railroad managers to have their self-contained systems. Federal land grants had absolutely nothing to do with the massive overconstruction and overpurchasing following the depression of the seventies.

System-building in the 1880's and the early 1890's brought overexpansion, bankruptcy, and financial and administrative reorganization for many roads besides the Santa Fe. During the 1880's far more railroad mileage was built in the United States than in any other previous or later decade. But by the mid-nineties a third of the mileage of American roads was involved in foreclosure or bankruptcy proceedings. It was then that J. P. Morgan played his major role in American railroading by financially and administratively reviving these roads. The reorganization of the nineties brought most American railroads under the control of a relatively small number of great systems. After the turn of the century these systems began to develop "communities of interests" in each major region by purchasing large blocks of stock in nearby roads. By 1904 one business analyst could report that less than ten major groups dominated the American transportation network.

The story of competition, rate-making and -breaking, federation, and consolidation is described and analyzed by contemporaries in the following three selections. In the first, Arthur T. Hadley, a prominent writer on railroads who later became the president of Yale, explains the economics of rate-making and competition as it appeared to the most knowledgeable analysts in the mid-1880's. In the second selection Albert Fink describes the associations he helped to form and administer in testifying before a Congressional committee in January, 1880. The testimony was published in 1882 under the title of "The Railroad Problem and Its Solution." The solution was, Fink insisted, legalized pooling. In the final selection S. F. Van Oss, a British financial expert, tells British investors about the motives and methods of the great consolidation movement among American railroads. Writing in the mid-nineties Van Oss still sees agreements and associations as methods of control; for even after the passage of the Interstate Commerce Act, the earlier associations continued to set rates and classifications although they no longer pooled traffic or income. In 1897, when the Supreme Court decided in the Trans-Missouri Freight Association case that such activities violated the Sherman Antitrust Act, the value of agreements and associations was further weakened and the movement to legal and administrative consolidation further strengthened.

THE READINGS

1] Competition and Competitive Rate-Making
Competition and Combination

. . . .

THERE is a marked difference of principle between mercantile competition, such as Ricardo had in mind, and the competition of railroads or factories, such as we have been considering. In the former case its action is prompt and healthful, and does not go to extremes. If Grocer A sells goods below cost, Grocer B need not follow him, but simply stop selling for the time. For: (1) This involves no great present loss to B. When his receipts stop, most of his expenses stop also. (2) It does involve a present loss to A. If he is selling below cost, he loses more money the more business he does. (3) It cannot continue indefinitely. If A returns to paying prices, B can again compete. If A continues to do business at a loss he will become bankrupt, and B will find the field clear again.

But if Railroad A reduces charges on competitive business, Railroad B must follow. (1) It involves a great present loss to stop. If a railroad's business shrinks to almost nothing, a large part of its expenses run on just the same. Interest charges accumulate; office expenses cannot be suddenly contracted; repairs do not stop when traffic shrinks; for they are rendered necessary by weather as well as by wear. (2) If B abandons the business, A's reduction of rates will prove no loss. The expense of a large business is proportionately less than that of a small one. A rate which was below cost on 100,000 tons may be a paying one on 200,000. (3) Profitable or not, A's competition may be kept up indefinitely. The property may go into bankruptcy, but the railroad stays where it is. It only becomes a more reckless and irresponsible competitor.[1]

The competition of different stores finds a natural limit. It brings rates down near to cost of service, and then stops. The competition of railroads or factories finds no such natural limit. Wherever there is a large permanent investment, and large fixed charges, competition brings rates down below cost of service. The competitive business gives no money to pay repairs or interest. Sometimes the money to pay for these things comes out of the pockets of other customers, who do not enjoy the benefit of the competition, and are charged much higher rates. Then we have the worst

---

1 [C. F.] Adams, [*Railroads and the Railroad Question* (New York, 1878)] pp. 148 ff. Testimony of E. D. Worcester before the Hepburn Committee, p. 1074; of Albert Fink, p. 564.

FROM Arthur T. Hadley, "Competition and Combination" and "Railroad Charges and Discriminations," *Railroad Transportation* (New York, 1885), pp. 73–77, 108–22.

forms of discrimination. Sometimes the money cannot be obtained from any customers at all. Then we have bankruptcy, ruin to the investor, and—when these things happen on a large scale—a commercial crisis.

There is but one way to prevent these results. If competition is ruinous to all parties, all parties must stop competing. If it finds no natural limit, it must be artificially limited; it must end in combination. And the moment you have established an effective combination, you have introduced the principle of monopoly. You have determined prices not in open market, but by an agreement among all the sellers.

This agreement may take any one of four forms. (1) Agreement to maintain rates. (2) To divide the field. (3) To divide the traffic. (4) To divide the earnings. The last three are commonly known as pools.

The first is the simplest, but least effective. There is scarcely an organized industry where the dealers do not meet and settle upon a schedule of rates and discounts, agreeing that no one shall sell below these prices. Such agreements are rarely kept. It is for the interest of all that rates in general should be maintained; but it is for the interest of each concern to secure business for itself by not quite maintaining them. This constitutes a great temptation to depart from schedule prices; a temptation all the stronger because it is so easy to violate the agreement indirectly, and so hard to detect any such violation. The result is apt to be a system of underhand competition, worse in many respects than the open competition which existed before there was any agreement at all.

This is why it is found necessary to divide the business among the different competitors, by a pooling agreement. Such agreements are hard to arrange. There is almost always a dispute about their terms. But as long as they are in force, it is hard to violate them without actual fraud, and it is comparatively easy to detect such violations and deal with them severely.

When it is possible to "divide the field" this course is usually the simplest. We see it illustrated where different gas or water companies parcel off the different districts of a city to one another; or where manufacturers in different cities agree to leave one another in undisturbed possession of the home market. We see it not infrequently in agreements between railroads. But in the majority of cases this arrangement is impracticable, and the rival concerns agree upon the proportion of business which each is to do. The companies in the Anthracite Coal Combination have arranged how much coal each company may mine. Factory combinations determine how much each concern may manufacture. Railroads agree just what percentage of competitive traffic each road shall carry.

When one railroad receives more than its agreed share of business, it is generally inconvenient to send the goods by a rival route, and easier to arrange matters by a money payment.[2] This brings us to the fourth and closest form of combination, where there is a division of earnings. The machinery for securing this division may have any degree of organization up to the point of actual consolidation of the competing interests.

The dangers of a pool lie in the arbitrary power which it places in the

2 For the question of traffic *vs.* money pools, see Fink: Argument before the Select Committee of the U.S. Senate, May 21, 1885, pp. 33-35.

hands of a few men to deal as they will with the business of the country. Even granting that the actual abuses of combination are less than those of competition, it seems like taking refuge from the excesses of democracy in an enlightened despotism. There is some slight truth in the analogy, but we are likely to carry it too far. Combination does not produce arbitrary results any more than competition produces uniformly beneficent ones. We hear a great deal said about charging "what the traffic will bear"; and the man who avows this as his principle is compared by anti-monopolists with the robber barons of the middle ages. He is represented as fleecing a helpless public out of all its hard-won earnings. In the proper meaning of the principle the case is just the opposite. Charging what the traffic will bear is a very different thing from charging what the traffic will *not* bear. It is a hard principle to apply intelligently; but when it is thus applied it adjusts the burdens where they can be best borne, and develops a vast amount of business which could not otherwise exist. Our railroad management has many faults and abuses in detail; but, taking its work as a whole, it has brought down rates to a cheapness which is unequalled elsewhere, and has developed the business of the country on a scale which would have been impossible under any system of rates based on cost of service. Nor does it leave the door open for inordinate profits. The moment a combination places its figures so high as to do this, other capital will seek investment in the same line; and though these new investments are apt, before long, to come into the pool at the old rates, yet they have cut down the profits by their entrance. An amount of business which would richly support one railroad or factory, yields but a scant income to two railroads or factories at the same rates. Witness what the "Nickel Plate" Railroad has done for the Lake Shore, or the West Shore Railroad for the New York Central. Parallel roads do not lower rates permanently, but they make havoc with profits. It is usually far-sighted policy for a combination to put its rates so low as not to tempt new capital too rapidly into the field. If that lesson is learned, the public gets the benefits of competition without its disadvantages. Unluckily, we place these combinations outside of the protection of the law, and by giving them this precarious and almost illegal character we tempt them to seek present gain even at the sacrifice of their own future interests. We regard them, and we let them regard themselves, as a means of momentary profit and speculation, instead of recognizing them as responsible public agencies of lasting influence and importance.

.   .   .   .

Railroad Charges and Discriminations

. . . But the fact that the charges are so low does not make *differences* in charge bear any less severely upon business. A difference of five cents per bushel in the charge for transporting wheat a thousand miles is a small matter, taken by itself. It would be weeks before it would make a difference of one cent to the individual consumer of bread. But if a railroad makes this reduction for one miller, and not for another, it will be enough to drive the latter out of business. Competition is carried on with such a narrow margin of profit that the railroad has it in its power to ruin either competitor. The fact that charges in general are so low only puts men more completely at the mercy of the railroad authorities, because it is impossible to find any other means of transportation equally good and cheap.

A difference in rates not based upon any corresponding difference in cost, constitutes a case of discrimination.

Even when a railroad tariff was originally based on differences of cost of service, it does not continue so. It never remains long unchanged. Every day special circumstances arise which were not foreseen, and which seem to demand a change. The question in every such case is: what will be the effect of the change? If rates are reduced on certain lines of business, gross earnings will probably increase on account of increased volume of business obtained. But will net earnings increase? That is to say, will gross earnings increase faster than operating expenses?

This is the real question; and its answer involves two elements. One is, the expense of hauling each additional car-load; in so far, rates are based upon cost of service.[3] The other is the increased development of business by lower rates; this is quite independent of cost of service.

Suppose that the expense of loading and hauling each additional car-load of wheat from A to B is $10. Present rates are $15, and at that rate the road obtains 1,000 car-loads a week—gross earnings, $15,000, profit above operating expenses, $5,000. The question comes up whether they shall reduce to $13. If by so doing they can double their traffic and get 2,000 car-loads, it will be good policy; they will make gross earnings $26,000; expenses $20,000; profit $6,000. If it only increased the traffic one half it would be bad policy—giving gross earnings, $19,500; operating expenses, $15,000; profit, $4,500. But, to show how cost of service comes in, if the operating expenses had been $12 per car-load, the reduction would be bad policy in both cases; while if they were only $8 per car-load it would be good policy in both cases.

To a certain extent both these elements have acted in combination to secure the great permanent reduction in rates.[4] But in each particular case of reduction, cost of service has played but a minor part, and possibility of developing traffic has been the main question considered. Thus there has gradually grown up a system of rates favoring certain classes of goods, certain localities, or certain individuals. It was found that by lowering the rates for cheap goods a large traffic was developed. It was found that by lowering the rates at competitive points a large traffic might be secured which would otherwise go by other routes. It was found—or at any rate,

3 An analysis of the elements which enter into cost of railroad service would carry us too far out of our way. The chief considerations are speed, bulk, risk, quantity, and regularity of shipment. The question whether a return load can be secured is also of great importance. For more detailed analyses see L. E. Morehouse: "Cost of Transportation on Railroads," N.Y., 1874. A. Fink: "Cost of R. R. Transportation" (1874), N.Y., 1882. O. Chanute: "Elements of Cost of R. R. Freight Traffic," 1874, 1885. Jos. Nimmo, Jr.: U.S. Internal Com. Rep., 1876. F. B. Herzog: "The Transportation Question," New York, 1883. Kirkman: "Railway Expenditures," I., 291–327.

4 Hepburn Com. Test., p. 47 (joint letter of Vanderbilt and Jewett). Vining on "Classification of Freight"

it appeared—that by lowering rates to certain individuals, a road increased its returns better than by a general lowering of rates.

This constitutes the system of charging "what the traffic will bear." The ordinary objections to it are obvious at once. It is generally believed that the less-favored shippers are taxed in order that the railroad may do business for others at unreasonably low rates; that in any other business the loss of competition would prevent such abuses; and that in the absence of any effective competition, laws should be passed forbidding the railroad to make a great deal more profit on one part of its business than it does on another. This is the aim of anti-discrimination bills.

On the other side, it is maintained by railroad men that this idea of a tax is not warranted; and that any such attempt to enforce equality, whether between classes, localities, or individuals, will diminish the profit and efficiency of the railroads, and not bring the expected advantage to the shippers, still less to the general public.

The effects of the three forms of discrimination—between classes of business, localities, or individuals—must be discussed separately.

1. Classification of business. Railroads divide their freight into four or more classes, the division being mainly based on the value of the goods. Thus, dry goods are placed in the first class, and lumber in the fourth; and the charges on the former are made two or three times as high as on the latter. There is a difference of cost of handling, and of risk; but nothing like as great as the difference in charge. The railroad does not base its classification upon cost of service, but upon what the traffic will bear. A ton of lumber has so little value that, if they attempted to charge the same rates for it which they charge for the dry goods, they would get none of it to carry; the traffic would not bear the higher rate.

A great deal of freight of small value is carried not merely at less than the average rates, but at less than the average *cost;* that is, at rates which, if applied to the whole business of the road, would not pay expenses. Many people assume that such business is an actual loss to the road, and that other business is taxed to make up for it. This is a fallacy. Any rate which will more than cover the expense of moving the cars and handling the goods is a paying rate, *provided the business can be had on no other terms.* If it is a question of filling cars that must otherwise be returned empty, any rate which more than covers the mere difference in expense between running them full and running them empty, is a paying rate.[5] If a manager should reject such business because it did not pay its share of the fixed charges (as distinct from train expenses) he would make a great mistake. He would reduce his business, and leave those charges the same. The fixed charges must mainly be borne by the lines of business that can best afford to pay them—that is, by the valuable goods.

The earliest freight tariffs involved little or no classification. Each step

5 See some striking figures in L. E. Morehouse "Concerning the Cost of Transportation on Railroads," New York, 1874, p. 15. These figures are better arranged for our present purpose than are the more comprehensive statistics collected by Mr. Octave Chanute (1874, 1885), or than those of Albert Fink in his report on "Cost of R. R. Transportation," 1874.

toward our present system has been accompanied by increased efficiency. It has made the cheap traffic possible, and has helped the high-class traffic more than it has hurt it. To do away with this would be a long step backward. If our railroads made it a rule to carry nothing at less than the average cost of doing the whole business, they would give up nearly all the coal trade and a great deal of the grain trade. It would give us dear food and dear fuel, and would injure both the railroads and the districts which they serve.

2. Local discriminations. Where a railroad is the only means of conveyance, it can charge what the traffic will bear, without restraint. But where it comes into competition with a water-route, or with another railroad, its charges are brought down to the lowest possible figure. The points where there is no competition are made to pay the fixed charges, while the rates for competitive business will little more than pay train and station expenses. It is better to have business on those terms than to have it go by the rival route. In a railroad war this competition is carried beyond the bounds of reason. There was a time when cattle were carried from Chicago to New York at one dollar a car-load.[6] These low rates develop the competitive point rapidly, while the higher rates retard the growth of the places where there is no such competition. When the competition is simply between railroads, a pool may do away with these local differences by raising rates at the competitive point. Where one place has the benefit of water competition, and another has not, it is hard to devise any effective means of getting rid of the differences.

We are apt to think that because these local discriminations are an evil, it must be the fault of somebody. In our anxiety to get rid of the evil, we are apt to overlook the natural causes which led to it, and which sometimes must lead to it almost of necessity. That local discriminations are a most serious evil, no one can doubt. That they are exaggerated, and in many instances flagrantly exaggerated, by the short-sighted policy of the railroad managers, is equally certain.[7] But there are many instances where the railroads are not responsible for them,[8] and where it is worse than useless to try to prohibit them by law. We are not arguing in favor of this system, but against the popular remedy—a statute.

Suppose it is a question whether a road can be built through a country district, lying between two large cities, which have the benefit of water communication, while the intervening district has not. The rate between these points must be made low, to meet water competition; so low, that if it were applied to the whole business of the road it would make it quite unprofitable. On the other hand the local business at intermediate points is so small that this alone cannot support the road, no matter how low

6 Hepburn Com. Test. (Vanderbilt), p. 1659.

7 Hepburn Com. Exhibits, p. 313. Joint letter of Vanderbilt and Jewett, Testimony, p. 56. Argument of John Norris before Penna. Senate Judiciary Com., Apr. 9, 1885. The general management of a railroad rarely appreciates local needs at their full importance. The plan of having advisory boards to represent such interests has frequently been suggested. The plan has been carried out in some parts of Europe. Mr. H. S. Haines has shown strong reasons for trying it in America.

8 E. P. Alexander: "Reply to Questions of the N. Y. Chamber of Commerce," p. 7.

or how high the rates are made. In other words, in order to live at all, the road must secure two different things—the high rates for its local traffic, and the large traffic of the through points which can only be attracted by low rates. If they are to have the road, they must have discrimination.

This point is so important and at the same time so hard to grasp, that it is worth while to take a detailed illustration. On the coast of Delaware, a few years ago, there was a place which we shall call X, well suited for oyster-growing, but which sent very few oysters to market, because the railroad rates were so high as to leave no margin of profit. The local oyster-growers represented to the railroad that if the rates were brought down to one dollar per hundred pounds, the business would become profitable and the railroad could be sure of regular shipments at that price. The railroad men looked into the matter. They found that the price of oysters in the Philadelphia market was such that the local oystermen could pay $1 per hundred pounds to the railroad and still have a fair profit left. If the road tried to charge more, it would so cut down the profit as to leave men no inducement to enter the business. That is, those oysters would bear a rate of $1 per hundred, and no more. Further, the railroad men found that if they could get every day a car-load, or nearly a car-load, at this rate, it would more than cover the expense of hauling an extra car by quick train back and forth every day, with the incidental expenses of interest and repairs. So they put the car on, and were disappointed to find that the local oyster-growers could only furnish oysters enough to fill the car about half full. The expense to the road of running it half full was almost as great as of running it full; the income was reduced one half. They could not make up by raising the rates, for these were as high as the traffic would bear. They could not increase their business much by lowering rates. The difficulty was not with the price charged, but with the capacity of the local business. It seemed as if this special service must be abandoned.

One possibility suggested itself. At some distance beyond X, the terminus of this railroad, was another oyster-growing place, Y, which sent its oysters to market by another route. The supply at Y was very much greater than at X. The people at Y were paying a dollar a hundred to send their oysters to market. It would hardly cost twenty-five cents to send them from Y to X. If, then, the railroad from X to Philadelphia charged but seventy-five cents a hundred on oysters which came from Y, it could easily fill its car full. This was what they did. They then had half a car-load of oysters grown at X, on which they charged a dollar, and half a car-load from Y on which they charged seventy-five cents for exactly the same service.

Of course their [sic] was a grand outcry at X. Their trade was discriminated against in the worst possible way—so they said,—and they complained to the railroad. But the railroad men fell back on the logic of facts. The points were as follows: (1) A whole car-load at seventy-five cents would not pay expenses of handling and moving. (2) At higher rates than seventy-five cents they could not get a whole car-load, but only half a car-load; and half a car-load at a dollar rate (the highest charge the article would bear) would not pay expenses. Therefore, (3) On *any* uniform rate for everybody, the road must lose money, and, (4) They would either be compelled to take the oyster car away altogether, or else get what they could at a dollar, and fill up at seventy-five cents. There was no escape from this reasoning; and the oystermen of X chose to pay the higher rate rather than lose the service altogether.

This is a typical case. The business of a railroad is of two kinds. Some of its business, like the oysters of X, must be done over this railroad or not at all. Of such business it is sure, even at rather high rates. The only limit is the value of the service; the excess of the selling price at market above cost of production at X. But a railroad may also do business like that of the oysters from Y, which can be sent to market by other routes. To do this it must make special concessions and lower rates.

Now many of the railroad expenses are the same, whether it does both kinds of business or only one. Repairs, salaries, and interest charges are mostly independent of the volume of business done. These must be paid somehow, just as the expense of the oyster car must be paid somehow. At the higher rate the road cannot get sufficient volume of business. At the lower rate it cannot get sufficient profit. It must do as the oyster car did, get what it can at high rates, and fill up at the lower ones. If you prohibit this by law you quickly cut away the margin of profit. And if by so doing you make it impossible to run the road, who is most hurt? Not the oyster-growers of Y, who had the low rates. They still have the other route. It is the oyster-growers of X, and men in like situations, who now cannot do business at all.

There is one difference. The oyster car will be taken off as soon as it is unprofitable. The bankrupt road may run on almost indefinitely. But the indirect effect is the same. Witness the history of Granger legislation. The farmers had moved so far west that they were wholly dependent upon the railroads. Where there was but one road it charged what it pleased. Where there were two, they fought for the traffic, and brought rates down very low. A distant competing point paid much less than a near local one. The Potter law [9] attempted to make the rates per mile for local points nearly the same as they had been for competing points. The result was disastrous. The old roads struggled on as best they might, losing money all the time. But no new ones were built, and the local points could not get the service they needed. They suffered severely; and after two years' trial the law was repealed.

3. Far worse are the discriminations made between individuals. The system of carrying under special contracts, below schedule rates, is the most serious evil connected with our present methods of railroad management. Trade adjusts itself to almost any system of classification, and sometimes even to local discriminations. But where two individuals, under like circumstances, receive different treatment, no such adjustment is possible.[10]

9 [Passed the Wisconsin legislature in 1874 and was repealed in 1876.]

10 The old theory that a rate should be reasonable in itself, and that, if that is the case, it makes no difference to A what B may be paying, can no longer be held. The chief thing which A has a right to demand is that he should not be unfairly handicapped in competition with B. Any such inequality is a real grievance. Hepburn Com. Test. (Fink), p. 513.

A mere "allowance for quantity," if granted to all without partiality, hardly comes under this head. If a man receives a reduced rate because he ships in large quantities, or at stated times, there is good ground for making a certain difference in his favor. But such allowances are not always given impartially; they are frequently kept secret,[11] and are often quite unreasonably large in amount.

If the object of a special rate is to develop business which could not otherwise exist, it may possibly be justifiable. Much good is often done in this way. But there is always a presumption against special rates of this kind. They establish one shipper; but they handicap others. The good they do is seen and felt. The evil they do is unseen, and, for a time, unfelt. This makes the temptation to grant such rates all the more insidious, and their actual effects all the more dangerous.

A special contract, for instance, is given to millers at Niagara. It produces new business at that point. But if it discriminates unfairly against the millers at Rochester or Buffalo, the gain of business at one place is made up by a loss at the other. Not a direct loss, be it observed; the mills will not shut down; but the natural growth of business will be checked. The railroad manager sees the mill at Niagara with its new traffic; he does not see how he may have prevented the growth of the old traffic at Rochester.

What makes matters worse is that, where the system of granting special rates becomes deeply rooted, a great many are given without any principle at all, through the caprice or favoritism of the railroad companies and their agents.[12] The revelations made before the Hepburn Committee,[13] as to the practice of railroads in the matter of secret rates were simply appalling. The fact that railroads had responsibilities to the public seemed to be completely lost sight of. There was, in many instances, scarcely a pretence of regular charges.[14] Everybody received favors as a matter of course; [15] the only question was how many such favors he could obtain.

An unfortunate result of the system is that special rates are granted to the very persons who need them least. Any concern which does not charge fixed prices—from the largest railroad down to the pettiest shop,—gives lower rates to two quite distinct sets of people, and for two quite distinct reasons. Some people get low rates because they are too poor to pay the

11 Hepburn Com. Rep., p. 48. Even where the railroads themselves would like to do away with them it is not always easy. The diversion of freight (by pools) from one line to another, so bitterly complained of by shippers, is resorted to to prevent secret rebates or drawbacks. One of the worst abuses is the practice of "underweighing"; where full rates are charged, but the shipper is allowed to send more goods than he pays for.

12 This is the most indefensible part of the whole system of railroad management. It is characteristic that Bismarck, who always chooses his fighting-ground with skill, made this a main base of operations in his contest against private railroad policy in Prussia. . . .

13 Hepburn Com. Rep., pp. 49 ff.

14 Hepburn Com. Test. (Goodman), pp. 120 ff. It was estimated that ninety per cent of the Syracuse business and fifty per cent of the whole business of the New York Central Railroad was done at special rates.

15 Goodman, Testimony, p. 159. "Question: 'Then the condition of getting the special rate is making the application?' Answer: 'Yes, sir.' "

high ones; others, because they are too shrewd to pay the high ones. The
very poor man perhaps gets the low rate, because he otherwise cannot buy
at all; the rich man gets the low rate, because he can go somewhere else,
and his large custom is worth making special efforts to secure. The more
justifiable forms of discrimination are those in favor of the weak. Classification, giving low rates to low-priced articles of prime necessity, like fuel,
lumber, or provisions, comes under this head. On the other hand, the great
majority of local and personal discriminations are in favor of the strong.[16]
As such, they do great harm to the community by increasing inequalities
of power; and in the end they are apt to do harm to the roads themselves.
The Standard Oil Company was fostered by a system of special rates until
it became strong enough to dictate its own terms.[17]

This was an extreme case; but there is almost always a certain opposition
between the present and future interests of a railroad. If a company's object
simply is to make as good a dividend as possible for the current year, that
object is best obtained by squeezing the local business of which it is sure,
and securing competitive business on almost any terms, however low. But
for the permanent interests of the road this is bad policy. The local business
may bear the squeezing for a year or two, but it will gradually die under
the effects. Such a policy destroys a road's best customers, and strengthens
the hands of those who are in a position to dictate their own terms. A
special rate to a favored customer means temporary gain. To make the
low rate general means temporary loss. Yet, where there is any doubt felt,
the latter policy is almost always the wise one.

.   .   .   .

2] Federation

.   .   .   .

THE QUESTION before this committee, if it desires to deal effectively
with the railroad problem, is, therefore: How shall this unity of management be attained in this country, consistent with the public interests,
and in accordance with the peculiar institutions and the practical working
of this government? That it cannot be obtained through governmental
ownership of the railroads is a self evident proposition.

Before considering this question further, it may be of interest to your

16 The more plausible arguments in favor of personal discrimination are made by
selecting special instances, where they were given in favor of the weak, and ignoring
the fact that such instances are by no means the rule.—E. P. Alexander: "Reply to
Questions of Chamb. of Com.," p. 9.

17 Hepburn Com. Rep., 40–46. Exhibits, p. 182. Testimony (Rutter), p. 2549. See
references in previous chapter.

FROM Albert Fink, in "The Railroad Problem and Its Solution." Testimony before the
Committee on Commerce of the United States House of Representatives, January 14, 15,
and 16, 1880 (Washington, D.C., 1880), pp. 18–24.

committee to know the work that has already been accomplished without the aid of government, by the railroad companies themselves, toward the solution of the railroad problem.

The railroad companies have endeavored to secure unity of action by voluntary co-operation in all matters in which it is absolutely necessary for the proper management of the roads, in the interest of the public, as well as in the interests of the proprietors of the roads. But this co-operation has been most inefficient in all matters relating to the uniformity, equality and permanency of railroad tariffs, although in other respects, as already mentioned, it has been very successful.

It is on account of the great complexity of the tariff problem that this voluntary co-operation has not met with better success, and not for want of effort or desire on the part of the railroad companies to control it, although the public, ignorant of all the difficulties to be overcome, presume to hold each separate road responsible for the working of the whole system. The difficulty, however, has not been so much in agreeing upon the proper tariffs, but in carrying them into practical effect. The necessary means and machinery for that purpose have not been adopted, and there is no authority to enforce such agreements.

The managers of roads meet in convention, and make agreements which are broken before they disperse. Every one who has paid the least attention to this subject is familiar with these unsuccessful efforts. The press of the country chronicles almost daily some conference held by officers of railroad companies, or some agreement made, and on the following day it chronicles its violation or discontinuance.

During the last few years, however, some progress has been made toward a closer and more effective co-operation. Associations of railroad companies have been formed, with a proper organization, through which it was made at least possible to control the important tariff question. The first complete organization of this kind, and to which I shall refer hereafter more particularly, and explain fully its object and its methods, was the Southern Railway and Steamship Association, formed in October, 1875, and which is still in effective operation.

In 1877 the four Trunk Lines—the New York Central, Erie, Pennsylvania, and Baltimore and Ohio Railroads—entered into a similar compact, by which all the Westbound traffic from the seaboard was managed under one organization. In April, 1878, the Grand Trunk and Vermont Central companies commenced to co-operate with the four other Trunk roads. Through this compact it has been practicable to control the tariffs on the whole of the Westbound traffic from the seaboard to all points West of the termini of the Trunk Lines. Like charges have been made to the public for like service. The tariff has been permanently maintained for a period of two and a half years with only one change during that time—something that has never been accomplished before; thus securing practically to the people the object of the proposed measure now being considered by your committee, viz.: reasonable, just and permanent rates of transportation. I do not mean to say that perfection has been reached in this respect, because much remains to be done; but cases of violation of the tariff rates, as far as the Trunk Lines can exercise their influence, are now the exception, and not, as heretofore, the rule.

Similar efforts at closer and more effective co-operation have been made by the railroads west of Chicago and St. Louis, which have been in a great measure successful.

During the last year the principal roads embraced in the territory east of the Mississippi and the Atlantic seaboard, including the Trunk roads, and the Grand Trunk, have formed an organization known under the name of the Joint Executive Committee, for the purpose of securing uniform and equitable rates on the whole of their Eastbound traffic. This organization is of the same character as that of the Southern Railway and Steamship Association. . . . Acting as chairman of that committee, I beg leave to read an extract of the report which I was able to make at its first annual meeting in Chicago, in December last.

"It may not be out of place here to refer briefly to the past operations of this committee, which has now been established one year this day, although its organization was not fully perfected and put into working order until June last. Since then the committee has accomplished, in a great measure, the object for which it was created, namely, to establish reasonable and just tariffs for the competitive traffic, and to permanently maintain such tariffs, securing thereby reasonable compensation to the companies and remedying the great evils that have resulted from want of co-operation between the railroad companies, to the serious injury of their own and the interests of the public."

"You have now for the first time established a practical method by which the competitive traffic of your roads can be properly managed and controlled. Heretofore this was impossible; the mere holding of conventions of railroad managers, passing resolutions, and then dispersing and letting things take care of themselves, each party acting as it sees fit, will not accomplish the purpose of intelligent joint management of the large property under your charge. You have now added to the legislative department—your conventions—also a permanent executive department, the duty of which is to see that the resolutions passed and agreements made are faithfully carried out. In addition to this you have also established a judiciary department, consisting of a board of arbitration, whose duty it is to settle peaceably any question of difference, without resort to wasteful warfare, with all its injurious consequences. You have thus formed a complete government over this large competitive traffic over which it has heretofore been found impracticable to exercise intelligent control."

"It must be remarked, however, that the only bond which holds this government together is the intelligence and good faith of the parties composing it. To give greater stability and permanency to the operations of this committee, it would be desirable to make its operations legally binding upon all parties by legislative action, provided it can be shown, as I believe it can, that its operation is beneficial to the public interests. I consider that no other legislative action would be necessary to remedy the evils which it has been attempted unsuccessfully to remedy by State legislation, and which may be attempted by congressional legislation, I fear, with like results."

"The companies composing this association have already, by their voluntary action, abolished the pernicious system of special contracts, and all shippers are now put upon an equal footing. Rates for the last few months have been everywhere (in the territory in which these roads are located) maintained, and the great disparity between the local rates and the competitive through rates, which has heretofore been so great a source of trouble and complaint, has ceased to exist. Had such a result been sooner reached, we would have heard nothing of legislative control of railroads."

"I express it as my opinion, the result of the most careful consideration, that the only legislation required to accomplish the object which the most zealous advocate of the public interests can desire to accomplish, is to legalize, and even to enforce, the co-operative system of the railroad companies, so far as it is necessary to establish and maintain reasonable rates of transportation upon a uniform and equitable basis, treating alike all parties situated alike—in other words, to carry out the plan adopted by the committee, and which has been so successfully practiced during the last few months. I know that objection will be made by parties not conversant with all the conditions of limitation and restriction which are enforced upon railroad companies in establishing their tariffs, that such co-operation or combination, as it is generally called to make it appear odious, would lead to extortion on the part of the combined railroad companies. The past action of this committee is the best proof that such fears are unfounded. The committee, during its existence, has established rates lower than they have ever existed before, and even the highest rates charged have not exceeded those of the last few years, but have been considerably lower, although the conditions for high rates have been more favorable this year than they have been for years past."

"The only thing which the co-operative system has accomplished, is the maintenance of the established tariffs and the abolishment of the contract and rebate system. It is only when agreed rates are maintained, no matter by what means, either by the voluntary action of the railroads or by direct legislative enforcement, that the evils of the transportation business complained of by the public can be remedied."

"If, therefore, our work is to be judged by its fruit, it should recommend itself to public favor."

From this, it will appear that, in my judgment, the only measure now wanted in order to give permanency to the operations of these associations, is to recognize the same as necessary and beneficial, to give legal force to the voluntary agreements that may be made between its members, with the view of carrying out the objects of the association, namely, the establishment and maintenance of reasonable and nondiscriminating transportation tariffs; in fact, the object of your proposed legislation. If Congress would pass a law to this effect, I would consider the whole railroad problem in this country settled, and settled upon truly American principles. It would allow the proprietors of the railroads to manage their own affairs, which they are much better able to do than it could be done under a centralized government, and at the same time it would restrict the operation of each individual road under the legalized co-operative system, to the extent that it is necessary, in order to carry out the intent and spirit of the law which regulates the conduct of common carriers in their capacity as public servants.

I regret that I have not sufficient time to point out at length the great merits and advantages of this American plan of governing the railroads, as compared with the European plans, to which I have referred. It accomplishes fully the object contemplated by the centralized government of the railroads in Germany. It brings unity in the management of the roads, as far as that is desirable or necessary; and at the same time, it preserves the individuality of each road, and reserves to it the management of all its local affairs, in which it and the country through which it passes is alone concerned. Co-operation of the roads is only required in so far as the interest of the whole system of roads and the public interest requires it—no further. In this respect, the government of the railroads would be based on the same principle that underlies the government of the United States—the general government taking cognizance only of matters in which the several States are jointly interested, leaving to each individual State—and, in this case, each road—to manage its own local affairs as it thinks best, in accordance with the laws of the State which created it.

Is it necessary to point out the great advantage of such a government as compared with that of a centralized government? Considering the extent of this country and the extent of its railroad system, a government of the railroads, such as is contemplated in Germany, would be utterly impracticable here. Government ownership accomplishes only one purpose—the same as the co-operative plan, it secures unity of management—in other respects the difficulties of the tariff question arise and would have to be dealt with, whether the roads are the property of the State or of private individuals; and State ownership would necessarily bring with it many new difficulties not experienced or even thought of under the management by private owners.

The plan which I propose prevents that very centralization and absorption of the roads under the absolute control of one or few persons. It makes the separate, individual existence of these roads possible, and puts a check upon the consolidation of roads, which is regarded with so much alarm by the people in this country, but which is the natural result of the struggles of the railroad companies: the stronger must at last absorb the weaker. The proposed government of the road secures all the advantages of consolidation, without its disadvantages. Instead of conferring upon and concentrating great power in the hands of a few, it has the contrary effect—it will leave that power distributed among a great many separate corporations.

3] Combination and Consolidation

· · · · · · · · · · · · · ·

I SPOKE just now of consolidation, and no doubt this is one of the most
prominent characteristics of the American railway system. Numerous
small lines are continuously absorbed by larger systems, and sometimes
great corporations amalgamate with each other. The phenomenon in itself
is neither wonderful nor isolated. In England and on the European Continent consolidation of railways commenced years ago; it was carried on almost to its utmost limits, and in Great Britain, France, Belgium and Hol-
land a few great companies which have parcelled out the transportation
business of their respective countries have taken the place of scores of minor
corporations formerly leading a separate and independent existence. Nor
is consolidation of business interests confined to railways alone. Shops,
banks, manufactories, steamship, telegraph and mining companies amalgamate with their fellows, either voluntarily because in union lies strength,
or what we may call involuntarily, largely because of ruin threatening to
result from the competition of vast and wealthy interests. In almost every
country the rise of giant corporations is one of the most conspicuous features of modern business life, but in none has it assumed such vast proportions as in the United States. The complaint that in the Great Republic
the large interests crowd out the smaller is heard daily, and in almost every
branch of trade and industry we see control vested in a few great enterprises.

The fact that amalgamation is carried on in America is well known to
English readers. That which to-day is the Pennsylvania system, embracing
8,000 miles of railway, is an amalgamation of more than a hundred smaller
lines. The Erie owns, leases, and operates more than forty smaller railways,
now merged into one homogeneous whole. The Richmond Terminal system
consists of scores of Southern lines all of which at one time or another had
a separate existence. The Southern Pacific, the Illinois Central, the "St.
Paul," the Missouri Pacific, in short, all great systems of to-day acquired
their quality as such by gradual absorption of or amalgamation with other
lines. The Vanderbilt system, now comprising some 25,000 miles of railway
in the United States, originated in the New York Central, itself an amalgamation of seven small roads between Albany and Buffalo, effected by
Commodore Vanderbilt.[1] The Atchison [2] system grew from a small line, connecting two obscure townships in Kansas, some ninety miles distant, into
a giant network of lines traversing a dozen States and comprising over
9,300 miles of railway. Amalgamation has been at work everywhere, and
there are no indications of abatement. Just as there are some people who

1 [The Central was formed in 1853, and fifteen years later, in 1868, Vanderbilt obtained
control of it.]
2 [The Atchison, Topeka and Sante Fe.]

FROM S. F. Van Oss, "Consolidation," *American Railroads as Investments* (New York,
1893), pp. 64–67, 69–75.

predict that the entire world will ultimately be divided into a few great Empires, so in America we find people who forecast that consolidation of railroads will cease only when all lines are combined into a few vast systems. Whether such a result is to be anticipated or not it would be somewhat venturesome to say; but there can be no doubt that amalgamation of railway interests in the United States has been carried to an extent which fifteen or twenty years ago nobody could have foreseen. At the close of 1889 there were approximately 2,450 minor companies which had ceased to lead a separate corporate existence and were merged in others, mostly into one of the 33 vast companies to which nearly one half of the American railways belong. In 1889 these 33 companies had a total length of 77,000 miles, but since that date, later than which no statistics are available at the time of writing, numerous other consolidations have been effected. For instance, the St. Louis and San Francisco RR. and the Colorado Midland have become parts of the Atchison, the Ohio and Mississippi and Pittsburgh and Western have become members of the Baltimore and Ohio system, the Rome, Watertown and Ogdensburg has joined the New York Central, while control of hundreds of smaller lines has been acquired by larger systems; and I believe it is no exaggeration to say that to-day, counting all Vanderbilt lines as one system, there are in the United States twenty-five systems controlling at least 100,000 miles of railway, while 150,000 miles are in possession of not more than 75 companies. And of these systems there are some of great magnitude controlled by a few men. The Vanderbilts hold sway over upwards of 25,000 miles of the best lines; Jay Gould controls the two principal systems in the Southeast and Southwest, the Richmond Terminal and the Missouri Pacific. Huntington owns the Southern Pacific, Rockefeller the Northern Pacific, Wisconsin Central, and "Maple Leaf," and men like Pullman, Leiter, Armour, Swift etc. are said to form a clique controlling most railways in the Northwest, while Astor and other millionaires command other systems. What are the causes of this concentration of power, by what means is it accomplished, and how does it affect the railways?

First, as to causes. It is quite obvious that the principal purpose of consolidation is the abolition of excessive competition. Competition led to most of the evils that befel American railways; it caused constant rate wars and a reduction of revenue. There were too many railways, too many hostile interests; and it is quite natural that a reduction of their number was aimed at. This was attempted first by pooling, but, as we have seen, pooling was a failure, and other means had to be found which would prove more successful. Another motive was the thirst after power characterising most railway managers. War was not only conducted openly by means of competition and rate cutting in order to secure business, it was also carried on secretly; and managers were scheming and intriguing one against the other with the object of obtaining power. Every "railroad boss" was permeated with a desire to make his system great, to oust his rivals; and this desire prompted his every action. Consequently railroad presidents were always attacking others and defending themselves. There was a constant struggle not only for life, but also for supremacy. Every one was attempting to crush his rivals and to conquer them; but at the same time every company had to be protected against being destroyed and defeated itself. It was plainly seen that consolidation was desirable in the interest of railways; but it was also furthered because of personal motives.

.   .   .   .

There are, in the main, four methods of effecting consolidation:

1. By acquiring ownership.   3. By traffic agreements.
2. By leases.   4. By Associations.

The limits of the present work do not permit entering into exhaustive details with regard to these means, there being various ways of purchasing and an endless variety of leases and agreements, which, wherever such is necessary, will be described when individual lines are dealt with. Some general observations, however, seem pertinent at this juncture.

Ownership can either be absolute or partial. A company may own all the stock of a subsidiary railway, as for instance in the case of the Erie, which owns all the shares of the re-organised Chicago and Atlantic. It may own only a controlling interest, a method adopted by the Atchison in its relations with the St. Louis and San Francisco RR., the former company owning $15,861,000 in shares of the $30,000,000 issued by the latter. It may own a railway jointly with another company, as is exemplified by the joint ownership of the Great Northern and International RR. by the Missouri Pacific and the Missouri, Kansas and Texas railroads. Lastly, a majority of stock of two or more companies may have a common owner, a principle underlying the control of the Vanderbilt lines. In all cases absolute control must be an inevitable result. The latter method seems the most desirable, because it affords very few opportunities for frauds; the former are open to several objections. Purchases have been known to be made chiefly because the acquired property had first been bought by gentlemen who happened to be very intimately connected with the purchasing company; part ownership has led to speculations before the purchase in which, needless to say, some people "in the know" were involved; and joint ownership is unsatisfactory because it is apt to lead to squabbles, the more so since the joint owners are frequently competitors. Of all forms of ownership that to be found in the case of the Vanderbilt lines seems the best. With this method frauds are impossible; the New York Central for instance can never be accused of having paid too much for the Lake Shore. Further, common ownership leaves combined railways independent of each other so that the strong parts of a system are not impaired by the weakness of others; on the other hand it has this disadvantage that, as a tie between two railways, it is theoretically liable to dissolution at any time.

Of leases the variety is far greater than of forms of ownership. There are some that can be dissolved "while you wait," and there are others that will hold good until the crack of doom; some railways are satisfied with securing subserviency of the subsidiary railway for ten years, and others will not take it for less than 999, as we are reminded of by the firm ties

by which the St. Paul and N. P. is linked to the Northern Pacific. Some
leases stipulate that a fixed annual rental shall be paid, and others fix a
progressive rental, or make it proportionate to either gross or net earnings
of the leased line. Now the lessee guarantees nothing, then everything; in
some instances he undertakes to make up any deficiency below a minimum
sum, and in others he gobbles up all earnings above a certain maximum.
In some cases even, as was the case with the "lease" between the Missouri
Pacific and the Missouri Kansas and Texas railroads, stipulations are so
loose that the lease can practically be dissolved at will, and that the lessee
can either pay a certain sum or not, as he sees fit. But in the vast majority
of cases the lessee guarantees to the leased road the annual payment of a
rental, frequently regulated by its earnings, i.e. by its performance, certainly the fairest method of all. In many other cases interest upon bonds or
a dividend upon shares is guaranteed, but this method is hardly as fair as
the other because it does not give the leased company the benefit of improved business. But even in the most common form of leases there prevails such a variety that it is neither possible to enter into particulars, nor
to generalise.

.   .   .   .

Consolidation being, as has abundantly been shown, one of the most
pronounced features of the American railroad of to-day, the question
naturally arises whether its results have been detrimental or beneficial to
the railroad interest, and whether from a general point of view it is desirable or not. Although we shall have to consider the interests of the investor first, and those of the public afterwards, it would be injudicious to
altogether ignore the latter, since, as we have seen before, the people of
the United States have a word to speak in railroad matters. But whatever
may be said of amalgamation, there can be no doubt that to the railways
it has been beneficial, and that this has been so can cause no surprise
whatever.

Economy and a decrease of hostilities have been the principal results of
railway consolidation. It is quite evident that amalgamation enables railways to effect great savings. If we will but think of any of the great systems,
and imagine how different matters would be if a large number of small
companies continued to lead a separate corporate existence instead of being
united into one homogeneous system, the great economy effected by amalgamation will be at once apparent. Instead of scores of main offices with
a corresponding number of sets of officials there is but one, larger, it is
true than any of the small companies would require, but considerably
cheaper than the total that would have been required by numerous smaller
companies; and in addition the facts that a great system can command
the services of better and more efficient men than a small one and that its
power as a factor in transportation business increases with its size should
not be lost sight of. Further, there must be an important saving in the purchase of supplies; they are bought in large quantities, and the large company can have its own coal mines, its own workshops, and its own locomotive works, while it can maintain permanent staffs of labourers and

employees. That all this is impossible for small companies, and that both economy and earning power must result from such advantages needs no emphasising.

In the second place consolidation produces harmony. The greater Empires become the less frequent are wars; and with railways it is the same. Rate war between giant systems is no trifling matter; and hostilities between the two great systems known as the Pennsylvania and Vanderbilt lines naturally are far less frequent than they were in the days when over a hundred small lines occupied the places of the present two. War has become more formidable, more destructive, and in addition the generals who conduct it have a higher sense of their responsibilities than the petty presidents of bygone days. And as a result rate wars are fortunately far less frequent than they were of yore.

Greater facility in the working of railroads is also one of the wholesome results of combination. Formerly many a small road either had too much *personnel* and rolling stock or not enough, and the result as a rule was extravagant expenditure. With consolidation it is different. On a large system business varies according to divisions, seasons and periods; but staff and rolling stock can always be profitably employed somewhere and the strain sometimes placed upon special parts can be relieved without additional expense or loss of business. Thus a waste of energy is prevented, a better service maintained, and great savings are the result.

The effects of consolidation therefore have been most wholesome from the investor's point of view. As yet it would be less correct to say that peace reigns supreme than that war still is the device, but harmony is steadily increasing, and there can be little doubt that amalgamation is the cause; for that reason it should be noted with satisfaction that consolidation continues to progress. Upon the extent to which it is likely to be carried it would be idle to speculate. Of greater importance is the undisputed fact that with the progress of amalgamation the average returns of American railways have increased if we make due allowance for the constant decline in rates.

As far as the public is concerned, the consolidation of railroads has been viewed with a considerable amount of apprehension, chiefly, however, in connection with the increase of monopolies. Some writers, like Mr. Cook in his *Corporation Problem*,[3] foresee general disaster as a result of the growth of monopolies in general, and of railway systems in particular, and urge the necessity of State interference. But against such objections a very forcible argument can be advanced: For at least fifteen years consolidation has been in constant and rapid progress, and during that period the average rate for all freights in the United States has fallen more than $33\frac{1}{3}$ per cent; and in spite of consolidation the rate of interest paid on bonds and stock declines year by year. With rates and returns constantly falling off it is difficult to see why the public should object to consolidation of railway interests.

. . . .

3 [William W. Cook, *The Corporation Problem* (New York, 1893).]

PART VI

The Beginnings of
Modern Governmental
Regulation of Business

INTRODUCTION

❲ ALTHOUGH few federations of manufacturers were organized as carefully and on so broad a scale as the Southern Railway and Steamship Association or the Eastern Trunk Line Association, American industrialists soon began to follow the ways of competition and cooperation that the railroads had initially worked out. In industry as in railroading, failure of federation led to combination and consolidation; and in industry as in transportation, federation and combination created demands for government regulation. Thus, the Federal Trade Commission, formed in 1913, was patterned on the earlier Interstate Commerce Commission. It was to supervise corporations in manufacturing and commerce in much the same way as the latter had begun to regulate the railroads in 1887. Later in the twentieth century, utilities, airlines, communication networks, securities exchanges, and even labor-management relations came to be supervised by similar bodies. The regulatory commission has become as significant an institution in the American economy as the investment banking house, the large corporation, and the trade union.

The demands that brought the first permanent regulatory commission to the United States resulted directly from the railroads' discriminatory pricing policies. Farmers, merchants, and small manufacturers whose livelihood was so intimately related to the costs of transporting their products to market spear-headed the protest against discriminatory rates. They were quickly joined by many who, like Charles Francis Adams, were outraged by the exploitative and speculative practices of Wall Street and disturbed by the alliances between railroads and politicians. By the 1880's many Americans whose livelihoods were not directly affected by the costs of transportation viewed the concentrated economic power wielded by a few railroad directors and managers as a threat to political democracy as well as to economic opportunity. All agreed that only public power could control such private influence.

The first object of regulation was, then, to assure all Americans equal transportation facilities at reasonable prices. A second was to bring the railroad corporation under closer public surveillance. Initially, the advocates of regulation looked to the state governments. Only when the states proved unable to handle these tasks did they turn to Congress. In the West, where the pressure for regulation came from farmers' organizations, particularly the Granges, states passed laws that prohibited discrimination and even set the rates the roads could charge. Here an Illinois law was the model. In the East, where boards of trade, chambers of commerce, and other groups of merchants led the drive for regulation, the legislatures preferred to require publicity of rates and accounts from the railroads rather than actually to set rates by law.

Here Massachusetts pioneered. In both
Illinois and Massachusetts the legislatures created commissions to carry out
their laws. Of the two the Massachusetts
"advisory" type of commission with its
broad powers of investigation had the
greatest opportunity to develop techniques of collecting and analyzing data
on rates and rate-making.

By the mid-seventies the inadequacies
of any type of state regulation were becoming clear. The primary difficulty was
that so much traffic crossed state borders. Even though the Supreme Court
in the case of *Munn* v. *Illinois* (1876)
permitted a state to regulate interstate
commerce, neither its laws nor its commission could be effective beyond its
own boundaries. Then in 1886 the Supreme Court reversed its earlier decision. In *Wabash, St. Louis and Pacific
Railroad Company* v. *Illinois,* it ruled
that the federal Congress had exclusive
control over interstate commerce.

This decision brought to fruition a
long agitation for national regulation.
In the 1880's few issues were argued
more hotly and excitedly than railroad
regulation. Many of its supporters saw
it as an essential way to preserve democracy and freedom, while its opponents
insisted that it was the first step toward
a socialistic state. At first the most popular proposal for national regulation
was embodied in a bill advocated by
John H. Reagan of Texas, which forbad
rebating, discriminatory rates, and pooling and which was to be enforced in
the courts rather than by a commission.
The bill that finally passed, one proposed by Senator Shelby C. Cullom of
Illinois, also prohibited rebates, out-
lawed discrimination between persons
and places, and forbad variable and unreasonable rates. Despite the protests of
railroad presidents and state commissioners, it forbad the pooling of traffic
or income. This bill differed, however,

from the Reagan proposal by providing
for a commission of five men who were
to enforce the Act by obtaining regular
reports, investigating and hearing complaints, and then, on the basis of this
information, adjusting rates.

At first the railroads cooperated with
the Commission. Then they soon found
they could avoid its more unpalatable
rulings. This they accomplished by ap-
pealing these decisions to the federal
courts, which tended to uphold the railroads against the Commission. In 1897
the Supreme Court in two separate decisions sharply curtailed the Commission's
power and effectiveness. In the so-called
Maximum Freight Rates case the Court
decided that the Commission "has no
power to prescribe the tariff of rates
which shall control in the future." In
the Alabama Midlands Railroad case it
prevented the Commission from disal-
lowing certain discriminatory rates.
These powers were returned by the passage of the Hepburn Act in 1906, which
gave the Commission the authority to
set maximum rates and to prescribe
uniform methods of accounting. The
Hepburn Act further provided that the
ICC's rulings were binding on the carriers until the courts had decided on
their validity.

Nevertheless, as Edward Kirkland has
suggested in his *Industry Comes of
Age* (1961), the Interstate Commerce
Commission did play a significant role
in American railroading from 1887 on.
A large number of the Commission's
rulings were not appealed to the courts.
Moreover, the Supreme Court's emas-
culating decisions did not come until
almost ten years after the Commission
went into operation. The commissioners
began their work immediately. In 1887
they called for reports on finances and
rates from the railroads and began thorough investigations and hearings in
order to develop a more reasonable and

uniform rate structure. From the start, too, the commissioners realized the complexities of their task. They appreciated that discrimination often resulted from the economics of railroad transportation rather than from any personal favoritism, and that changes in rates usually affected two groups of shippers as well as the railroad. The adjustment of rates on the complaint of one set of shippers in one community often led to a strong protest from another set in another community. Because the commissioners came to their problems with the same assumptions as railroad managers and analysts, and the most important of these assumptions was that the roads were entitled to a return on their investment, they soon analyzed the problems of costing, pricing, and competition in much the same way as Fink, Hadley, and others had done earlier. For example, by the mid-nineties a majority of the Commission favored legalized pooling to unrestricted competition. Possibly because of its flexible pragmatic approach, the Interstate Commerce Commission had come to have a meaningful voice in the determining of the nation's rate structure even before the passage of the Hepburn Act.

The three selections in this section were chosen to illustrate and to assist in the analysis of three points: the nature of the demand for government regulation of business, the reasons for the formation of a new type of institution to meet these demands, and the ways in which this institution operated. The first brief passage lists grievances of Western farmers and the remedies they proposed. In the second, a representative of the New York merchants spells out both specific and more general complaints against the railroads and then presents a reasoned plea for a national regulatory commission. The last set of readings, from the first annual report of the Interstate Commerce Commission, outlines the provisions of the Act and then considers the difficulties involved in carrying out two of its principal stipulations. In reviewing the final selection, the reader should try to determine the common values, assumptions, and economic concepts held by all men connected with the railroads—commissioners, managers, financiers, outside experts, and union members. How did these common views limit the possible alternatives to the "railroad problem"? What was the precise nature of the disagreement? And how did this disagreement help to define the different solutions that were proposed and that were finally accepted?

THE READINGS

1] The Farmers Demand Regulation

B Y COMMITTEE on the Railway System—WHEREAS, we recognize the railways of the country as an effectual means of developing its agricultural resources, and as having an interest, common and inseparable, with the country through which they pass; and, whereas, we have in times past fostered and aided them by liberal charters and concessions, made by public and private parties, and still desire to encourage further development of the railway system; therefore,

Resolved, that a fair degree of reciprocity would suggest that corporations having a common interest and public aid, should, in their turn, endeavor to subserve the interest of the country through which they pass, by charging fair rates of freights, and by the equitable and just treatment of all localities along their lines.

Resolved, that, on the contrary, railroad corporations in many instances have been exorbitant in their charges, have discriminated unjustly between localities, and have failed to respond to the generous grants of powers and moneys that have been given them by our national and state governments.

Resolved, that the system adopted and now practiced in the building of railroads, viz: the soliciting of stock subscriptions from individuals, corporations, and counties, and after receiving these subsidies to depress the value of said stock by forcing it upon the market and depreciating its value to such an extent as to enable a few speculators to secure control of the road, thereby depriving those who aid in its construction of all voice in its management; increasing the cost four or five times above the amount it would have cost if those managing it in the outset had had the foresight to have the funds on hand at the start to build and equip said road; then requiring the producer and shipper to pay dividends upon the fictitious cost by charging excessive freight and passenger tariffs—operates most injuriously to the best interests of the farming class, and calls loudly for reform and restraint by adequate legislation.

Resolved, that we recommend all farmers to withhold their voices and their aid from railway corporations, unless it be fully conceded and agreed that corporations so aided are subject to regulation by the power incorporating them, and will not, after receiving the advantages conferred by the public authority, claim the immunities of a private corporation.

Resolved, that we indorse and will support the doctrine promulgated by some of our courts, that a railway corporation in receiving and exer-

FROM "Resolutions of the Second National Agricultural Congress," May, 1873, in Jonathan Periam, *The Groundswell* (Chicago, 1874), pp. 335–37. (The congress was held at Indianapolis on May 28, 1873.)

cising the state's right of eminent domain, and receiving aid raised by taxation from public authorities has thereby accepted and admitted itself to be a corporation with a public function, and subject to the power from which it has received its charter, in the limitation of its rates.

Resolved, that a railway being practically a monopoly, controlling the transportation of nearly all the country through which it passes; and that as competition, except at a few points, can not be relied upon to fix rates, therefore it becomes the duty of the state to fix reasonable maximum rates, affording a fair remuneration to the transporter, and without being an onerous charge to the producer and consumer.

Resolved, that, inasmuch as Belgium has succeeded in regulating the rates upon railways by government lines, we ask an investigation of the proposition to control the rates upon existing railways by trunk lines built and controlled by the states authorities and run at fixed uniform and cheap rates.

Resolved, that the consolidation of parallel lines of railway is contrary to public policy, and should be prohibited by law.

Resolved, that wherever a railway corporation owns or controls a line or lines in two or more states, it is the right and duty of the general government to regulate the rates of freight and fare upon such lines, under the constitutional power to regulate commerce between the states.

Resolved, that we commend the thorough organization of the farmers of the country in local, county, and state organizations, for the purpose of reforming the great abuses and dealing out equal and exact justice to all men.

2] The Merchants Demand Regulation

M R. THURBER,[1] of New York: I desire to offer a resolution which I have drafted, to this effect:

Resolved, That in the opinion of this Board it is desirable to secure national legislation upon interstate commerce by railroad, and that said legislation should embody the following provisions: First, to raise a special commission or tribunal to secure uniformity and publicity in railway accounts, and publicity of railway contracts and transactions; Second, to enforce provisions securing uniformity of rates and classifications under like circumstances, and relative quality where circumstances differ; Third, to secure publicity of rates and prohibition of sudden

1 [Both Sterne and Francis B. Thurber, a partner in one of New York's largest wholesale grocery firms, had long been active leaders of the New York Cheap Transportation Association, the forerunner of the New York Board of Trade and Transportation.]

FROM Simon Sterne, "An Address on Interstate Railway Traffic," Tenth Annual Meeting of the National Board of Trade, December 11, 1879 (New York, 1880), pp. 3–12, 17–21. (This session of the National Board of Trade was held in Washington, D.C., on December 10, 11, and 12, 1879.)

and arbitrary changes; Fourth, to secure the prevention of extortionate charges, and of personal or local favoritism.

I should have been glad under some circumstances to speak upon this subject; but Mr. Sterne, a member of the New York Board of Trade and Transportation, who has for several years been doing excellent work in connection with this subject, and in the most disinterested manner has advocated legislation designed to secure substantial justice to the public, has been induced by us to come here, very much against his inclination and at great personal inconvenience. I would therefore ask Mr. Sterne to touch upon the various points mentioned in my proposition, instead of doing so myself.

Mr. STERNE, of New York: *Mr. President:* Mr. Thurber has quite truly stated that I came here with considerable reluctance. I am a member of the Board of Trade and Transportation, and have been so since its organization; but I felt that it would be regarded to some degree as an intrusion for a man not strictly related to trade, but connected with the legal profession, to present his views at large here, except upon a special occasion, or when a special question, such as this, is under consideration.

Some of you, gentlemen, are probably aware that on behalf of the Chamber of Commerce and Board of Trade, I represented, as counsel, before a Legislative Committee of Investigation, the views of the New York merchants upon railway policy in the State of New York. This enquiry extended over a period of eight months, and has been described by railway people as the most thorough and searching investigation that has ever taken place in this country, upon any subject relating to trade or commerce. Therefore, even if I had not been prepared by previous study to speak upon a matter of this character, the experience and buffetings that I have had and met with for the past eight months upon this subject would, of themselves, to a considerable degree, fit me to say a few words upon the question which is now before the Board.

Why is it that we have a railway problem upon our hands while we have not a breadstuff problem, a petroleum problem, nor, indeed, a problem in reference to any other occupation or private enterprise? The answer is, that we have from the very outset, from the time the railway system took its origin in this country and in England, misunderstood as a people the bearing, the power, and the consequences of giving a public highway into private hands; and we did not suppose—and very naturally we did not suppose—that in granting railway franchises we were in reality not only giving a public highway into private hands but also the exclusive transportation over it. We had nothing to guide us. There had been nothing like it in the history of the world; and it was for the first time that the owner of a road became the sole transporter over that road, because all other highways that had been built, whether by Government or in part by Government, and in part or wholly by private enterprise, were built simply for the ownership and control of the highway; and the vehicles that travelled thereon, belonged to private owners and became subjects of private competition, to transport the goods over the highways, so that the analogy of the turnpike did not help us, because the turnpike was simply the ownership of the road, while the goods that were transported over the turnpike went over it in private wagons or vehicles over which the turnpike company had no control except to fix uniform tolls for the use of the road only.

The analogy of the canal gave us no light, because there again the canal company, when it was in private hands, became simply the owner of a canal, while the boats that passed through the canal were provided and propelled by private enterprise, remained private property, and were entirely separate from the canal company. So we, in utter ignorance of the consequences of chartering corporations which would at the same time be the sole transporters over the road, legislated upon the basis or plan as if private carriages could go over the new road, and that heavy freights never, by any possibility, would be carried over it. You will find, Mr. President, in all the early railroad charters in this country, and in England, provisions incorporated by which the right of a citizen to put his private carriage upon the new roadway was secured, on payment of certain tolls; and you will also find, by a report made in 1833 by four of the then leading engineers in the State of New York to the Legislature of the State, in answer to an enquiry in reference to the future development of this form of highways, these engineers substantially said that they would be exceedingly useful for the carrying of passengers over level plains, but that for the purpose of carrying freight they were not at all to be considered in comparison with the water-ways, and that there was, therefore, no necessity for fixing any limit in regard to freight charges which would never be made. It is not to be wondered at, therefore, that our legislators went wrong, and our people went wrong, and that we have now upon our hands a railway problem of the first magnitude. I do not propose in what I have to say, to utter an unkind word of the men who control our great public highways called railways, which have, according to Mr. Nimmo's report of 1877,[2] carried over eighty per cent of the traffic going from the West to the East, and which now carry about seventy per cent of the traffic East bound, and even a larger percentage of West bound traffic (because the West bound traffic being first-class is almost exclusively and wholly in the hands of the railways).

That that condition of things was not provided against is the fault of our people and our legislation—a fault which is easily explainable by the misapprehension already referred to—that we had nothing to guide us. Our ignorance was, therefore, very naturally taken advantage of by strong and intelligent men, who went into railroading as a business, in which to make as much money as they could, paying no more attention to the public than any man who goes into a private business; and, therefore, the railroad man is not to be blamed for making whatever he could out of his investments. Consequences to the public of the most serious and grave character have flowed from this, and have become aggravated to a degree no longer to be borne; but in legislating upon the subject we must bear

2 [Joseph Nimmo compiled the *Annual Reports on the Internal Commerce of the United States* for the Treasury Department's Bureau of Statistics.]

in mind that we must be just to the citizens who have, through our own neglect, invested their moneys in these great enterprises upon a different theory than that which will hereafter prevail, and done so at our invitation as a people, to regard it exclusively as a matter of private enterprise. Therefore, the legislation that we want in the first instance is of the most conservative character, because we should avoid the bringing about of any condition of affairs which will permit private interests to say with justice to the public: "We were invited to enter into this business and put our money into it as a private enterprise, and you now put the whole burden upon our shoulders and take the whole benefit to *yourself*. We shall put no more money into enterprises which are subjected to that kind of control." Such was the consequence of some of the Western legislation which decided to embody a hard and fast tariff in the bills creating a board of railroad commissioners, and which attempted to apply the strict rule of a *pro rata* freight toll for the shorter, compared with the longer distance. Now I believe that the adoption of provisions in any bill which would, in the first place, put into the law a hard and fast tariff, not to be changed under any circumstances until the law-makers could again convene and be persuaded, or which would directly apply a *pro rata* freight schedule, without the slightest regard to terminal advantages, or without the slightest regard either to gradients or superior facilities between railroads, or any other questions which determine a freight charge, would necessarily be dangerous legislation, not only to the interests affected, but to the people at large, because it would work so badly as to cause distrust with it and thereby ensure its repeal, thus putting us back again to a condition worse than we were in at the outset, since it will create a feeling that legislation upon that subject is useless.

The reason why the railway question or the railway problem differs from every other problem, and why railroading can never be considered a private business is this: Competition applies in every case where, for the time being, in the individual instances, the supply is larger than the demand. To explain what I mean by this, I will give you an example:

If I want a hat, although all the hats that are wanted by the people, and all the hats the people want, may counterbalance each other (I mean the supply and demand be about equal); yet to each individual man who wants a hat there are practically a million more hats offered to him than he wants, and he therefore is perfectly free to choose. A man who wants a railroad train, or fifty men who want a railroad train from any one point to a given point, have not a million railroad trains to choose from. They generally have but one, which leaves at a stated period of time, and they must take that or none; and, therefore, the supply in that case is the very reverse of what it is in the instance of the demand for a hat. For in the case of the railroad there is but one to supply the want, and a million who want that particular service. In addition to that fact, in almost every other business the conditions are absolutely different. In every private business, the moment that excessive profits can be made, a very limited supply of additional capital drawn from other occupations would tend to create a competition. In a railroad you never can create competition without attempting to raise a sum of money so large as to make it a very serious question whether or not it can be raised, if a railroad to supply such a demand is already in existence; and then, when you have two or three, or even four or five, railroads from any point to another given point, they never can be so multiplied but that the presidents of such railroads can get around a single table and determine upon either a pool or a combination which will fix a rate of freight from one point to another given point, which will pay an interest on all the capital invested in all the railways, thus imposing a burden in addition to that which had been already imposed by the existing railway, four times as great as would otherwise be necessary, simply because additional railways not demanded by the necessities of the case had been built.

Statistics gathered both in this country and in England, show there is not a single line of railway in the world (except those exclusively passenger railways in dense populations, such as the elevated roads in New York, or the underground railways in London), which is operated to a large percentage of its capacity. For instance, the New York Central Railway or the Pennsylvania road—the two roads operated more than any others in this country—are operated not above fifteen per cent of the actual capacity of the roads for the carriage of trains with safety. Therefore, quite independent of the fact that the roads exercise the right of eminent domain which gives them a *quasi* public nature, the character of their business is such that we cannot expect competition for any long period of time between them, because combination is easy, and combination is more profitable than competition; and there is not the same freedom on the part of the buyer of the commodity of transportation as there is of the seller; consequently, the condition of freedom which lies at the very basis of competition does not exist; and, therefore, quite independently of the exercise of the right of eminent domain, and of the correlative duties that flow therefrom, the nature of the business requires regulation to secure the freedom which without regulation is denied. Strangely enough the railways themselves have, within the past few years, publicly abandoned even the pretence of competition between themselves, and have cast aside the whole basis of American legislation which proceeded on the principle of competition, and was founded upon that idea. Our free railway acts throughout the States, commencing with the State of New York in 1850, copied in all the States of the Union, were based upon the theory that there would be competition in railway management and railway building, precisely as in all other enterprises in this country, and that that competition would result in the most efficient service at the lowest possible prices to the consumer. By a pooling and arbitrary division of the freights to be carried, and agreement as to rates, the twenty-seven leading railways of this country, combined under the management of Mr. Fink, have made a combination as close as though they had for all practical purposes become amalgamated under one board of control. Each railway company has thereby abandoned not only the right to make individually its own traffic rates, but also the right to carry such freights as may be offered to it; so that if I choose to send a particular package by the Erie Railway Company to a western point, whether it shall go to such particular point by the Erie Railway depends not upon my direction, but upon whether that road has already shipped freight to its allotted amount and reached the maximum, when it must send part of its traffic which comes to it under the pooling arrangement to some other road. Therefore, that important part of the whole railway system of this country which runs east and west from St. Louis to the sea shore, is combined under one arrangement, which has resulted in an absolute abandonment of competitive traffic by the railways themselves.

This confronts us with a power as great as, and indeed greater than, any of which we have any record; greater by far than has ever been permitted to exist unchecked and uncontrolled by proper legislation. Our Secretary, in his annual report, read yesterday, stated that there are now upwards of 80,000 miles of railway in this country, representing a capital of over $4,500,-000,000, which, when aggregated under one head, or a few heads and practically under one management, represents a power so formidable and so above and beyond the power of legislators, either State or national, as they are now organized, that it will break through and defeat any law which we may see fit to make, unless the people in their turn accumulate power to meet power. The railroad has outgrown all State limits and swept them (in so far as the railroads are concerned) out of existence, not only by the leasing of parallel lines and the leasing of lines running in conjunction,— lines running from Boston, Baltimore, Philadelphia and New York, to St. Louis, Cincinnati, Chicago and Louisville,—but by the traffic between them being so controlled by an arrangement as substantially to be equivalent to a pooling of the capital stock; so that in the place of five or six competing lines there is, practically, but one company, having five or six different sets of parallel rails, having different local but the same through traffic; and, therefore, in each one of the States each State finds itself powerless to control anything but a mere section of this vast body of roads. This condition is the basis of an argument that is constantly made, and made by the railroad managers themselves, against legislation in any particular section of the country, that it submits certain portions of a through line to a control which may place it at a disadvantage compared with other through roads; and that, therefore, there should be some sort of simultaneous action, so that they shall be treated as a whole; treated as they have practically become,—one body.

.   .   .   .

To such an extent has this matter of personal rates gone, that one witness whom I examined in New York, a very intelligent merchant, and I believe one of the largest foreign shippers of grain from New York to European cities, when under examination by me as to the rates he was paying, said: "I do not know what rates I have paid for the last three years, on the shipment of grain from the west to the east, because each shipment rested on its own contract." "Why," said I, "isn't there a tariff?" to which he replied, "I have heard of such a thing. The railways sometimes amuse themselves by making a tariff; but I make my own rate, and at my own time, and in my own way, for every shipment which I make." Here was a large shipper (that case is a sample of the rest) who utterly disregarded the tariff. He never paid any attention to it, but went into the railroad office and made his own personal rate; and whether it differed from the rate to anybody else he did not care, although, no doubt, he endeavored, if possible, to get the lowest rate. If he succeeded in getting a lower rate than other people, it placed him in a position of particular advantage in the markets of the world in the shipment of grain.

As to the local traffic, the evidence showed a condition of the freight office which is still worse, and that is, that one set of men, situated side by side with men in similar business in the interior towns of New York, would be compelled to pay thirty, forty and forty-five cents a hundred on the different classes of first, second, and third class freights, while their neighbor obtained a rate of ten or twelve cents a hundred upon all classes. Of course the difference was so great that it represented a commercial profit, and the man who did not know at what rates his neighbor was getting his goods transported, finding his business languishing and his neighbor growing rich, attributed it to superior business advantages on the part of his neighbor, abandoned his occupation, or stayed in it until he was by the railway taxed out of existence, while the other man continued to flourish more and more as the business light of his neighbor was being extinguished. Here we see the development of an absolute power on the part of the railway, precisely analogous to and partaking of the same character as the taxing power when it is unequally distributed, of crushing out one man and building up another. I venture to say that such a power as that, exercised capriciously and with favoritism, makes it possible to the freight agent of a railway to constitute himself a special partner in every line of business in the United States, contributing as his share of capital to the business, the ability to crush out rivals. This is a power so great, and the consequences of it are so widespread, particularly for evil, that no community can prosper with such a power as that irresponsibly lodged in private hands, no matter who the men are who wield that power.

One of the justifications of the French revolution was the system known as *Fermiers Généraux,* which prevailed prior to the revolution, and by which a speculator purchased from the treasury of the French Government on the payment of, say, a million francs into the treasury, the right to tax a particular community in France. He invested his money in the right to tax, and he taxed them at his own sweet will, seeing to it that he did not tax them so utterly out of existence that the following year he could not make a good speculation in taxing them again. A power of the same character we have without stint, and without restraint, placed in the hands of our corporations. It is the power to tax, limited only by their own sense of personal interest not to tax to such a degree that they dry up the sources of taxation. And that is what railway men mean when they talk about charging what a thing will bear; and that is what they mean when they say, we charge arbitrary rates because we have no competition; and that is what they mean when they say that their rates go down by reason of competition, although they do not go down correspondingly to the changes that have taken place in prices in this country within the last eight or ten years.

.   .   .   .

The resolutions before the Board provide that there should be a special commission, or tribunal, to secure uniformity and publicity in railway accounts, and publicity of railway transactions. One of the defects of the Reagan Bill, and a defect that is shown in almost all legislation I have seen originating here in Washington, is the absence of provision for the creation of a proper Board of Commissioners. We cannot here adopt the paternal policy of continental European countries. We must adopt something a little more slow, possibly, and a little less radical,—but better adapted to our institutions. Publicity and investigation are thoroughly American methods of dealing with subjects, and I do not know whether we would require much additional legislation if that were secured. Be that as it will, in that you would have the basis for all further legislation. There are serious constitutional questions as to how far the National Government may interfere with organizations created by state authority, and which only exist and have their being under state laws, and are responsible to state organizations; but there cannot be any question that the clause in the Constitution of the United States giving Congress the power to regulate commerce, gives it the power to investigate, and the power to insure publicity, and the power to have returns made to Congress, or to any tribunal that it may organize as to interstate commerce. If there is any portion of the power conferred by the Constitution on Congress which I would be content to see stretched to its limits, it is that of regulating interstate commerce, under which Congress may create a Board of Railroad Commissioners and give to them the power to call for books and papers, and to enter upon an investigation of the whole subject so as to secure publicity of accounts and uniformity of accounts. In my opinion that power is within the limits of the Constitution, and will remain as a protection, and as a safeguard to the people of this country. It seems to me that a bill which fails to provide for a Board of Railroad Commissioners to gather and to disseminate information, and to hear complaints, even if the power to adjudicate be denied, is defective in form, and does not give us the sort of information we should have for a future sound and wholesome railway legislative code.

The second part of the resolution offered by Mr. Thurber, provides that such a commission shall enforce provisions securing uniformity of rates and classification under like circumstances, and relative equality where circumstances differ. Upon that subject I have already spoken. The four volumes of testimony which we took in the State of New York overwhelmingly bear witness to the necessity of such provisions, and show the utter absence of either uniformity or equality of rates as to local traffic, and, until recently, as to the through traffic. The first assistant General Freight Agent of the New York Central Railroad Company, testified that ninety per cent of the local traffic of the New York Central Company was carried at special rates, and that any tariff which claimed to be put in force was a non-existing thing which no one paid any attention to, and which did not exist at all so far as east bound traffic was concerned.

I have drawn the attention of this Board to the necessity of publicity of rates, for, in my opinion, it is better to have rates of freight high and known to all, than to have them lower but subject to sudden, personal, and arbitrary changes. For that reason it is absolutely essential that such a law shall contain a provision in regard to the publicity of rates. The next part of the resolution deals with the question of extortion. I am a little apprehensive that extortionate charges, if equal to all, are not within the control of general legislation. They generally take place where the railway, being a single line, has the absolute power to make the charges such as it may see fit. Wherever competition prevails, there the charges are either run down by railroad wars to a very low figure, or by combination maintained at an average one.

Where the railway competes with the water way, there the interest of the railroad is to keep from charging what is called extortionate charges. Now this brings me to a question, with which I think I shall close. It is one of considerable importance. It has ordinarily been supposed that when a railway has said, "Why, we have reduced our charges far below what they have been in years past," they have made a complete answer to the claim for fair dealing on the part of the community. I do not want to state it too broadly—but it may be stated quite broadly—that within certain limitation it does not much matter what the railway charge is so long as it be uniform, and so long as the whole public are treated precisely on the same basis. We have found everywhere in this country that we were very much worse off when the railway rate went down than when it was maintained; for the rate not being calculable, resulted in converting every merchant into a speculator, and made the prices of commodities in the wholesale market absolutely without limit in fluctuation, while, when the rates were maintained, the price was governed by supply and demand. Hence it is, that an event which once would have struck this community with fear,— the combination of the railway interests which absolutely abandoned competition—was hailed with delight from one end of the land to the other, simply because it took the place of a condition of things which was absolutely and utterly intolerable.

When the rate went down to ten cents a hundred from Chicago to New York, or fifteen cents from St. Louis to New York, the rate was to some few fifteen, to some few others ten, but the main body of the commercial community were compelled to pay twenty, twenty-five and thirty cents a hundred, and the standard rate was forty and forty-five; thus inaugurating a wide-spread system of uncertainty, chicanery, fraud and personal favoritism, demoralizing trade and commerce even worse than the demoralization due to an uncertain currency, because the freight charge fluctuated more frequently, even from hour to hour and day to day. Consequently, the combination which brought the rate to seventy cents a hundred, and maintains it there, is considered a God-send and a blessing, compared with the fifteen or ten cent fluctuating rates before, simply because the seventy cents is an equally distributed and calculable element.

. . . .

Another question which has thrown considerable light upon the difference between the railway as a private interest and the railway as a public institution, is the fact that the railway managers themselves have discovered that they cannot carry on a competitive war in railroading with such results as prevail in ordinary commercial competition. In private enterprises, when you have carried your war to the uttermost and have ruined your rival, you have driven him out of the business, and there is an end to him; but in a railroad war, when you have ruined your rival, you have put him into the hands of a receiver, and the trains are dispatched and arrive in the same manner as before, with the difference that you have exempted your rival from the obligation to pay dividends, and have thus put him in a condition of greater and more effective rivalry than he was in at the outset of the fight!

In other words, the bankrupt roads "run wild," as the saying is, for they run to obtain operating expenses only; and the consequence is, the railway manager says: I have got to carry on this war not with a mailed hand but with a gloved hand. Because if I smash up this railway the broken pieces of it will batter in my own head. It is a boomerang of the worst possible description.

In view of these facts it is apparent that the conditions of competition in trade do not apply to an enterprise in which the results of competition are not only different from what they are in private enterprises, but in which the results are exactly the opposite.

Yet, with all these facts before us, we must be conservative in the recommendations which we make. It is unfitting this body to adopt any but conservative propositions. . . . Therefore, we must conservatively but surely reverse our policy and recognize the fact, and base our legislation thereon, that this is an interest not subject to the natural law of competition, but to the law of combination; that it represents a power which, as now aggregated together, is vastly larger than that represented by any other one interest in the United States; that it overshadows courts, and overshadows more especially legislative bodies, and that the community itself must, when such a power as that is consolidated, combine to meet it so that the community shall be at least as strong, in its combination known as Congress or State Legislatures, as that combination of railroads has become by its so-called pooling or traffic arrangements. Therefore, I most heartily endorse these resolutions, and trust that this Board will appoint a special committee on the subject of railway legislation, to present its views to, and press the principles contained in the resolutions on, the attention of the National Congress, or that a special committee may be appointed to meet the Committee on Commerce, which is, as I understand, to meet tomorrow, for the purpose of presenting its views to it.

. . . .

3] The Interstate Commerce Commission and the Problems of Regulation

. . . .

The Act to Regulate Commerce

THE LEADING features of the act are the following:

All charges made for services by carriers subject to the act must be reasonable and just. Every unjust and unreasonable charge is prohibited and declared to be unlawful.

The direct or indirect charging, demanding, collecting, or receiving, for any service rendered, a greater or less compensation from any one or more persons than from any other for a like and contemporaneous service, is declared to be unjust discrimination and is prohibited.

The giving of any undue or unreasonable preference, as between persons or localities, or kinds of traffic, or the subjecting any one of them to undue or unreasonable prejudice or disadvantage, is declared to be unlawful.

Reasonable, proper, and equal facilities for the interchange of traffic between lines, and for the receiving, forwarding, and delivering of passengers and property between connecting lines is required, and discrimination in rates and charges as between connecting lines is forbidden.

It is made unlawful to charge or receive any greater compensation in the aggregate for the transportation of passengers or the like kind of property under substantially similar circumstances and conditions for a shorter than for a longer distance over the same line in the same direction, the shorter being included within the longer distance.

Contracts, agreements, or combinations for the pooling of freights of different and competing railroads, or for dividing between them the aggregate or net earnings of such railroads or any portion thereof, are declared to be unlawful.

All carriers subject to the law are required to print their tariffs for the transportation of persons and property, and to keep them for public inspection at every depot or station on their roads. An advance in rates is not to be made until after ten days' public notice, but a reduction in rates may be made to take effect at once, the notice of the same being immediately and publicly given. The rates publicly notified are to be the maximum as well as the minimum charges which can be collected or received for the services respectively for which they purport to be established.

Copies of all tariffs are required to be filed with this Commission, which is also to be promptly notified of all changes that shall be made in the same. The joint tariffs of connecting roads are also required to be filed,

FROM "The Act to Regulate Commerce," "The Long and Short Haul Clause of the Act," and "Reasonable Charges," *First Annual Report of the Interstate Commerce Commission* (Washington, D.C., 1887), pp. 10–11, 14–17, 22–23, 36–41.

and also copies of all contracts, agreements, or arrangements between carriers in relation to traffic affected by the act.

It is made unlawful for any carrier to enter into any combination, contract, or agreement, expressed or implied, to prevent, by change of time schedules, carriage in different cars, or by other means or devices, the carriage of freights from being continuous from the place of shipment to the place of destination.

These, shortly stated, are the important provisions of the act which undertakes to prescribe the duties and obligations of the carriers which by its passage are brought under Federal control. Some important exceptions are made by the twenty-second section, which provides:

> That nothing in this act shall apply to the carriage, storage, or handling of property free or at reduced rates for the United States, State, or municipal governments, or for charitable purposes, or to or from fairs and expositions for exhibition thereat, or the issuance of mileage, excursion, or commutation passenger tickets; nothing in this act shall be construed to prohibit any common carrier from giving reduced rates to ministers of religion; nothing in this act shall be construed to prevent railroads from giving free carriage to their own officers and employés, or to prevent the principal officers of any railroad company or companies from exchanging passes or tickets with other railroad companies for their officers and employés; and nothing in this act contained shall in any way abridge or alter the remedies existing at common law or by statute, but the provisions of this act are in addition to such remedies.

These provisions, it will be seen, are not intended to qualify to any injurious extent the general rules of fairness and equality which the act has been so careful to prescribe, and the exceptions may all be said to be authorized on public considerations.

In the performance of its duties the Commission has had occasion to decide that the transportation of Indian supplies may be free or at reduced rates under this section (Interstate Commerce Commission Reports, I p. 15), as also may be that of the agents and material of the United States Fish Commission (*Ibid.,* p. 21). The question of what may be included under the exception made for charitable purposes has never come before the Commission in such form as to call for an expression of opinion. It will be noted that in terms it applies to property only, not to persons.

By the eleventh section of the act this Commission is created and established, and other sections prescribe its duties and powers. Those sections it will be necessary to consider somewhat at length further on.

The Commission was organized March 31, 1887, and entered at once upon the discharge of its duties. The other provisions of the act took effect April 5, 1887. The demands upon its attention were immediate, and some of them of a very perplexing nature. It will be more convenient to take notice of these under specific heads in connection with the provisions of the act under which they were severally presented for its action.

.   .   .   .

II. The Long and Short Haul Clause of the Act

Another question presenting itself immediately on the organization of the Commission was that respecting the proper construction of the fourth section of the act, which, after providing

that it shall be unlawful for any common carrier subject to the provisions of this act to charge or receive any greater compensation in the aggregate for the transportation of passengers or of like kind of property, under substantially similar circumstances and conditions, for a shorter than for a longer distance over the same line, in the same direction, the shorter being included within the longer distance,

proceeds to say—

That, upon application to the Commission appointed under the provisions of this act, such common carrier may, in special cases, after investigation by the Commission, be authorized to charge less for longer than for shorter distances for the transportation of passengers or property, and the Commission may from time to time prescribe the extent to which such designated common carrier may be relieved from the operation of this section of this act.

The provision against charging more for the shorter than for the longer haul under the like circumstances and conditions over the same line and in the same direction, the shorter being included within the longer distance, is one of obvious justice and propriety. Indeed, unless one is familiar with the conditions of railroad traffic in sections of the country where the enactment of this provision is found to have its principal importance, he might not readily understand how it could be claimed that circumstances and conditions could be such as to justify the making of any exceptions to the general rule.

It is a part of the history of the act that one house of Congress was disposed to make the rule of the fourth section imperative and absolute, and it is likely that in some sections of the country many railroad managers would very willingly have conformed to it, because for the most part they could have done so without loss, and with very little disturbance to general business. But in some other parts of the country the immediate enforcement of an iron-clad rule would have worked changes so radical that many localities in their general interests, many great industries, as well as many railroads, would have found it impossible to conform without suffering very serious injury. In some cases probably the injury would have been overbalanced by a greater good; in others it would have been irremediable. To enforce it strictly would have been, in some of its consequences in particular cases, almost like establishing, as to vested interests, a new rule of property.

　·　　·　　·　　·　　·　　·　　·　　·　　·　　·　　·　　·

But the lower rates on the longer hauls have not been due altogether to water competition; railroad competition has been allowed to have a similar effect in reducing them. But as the railroad tariffs are commonly agreed

upon between the parties making them, the necessity which controlled the
water competition was not so apparent here, and to some extent the lower
rates have been conceded to important towns in order to equalize advantages as between them and other towns which were their rivals, and to
which low rates had been given under a pressure of necessity. But they were
given also in many cases as a means of building up a long-haul traffic that
could not possibly bear the local rates, and which consequently would not
exist at all if rates were established on a mileage basis, or on any basis
which, as between the long and short haul traffic, undertook to preserve
anything like relative equality.

It would be foreign to the purposes of this report to discuss at this time
the question whether in this system of rate-making the evils or the advantages were most numerous and important. Some of the evils are obvious;
not the least of which is the impossibility of making it apparent to those
who have not considered the subject in all its bearings, that the greater
charge for the shorter haul can in any case be just. The first impression
necessarily is that it must be extortionate; and until that is removed it
stands as an impeachment of the fairness and relative equity of railroad
rates. But, on the other hand, it must be conceded that this method of
making rates represents the best judgment of experts who have spent many
years in solving the problems of railroad transportation; and its sudden
termination without allowing opportunity for business to adapt itself to
the change would, to some extent, check the prosperity of many important
places, render unprofitable many thriving enterprises, and probably put an
end to some long-haul traffic now usefully carried on between distant parts
of the country. It is also quite clear that the more powerful corporations
of the country, controlling the largest traffic and operating on the chief
lines of trade through the most thickly settled districts, can conform to
the statutory rule with much more ease and much less apparent danger
of loss of income than can the weaker lines, whose business is comparatively
light and perhaps admits of no dividends, and the pressure of whose fixed
charges imposes a constant struggle to avoid bankruptcy.

.   .   .   .

Where the practice of making the greater charge upon the shorter haul
has long prevailed, the effect of its abrogation upon some portion of the
business of the smaller cities of the country should perhaps be noted. Those
cities have generally been in position to handle goods of all kinds, purchasing them at importing, manufacturing, and producing points, and re-
selling to retail dealers in the more immediate vicinity. The rates of freight
have favored these distributing points, and have been so low that goods
could be taken to them and sent forward after handling, or even returned
for a certain distance over the same line, at a less aggregate rate of freight
than the smaller places could obtain on the same goods from the same initial
point. The ability to do this has developed very important business houses,
and has largely controlled business methods in some sections of the country,
but it no longer exists when the fourth section has been literally applied.
The rate from the initial point to the given city—as, for example, from

Baltimore or Philadelphia to Danville, Va.—added to the rate from that point to smaller points beyond, will then be more than the through rates from the initial point to the latter places, and at the same time the rate to the given city will be as great or greater than the rates to the inter-mediate points on the same line; and the natural effect is to depress the wholesale business at all such points and to throw the trade into the hands of metropolitan dealers. This fact is clearly seen in some of the cases now pending before the Commission. There are compensations for all such in-cidental injuries, and the question involved being one of legislative policy, the Commission deems it sufficient to state the facts as they exist, without comment upon them.

The Commission, on October 20, caused a circular letter to be sent to the various carriers subject to the provisions of the act throughout the United States, inquiring concerning the practical application of the fourth section in making the tariffs in use upon the lines of each respectively. This circular has been very generally answered, and the replies give full information in respect to the manner in which the provisions of the "long and short haul" clause are now being observed by the carriers. A very large number of railroad companies, lines, and systems, answer unequivocally that there are no points upon their respective lines to or from which inter-state rates for passengers or freight are greater than to or from more distant points in the same direction over the same line. Others, slightly misappre-hending the inquiry made, state that no such instances exist upon their own roads, but that joint tariffs are made by them to points upon other roads where variations from the rule exist. Still others state the points upon their lines which are exceptionally treated, and give the reasons which are claimed to justify them in the rates made.

The statements and explanations of the different companies so far as they are other than a simple negative reply, present the situation so clearly and directly, from the stand-point of the carriers, and show so distinctly the various circumstances and conditions found in different parts of the country which are claimed by them to affect their traffic to an extent war-ranting a departure from the letter of the statutory rule, that the Commis-sion has determined to lay the entire series before Congress as an appendix to this report. This appendix, which is marked E, contains the following documents:

1. Circular letter to carriers of October 20, 1887.

2. List of carriers which reply that they do not make interstate rates where a greater sum is charged for a shorter than for a longer distance in the same direction over the same line, to or from any point on their re-spective roads.

3. Letters and documents from carriers which accepted the invitation of the Commission to make a statement concerning the circumstances and conditions of traffic which they claimed made their case exceptional.

Reviewing railway operations during the period which has elapsed since the act took effect, the Commission feels warranted in saying that while

less has been done in the direction of bringing the freight tariffs into conformity with the general rule prescribed by the fourth section than some
persons perhaps expected, there has nevertheless been a gratifying advance
in that direction, and there is every reason to believe that this will continue. That substantial benefits will flow from making the rule as general
as shall be found practicable can not be doubted; and even when the circumstances and conditions of long and short haul traffic are dissimilar, the
desirability of avoiding any considerable disparity in the charges is great
and obvious. So far, therefore, and so fast as business prudence and a proper
regard to the interests of the communities which would be disturbed and
injured by precipitate changes will admit of its being done, such railroad
companies as do not now conform to the statutory rule should make their
rates on these two classes of traffic more obviously just and more propor-
tional than they have hitherto been or now are.

XI. Reasonable Charges

Of the duties devolved upon the Commission by the act to regulate commerce, none is more perplexing and difficult than that of passing upon
complaints made of rates as being unreasonable. The question of the
reasonableness of rates involves so many considerations and is affected by
so many circumstances and conditions which may at first blush seem foreign,
that it is quite impossible to deal with it on purely mathematical principles,
or on any principles whatever, without a consciousness that no conclusion
which may be reached can by demonstration be shown to be absolutely
correct. Some of the difficulties in the way have been indicated in what
has been said on classification; and it has been shown that to take each
class of freight by itself and measure the reasonableness of charges by reference to the cost of transporting that particular class, though it might seem
abstractly just, would neither be practicable for the carriers nor consistent
with the public interest.

The public interest is best served when the rates are so apportioned as
to encourage the largest practicable exchange of products between different
sections of our country and with foreign countries; and this can only be
done by making value an important consideration, and by placing upon
the higher classes of freight some share of the burden that on a relatively
equal apportionment, if service alone were considered, would fall upon
those of less value. With this method of arranging tariffs little fault is
found, and perhaps none at all by persons who consider the subject from
the stand-point of public interest. Indeed, in the complaints thus far made
to the Commission little fault has been found with the principles on which
tariffs for the transportation of freight are professedly arranged, while applications of those principles in particular cases have been complained of
frequently and very earnestly.

Among the reasons most frequently operating to cause complaints of
rates may be mentioned:

The want of steadiness in rates.

The disproportion between the charges for long and those for short distances.

The great disparity between the charges made for transportation by roads differently circumstanced as to advantages.

The extremely low rates which are compelled by competition in some cases, and which may make rates which are not unreasonable seem, on comparison, extremely high.

Some others will be mentioned further on.

The want of steadiness in rates is commonly the fault of railroad managers, and may come from want of care in arranging their schedules, or from want of business foresight. But more often perhaps it grows out of disagreements between competing companies which when they become serious may result in wars of rates between them. Wars of rates, when mutual injury is the chief purpose in view, as is sometimes the case, are not only mischievous in their immediate effects upon the parties to them, and upon the business community whose calculations and plans must for a time be disturbed, but they have a permanently injurious influence upon the railroad service because of their effect upon the public mind. When railroad companies determine for themselves what their rates shall be, it is not unnatural for the public to infer that the lowest rates charged at any time are not below what can be afforded at all times, and that when these are advanced, the company is reaching out for extortionate profits.

Now, there are few important lines in the country that have not at some time in their history been carrying freight at prices that if long continued would cause bankruptcy. But to a large proportion of the public the fact that the rates were accepted was proof that they were reasonable; and when advanced rates are complained of, the complainants, to demonstrate their unreasonableness, go back to the war prices, and cite them as conclusive proof of what the companies then charging them can afford to accept. Many popular complaints have their origin in the ideas regarding rates which these wars have engendered or fed, and the evils of the controversies do not end when the controversies are over, but may continue to disturb the relations of railroad companies with their patrons for many years afterwards.

It may be truly said, also, that while railroad competition is to be protected, wars in railroad rates unrestrained by competitive principles are disturbers in every direction; if the community reaps a temporary advantage, it is one whose benefits are unequally distributed, and these are likely to be more than counterbalanced by the incidental unsettling of prices and interference with safe business calculations. The public authorities at the same time find that the task of regulation has been made more troublesome and difficult through the effect of war rates upon the public mind. These are consequences which result so inevitably from this species of warfare, that it would naturally be expected they would be kept constantly in mind by railroad managers. It is inevitable that the probability that any prescribed rates will be accepted by the public as just shall to some extent be affected by the fact that at some previous time they have been lower; perhaps considerably lower.

The disproportion between the rate charged and the distance the property is carried is also important in its effect upon the minds of those who have not the time or perhaps the opportunity to study the subject and understand the reasons. There are grounds on which short-haul traffic may be charged more in proportion to the distance of transportation than long-haul traffic, some of which any one would readily understand and appreciate. Thus, it is seen that a considerable proportion of the carrier's service is the same whether the transportation is for the short or for the long distance; there must be the same loading and unloading, the same number of papers and entries on books, and so on. It is also seen that short-haul traffic is more often taken up and laid down in small quantities, and that for this reason the proportionate train service is much greater.

But when all these considerations are taken into account it will still appear that the long-haul traffic is given an advantage in rates which must be accounted for on grounds which are not so readily apparent. When the reasons are seen it may perhaps appear that there is in fact no wrong either to the shippers who are apparently discriminated against, or to the general public.

It is not uncommon that in railroad freight service the rates for the transportation of a particular kind of property, instead of being regularly progressive, shall be found arranged on a system of grouping, whereby the charges to all points within a defined territory shall be the same, though the distances will vary. Thus, at the present time the rates which are made from New York to Chicago are also made from New York to all points within a territory about Chicago, which includes some important towns in western Indiana and western Michigan. A question might be made by such towns whether grouping them with Chicago and making them pay the same rates is just; but the grouping system in general departs so little from the distance proportions that it is seldom the ground of complaint.

There are cases, however, in which the distance proportions are purposely disregarded, and the doing so is justified by the managers on the negative ground that no one is wronged by it, and on the affirmative ground that the public is benefited. Cases of the sort may perhaps be found about all our large cities in which the railroads, as to some particular agricultural production needed for daily consumption in the city, have gradually extended the area from which they would receive and transport it at the lowest rates, until they may be found carrying the article at the same price for 100 miles as for 20. The low rate for the long distance has extended the area of production and benefited the city; and it is possible to conceive of cases in which the opposite course, of taking distance into the account in all rate making, would have kept production so far restricted in territory that producers near the city could never have been given as low rates as they receive now, when they are charged the same as their more distant competitors. Where such a case appears, the failure to measure the charges from regard to distance could not dogmatically be pronounced unjust, if it appeared that the railroad on the one side, and the public on the other, was benefited by the course actually adopted. But to increase the rates to the nearer producers, or even to keep them at a point which, though fair in the first place, has in the course of events become unreasonably high, in order to be able to put those at a distance on an equal footing in the market with such nearer producers, would be manifestly unjust. Not even on grounds of general public advantage do we understand that this would be justified; for public benefits, when they are to be had at the cost of individual citizens, can not rightfully, nor we suppose lawfully, be assessed on one class of the people exclusively.

The great disparity in the charges of different roads for the transportation of the same kind of property is a prolific cause of complaint, sometimes justly founded and sometimes not. It is apparent sometimes, in the complaints which are made to the Commission, that the parties complaining hold the opinion, or at least have an impression, that the cost of transporting a particular species of property is substantially the same on all roads, and that consequently the charges made by one road may prove with tolerable certainty that the higher charges made by another road are unjust. If the circumstances and conditions under which the traffic is carried by the two roads are substantially the same, the comparison would be legitimate and the argument from it of very great force. But when any such comparison is made, there are some circumstances having an important bearing upon rates which can not be left out of view. Among these may be specified:

The length of haul. A thousand tons of wheat can be loaded, transported a thousand miles, and delivered much more cheaply in proportion to distance than the same quantity can be loaded, transported one hundred miles, and delivered.

The quantity hauled. A train load of coal can be transported more cheaply in proportion to quantity than a single car load, and a car load more cheaply than a hundred pounds. So if the business is large, though it be the transportation of many kinds of property, it can be done relatively more cheaply than if it were small.

Return freights. If lumber or other property in quantity is to be delivered at points where there will be return loads for the same cars, the delivery can be made much more cheaply than at points where return freights could not be expected.

Cost of moving trains. This is very much less on some roads than on others by reason of lighter grades, cheaper fuel, less liability to obstruction from storms, and other causes which may disturb the track or delay trains.

These are among the causes which have an important bearing on relative rates. Beyond these the relative cost of roads must be allowed force also, if the owners are to be permitted to charge such rates as will make their investments remunerative. A complaint that rates are unreasonable may therefore require for its proper adjudication a careful inquiry not only into the circumstances and conditions of the road which makes them and of the traffic upon it, but also into those of other roads whose lower rates are supposed by comparison to show the injustice of the rates complained of.

But there are reasons which make it necessary, in adjudicating a case of alleged excessive rates, to consider rates on other lines or at other points, even when the complaining party makes no argument or draws no conclusion from them. Questions of rates on one line or at one point can not be considered by themselves exclusively; a change in them may affect the rates in a considerable part of the country. Rates from the interior to New York necessarily have close relation to rates from the same points to Philadelphia, Boston, and Baltimore; rates from the sea-board to Toledo must have a similar relation to those from the sea-board to Detroit and other towns whose business men compete with those of Toledo in a common territory. Just rates are always relative; the act itself provides for its being so when it forbids unjust discrimination as between localities. This prohibition may sometimes give to competition an effect upon rates beyond what it would have if the competitive forces alone were considered.

The Commission has had occasion, where a railroad company operated lines which run parallel to each other, to hold that if the company yielded to competitive forces so far as to give the towns on one line very low rates, the effect of such low rates upon the business of rival towns on the other line could not be ignored when their rates came under consideration. The natural influence of just competitive forces ought to be allowed as it would be as between two lines owned by different companies; and if the rates on one line were made very low because of competition, keeping the others high because the absence of competition enabled it to be done might amount, within the meaning of the law, to unjust discrimination. Consolidation of rival lines, or the bringing them under the same management, can not justify ignoring on one line the effect of competitive forces on the other; those forces always, when not unnaturally restrained, have an influence which reaches beyond the points whose business is controlled by it, and by secondary effect modifies prices to more distant points. This is well understood in the transportation business; the modifying effect of rates by lake and canal is perceived in the charges on all lines from the Mississippi to the sea-board; the rates to and from Duluth affect all charges in the Northwest to and from Chicago. Any arrangement by consolidation or otherwise that should undertake to eliminate this influence would, if made on a large scale, be futile, because it would antagonize laws of trade and communication which would be too powerful for it, and on a small scale, affecting particular towns or small districts, it might be illegal from its manifest inequality or injustice.

Competition. A study of the act to regulate commerce has satisfied the members of the Commission that it was intended in its passage to preserve for the people the benefits of competition as between the several transportation lines of the country. If that shall be done the towns which have great natural advantages, or advantages acquired by large expenditures of money in establishing new thoroughfares of commerce, will have cheaper rates than can ordinarily be obtained by towns less favorably situated. New York with its noble harbor, its central location, the Hudson River, and the Erie Canal for interior water-ways, can not be deprived of the benefits which spring from these great natural and acquired advantages without altogether eliminating competition as a force in transportation charges, and by an exercise of sovereign legislative power establishing arbitrary rates over the whole country.

It might possibly be within the competency of legislative power to prescribe for the several interstate railroads equal mileage rates for the whole country; but this, if enforced, would put an end to competition as a factor in making rates, and to a very large extent deprive the great business centers of the country of their several natural advantages, and also of the benefit of expenditures made by them in creating for themselves new channels of trade. It would, in fact, work a revolution in the business of the country, which, though it might be greatly beneficial in some directions, would be fearfully destructive in others. Congress has not by the existing legislation undertaken to inaugurate such a revolution; nothing in the act to regulate commerce looks in that direction, unless it be the prohibition to charge more for a shorter than for a longer haul on the same line in the same direction, the shorter being included in the longer distance. But that prohibition is not absolute, and if it were, a strict enforcement would necessarily be at the expense of the competitive centers which have heretofore had the exceptionally low rates. The rates have made them centers for a valuable wholesale trade which they cannot expect to retain permanently in its entirety if they are deprived even in part of the advantages which they have hitherto had from the competition of rival carriers. The benefit which non-competitive points receive must be largely at the expense of the competitive. This is one of the inevitable consequences of perfecting the reform in the direction of basing rates upon distance more than has been the case hitherto. It is an incidental disadvantage to some which is supposed to be more than made up by the more equal apportionment of transportation benefits.

The competition by water is the most important factor in forcing rates to a low level at the points where the lines of land and water transportation intersect. Where there are good channels of water transportation, the cost of moving traffic upon it is so very greatly below the cost of rail transportation that the railroads would scarcely be able to compete at all if rapidity of transit were not in most cases a matter of such importance that it enables the railroads to demand and obtain higher rates than are made by boat. But even when compensated for the extra speed, the rates which the roads can obtain in competition with the natural waterways must be extremely low and in some cases leave little if any margin for profit. The experience of the country has demonstrated that the artificial waterways can not be successful competitors with the railroads on equal terms. If the effort is to make the business upon them pay the cost of their maintenance and a fair return upon the capital invested in them, its futility must soon appear. The railroads long since deprived the great canals of Ohio, Indiana, and Illinois of nearly all their importance, and the Erie Canal is only maintained as a great channel of trade by the liberality of the State of New York in making its use free; the State thus taking upon itself a large share of the cost of transportation which would be assessed upon the property carried if the canal were owned and held for the profit of operation as the railroads are.

In their competitive struggles with each other towns can not ignore the effect which the existence of natural waterways must have upon railroad tariffs; the railroad companies can not ignore it, nor can the Commission

ignore it if competition is still to exist and be allowed its force according
to natural laws. Neither can the great free Erie Canal be ignored; it influences the rates to New York more than any other one cause, and indirectly, through its influence upon the rates to New York, it influences
those to all other sea-board cities, and indeed to all that section of the
country.

Other considerations bearing upon the reasonableness of rates might be
mentioned, but enough has been said to show the difficulty of the task
which the law has cast upon the Commission, and the impossibility that
that task shall be so performed as to give satisfaction to all complaints.
The question of rates, as has already been shown, is often quite as much
a question between rival interests and localities as between the railroads
and any one or more of such localities or interests; but while each strives
to secure such rates as will most benefit itself, the Commission must look
beyond the parties complaining and complained of, and make its decisions
on a survey of the whole field, that either directly or indirectly, will be
affected by them.

CONCLUSION

BY THE coming of the twentieth century the railroads had ceased to be a creator of new economic institutions in the United States. Rising industries had replaced them as the instigators and shapers of economic change. For the decade of the 1890's marked the culmination of many developments in the railroad world. In that decade the new Interstate Commerce Commission began to work out procedures and processes to regulate rates and classifications. In the 1890's, too, consolidation generally replaced federation, so that by 1900 the huge self-contained systems that we know today had come to dominate the nation's railroad network. It was in the financial stabilization of these new systems that J. Pierpont Morgan played his most critical role in American private finance. After Morgan and others had helped to reorganize the vast railroad empires, many of their managers instituted rational administrative structures similar to the one that Charles E. Perkins had outlined for the Burlington in the mid-1880's. Finally, the nineties were years of labor unrest. But while reaction to labor protest helped to bring the failure of the Knights of Labor and to dash Debs' hopes for industrial unionism, it had little effect on the better organized railroad brotherhoods. In that decade these craft unions received full recognition by railroad managements, and together unions and management firmly established modern methods of collective bargaining.

In the same decisive decade many industrial enterprises were beginning to become big businesses and to follow the patterns of economic action that the railroads had first defined. The opportunities and the needs engendered by the great national market, which the railroads had done so much to create, encouraged the growth of integrated, self-contained enterprises that did their own buying and marketing as well as manufacturing. As in the case of the large railroad systems, competition brought consolidation. By the turn of the century such industrial consolidations were looking to J. P. Morgan and other lords of Wall Street for financial assistance. At the same time these new business giants began to adopt administrative structures similar to those earlier worked out on the railroads. They formed functional departments to handle manufacturing, sales, purchasing, finance, and legal affairs and a central office to coordinate, appraise, and plan for the work of all the departments. Again, as in the case of the railroads, combination and consolidation bred a demand for government regulation, and in a few years the Federal Trade Commission became the ICC for industry. Finally, when the growing craft unions encountered the new large industrial corporation, they began to use many of the collective-bargaining methods and procedures that had already been developed on the railroads.

The process of making and selling goods differed from the mere transporting of them, so that the new industrialists had often to alter, modify, and even radically change the ways of finance, management, labor, competition, and regulation in which the railroads were pioneers. Yet even these later changes served to underline the significance of the railroads and to demonstrate the decisive role they played as the nation's first big business.

SUGGESTED READINGS

(Books and articles from which the selections have been reprinted in this volume are not listed below.)

ADAMS, CHARLES FRANCIS, JR., *Railroads: Their Origin and Problems*. New York, 1878.

ALLEN, FREDERIC LEWIS, *The Great Pierpont Morgan*. New York, 1949.

BENSON, LEE, *Merchants, Farmers, and Railroads: Railroad Regulation and New York Politics, 1850–1887*. Cambridge, Mass., 1956.

CAMPBELL, E. G., *The Reorganization of the American Railroad System, 1893–1900*. New York, 1938.

CHANDLER, ALFRED D., JR., *Henry Varnum Poor, Business Editor, Analyst, and Reformer*. Cambridge, Mass., 1956.

CLEVELAND, FREDERICK A., and FRED W. POWELL, *Railroad Promotion and Capitalization in the United States*. New York, 1909.

COCHRAN, THOMAS C., *Railroad Leaders, 1845–1890: The Business Mind in Action*. Cambridge, Mass., 1953.

DAGGETT, STUART, *Railroad Reorganization*. Cambridge, Mass., 1908.

GATES, PAUL W., *The Illinois Central Railroad and Its Colonization Work*. Cambridge, Mass., 1934.

GRODINSKY, JULIUS, *Jay Gould, His Business Career, 1867–1892*. Philadelphia, 1957.

GOODRICH, CARTER, *Government Promotion of American Canals and Railroads, 1800–1890*. New York, 1959.

HANEY, LEWIS H., *A Congressional History of Railways in the United States*. Madison, Wisc., 1910.

KIRKLAND, EDWARD C., *Industry Comes of Age: Business, Labor, and Public Policy, 1860–1897*. New York, 1961.

———, *Men, Cities and Transportation: A Study in New England History, 1820–1900*, 2 vols. Cambridge, Mass., 1948.

McMURRAY, DONALD L., *The Great Burlington Strike of 1888: A Case History in Labor Relations*. Cambridge, Mass., 1956.

OVERTON, RICHARD C., *Burlington West: A Colonization History of the Burlington Railroad*. Cambridge, Mass., 1941.

RIEGEL, ROBERT E., *The Story of Western Railroads*. New York, 1926.

RIPLEY, WILLIAM Z., *Railroads, Finance and Organization*. New York, 1915.

———, *Railroads, Rates and Regulation*. New York, 1912.

SHARFMAN, I. L., *The Interstate Commerce Commission: A Study in Administrative Law and Procedure*, 4 vols. New York, 1931.

STOVER, JOHN F., *American Railroads*. Chicago, 1961.

TAYLOR, GEORGE ROGERS, *The Transportation Revolution, 1815–1960*. New York, 1951.

———, and IRENE D. NEU, *The American Railroad Network. 1861–1890*. Cambridge, Mass., 1956.

VERMONT COLLEGE
MONTPELIER, VERMONT

Please remember that this is a library book,
and that it belongs only temporarily to each
person who uses it. Be considerate. Do
not write in this, or any, library book.